To dear Terri:
With love and
respect

Vladan

7-25-05

AMERICA

For Luba, Jill and Olga

America

Sovereign Defender or Cowboy Nation?

Edited by

VLADIMIR SHLAPENTOKH
Michigan State University, USA

JOSHUA WOODS
Michigan State University, USA

ERIC SHIRAEV
George Mason University, USA

ASHGATE

Published by
Ashgate Publishing Limited
Gower House
Croft Road
Aldershot
Hants GU11 3HR
England

Ashgate Publishing Company
Suite 420
101 Cherry Street
Burlington, VT 05401–4405
USA

Ashgate website: http://www.ashgate.com

British Library Cataloguing in Publication Data
America : sovereign defender or cowboy nation?
 1.September 11 Terrorist Attacks, 2001 - Public opinion
 2.United States - Foreign public opinion 3.United States -
 Foreign relations - 2001-- Public opinion
 I.Shlapentokh, Vladimir II.Woods, Joshua III.Shiraev, Eric,
 1960-
 327.7'3'0090511

Library of Congress Cataloging-in-Publication Data
Shlapentokh, Vladimir.
 America : sovereign defender or cowboy nation? / by Vladimir Shlapentokh, Joshua Woods, Eric Shiraev.
  p. cm.
 Includes bibliographical references and index.
 ISBN 0-7546-4428-6
 1.   United States--Foreign relations--2001- 2. United States--Foreign public opinion. 3. Anti-Americanism--Case studies. 4. Anti-Americanism--History. I. Woods, Joshua. II. Shiraev, Eric, 1960- III. Title.

 E902.S55 2005
 327.73--dc22
                                                                      2004028606

ISBN 0 7546 4428 6

Typeset by Saxon Graphics Ltd, Derby
Printed and bound in Great Britain by TJ International, Padstow, Cornwall

Contents

Preface

Assembling a book about international attitudes toward the United States at the start of the twenty-first century has been a difficult task. Any study of America's image abroad must contend first of all with the ideological climate surrounding this topic. Critical audiences, including the editors of journals and publishing houses, may suspect, almost by instinct, a bias in an author's research and publications. Suspicions often lurk in a study's methods – including the preparation of questionnaires and codebooks, the training of researchers and aids, and the choice of sampling and statistical procedures – as well as in the presentation of the results. For those whose ideological predilections conflict with a study's findings, a justification for harsh judgment always seems readily available.

The same may be true of the research and publications on abortion, gay marriage, illegal immigrants, the division of church and state, social welfare programs and foreign policy. Indeed, the study of "anti-Americanism" ranks among the most controversial topics of our times.

In the wake of 9/11, the character of American society was on trial, and judgments from around the globe were split and divisive, including in the United States. The 2004 American presidential election only exacerbated the polarization of the Americans on all major issues, particularly on foreign policy and the high level of anti-Americanism in the world.

The deep ideological confrontation within and beyond America's borders existed even before 9/11. The dislike of America is as old as the country itself. In the twentieth century alone, the level of anti-Americanism abroad has been influenced by two world wars, the Cold War, the increased contact between nations, new technologies, and most significantly, by the collapse of the Soviet Union. The United States emerged in the 1990s as the most powerful country whose influence in culture, economics, and politics spread to each corner of the globe. Of course, there is not one history of America's image abroad, but numerous histories – one for each country in the world. Each nation has its own historical experiences with the United States as well as its own cultural, political and social context within which the people perceive these experiences. For this reason, the contributors to this book were asked to analyze not only their country's current attitudes toward America, but also the history of these attitudes and the events that changed them.

Without losing sight of the past, we used the events of September 11th as the backdrop for our research. Our initial intention was to take a snapshot of people's attitudes at a moment when the United States emerged as the victim of three spectacular acts of terrorism. While we focused on the days immediately following September 11, we extended our study to December 2001 in order to survey international views of the war in Afghanistan. Our basic objective was to create a record of how the various political figures, journalists, editors and opinion makers in foreign countries described the United States, its leaders, institutions and people in the aftermath of 9/11.

In the debates over America's image after 9/11, the terrorists themselves and their motives for attacking the United States played an important role. There was, in fact, little international agreement on who these terrorists were, or how they should be characterized. While many observers pointed to America's prime suspect Osama bin Laden as the perpetrator of 9/11, strong minorities in some countries speculated that other enemies of the United States, including domestic terrorists or even the United States itself, could have launched the attacks. The perpetrators of 9/11 were widely regarded as "international terrorists," "evildoers," fanatics inspired by Islamic fundamentalism, and committed enemies of Western civilization. At the same time, some people saw them as an oppressed class of "freedom fighters," or even "heroes" who had suffered for decades under unjust American foreign policies. Ideological lines divided the international reaction to 9/11 on several other issues, including the root cause of the attacks, the proper course of action that should be taken in response to 9/11, and the use of military force by the United States.

In discussing the ideological struggle in the world we deemed it necessary to distinguish between the "agents" who epitomized the enemy – whether Osama bin Laden or George W. Bush – and the "structure," or the principles of the inimical ideology – that is, Islam fundamentalism or the decadent individualistic philosophy of the West. Several past studies, and our project joins them in this respect, have stressed the importance of the enemy's image in the world, and how this image influences international and domestic developments. The image of the enemy, which is full of ideological fervor, is a very important factor that impacts the composition and strength of international alliances, as was the case, for instance, during the Second World War and the Cold War.

With the highly charged ideological climate in the world, we saw our task as not so much to please everybody, but to make an attempt at putting together a book as objectively as possible. We were particularly concerned about the objectivity of our study, because part of the funding for this project came from the United States government, a circumstance that can give ammunition to critics who dislike the results of the project. The quest for objectivity demanded three tasks from us: first, to minimize as much as possible the impact of ideology on the collection and analysis of empirical data; second, to guarantee that all ideological trends are described by these data and presented in the book; third, to minimize as much as possible the influence of the ideological position of our coders and other people who helped us in the collection of the data. In other words, the views of people who hold "anti-American" views, including those who see America through the eyes of Islamic extremists, should be adequately, and objectively, as much as contemporary social science permits, portrayed in the book. The aim of these efforts was to minimize in this book the ideological stance of the authors and editors – they were, as a matter of fact, not at all unanimous on various political issues.

We claim that in this respect our book is unique, since most publications that discuss foreign attitudes toward the United States disregard the differences in the views of various groups. Meanwhile, the ruling elites (political, economic and cultural) are the key actors in the formation of a nation's foreign policy and in shaping, via the media, the people's attitudes toward other countries. Of course, the views of the elites and the ordinary people are not identical and this book will devote a lot of attention to this issue. At the same time, it is the elites who control the media and effect the position of the masses, not vice versa. Indeed, during the Cold War the images imposed on the masses by the ruling elites with respect to America in the USSR and in regard to the USSR in America were filled with various absurdities about the two superpowers.

In our study of elite views, we used various sources but first of all the printed media. We faced the complicated task of trying to avoid any bias in the selection of newspapers. We selected in each country, using a random technique, the newspapers with the highest circulations, which means the greatest impact on the population.

At the same time, in order to guarantee the representation of all views of America, we also included in our sample the newspapers that reflect the views of the elites in the opposition as well as the radical groups in society on both right and left. In such a multi-linguistic and multiethnic country as India, we operated with newspapers in six different languages. We were also concerned about the study of the media in such countries as China and Egypt, where the media are controlled by the state. We resorted to additional sources of information such as interviews with the local people published in the Western media as well as Internet chat rooms and online forums.

We tried to protect ourselves as much as possible from being biased when we created the questionnaire (otherwise known as a codebook in content analysis, the quantitative analysis of texts, which was used in our project) for the study of the articles selected randomly from the newspapers. Each question used by pollsters contains various alternatives. In our codebook, we did our best to guarantee that the number of alternatives on the pro-American and anti-American sides were equal. We also trained our coders to be as objective as possible in the reading and coding of articles from the newspapers (the major stuff of our project).

With our desire to offer readers a reliable picture of the international attitudes toward America we tried to avoid simplifying this picture – a common flaw among those who strongly admire or dislike America.

We do not think that it is possible to create a general theory that explains the positive or negative attitudes toward America. In fact, in this book we advance the concept that attitudes toward America in each country result from a combination of internal and external factors influencing the various developments in the given country. Our point is that the role of America as the single superpower is so high in the world (for better or worse) that almost in each country people have to take some position toward it. In many countries anti-Americanism became a sort of ideology, which is used to explain the country's domestic and foreign policy. Among internal factors we point to the role that America plays in the political struggle in each country, which often divides the political and economic elites. Of no less significance are the people's perceptions of various sides of American society – its political and economic order, its culture and style of life. Negative attitudes toward America can be attributed to critical evaluations of many aspects of the American style of life. The factor of envy cannot be ignored if you try to explain the hostility toward the United States in Russia or in France.

The American foreign policy is, of course, a leading external factor that shapes the position of the ruling elites and then of the masses toward America. The political and economic conflicts with America and the reluctance to accept the hegemonic role of America in the world are among the most powerful motives for people who do not like the country.

Our book will show how the relative role of internal and external factors varies from country to country. Looking for an explanation of the attitudes toward America in various countries we studied the role of economic and political developments in each country, the religious composition of the population, the conflict of interests with America, and the country's distance from the Middle East. We hope that our comparison between the different countries will protect us from the ideological biases in favor of one or another theories for explaining anti-Americanism. It was particularly important to compare the positions of Russia and Germany as well as India and China.

As an important device to overcome the ideological biases of the editors we invited, as the authors of the individual chapters, scholars from very different backgrounds. We even tried to offer the readers the positions of authors with clearly different ideological leanings, as was the case with Germany. Some chapters were written by authors who currently live in the country they wrote about. The diversity of the authors' viewpoints, and the nonintervention of the editors are additional evidence of our willingness to make the book as objective as possible. But, of course, it is the readers who will make the final judgment about our good intentions, and decide whether they pave the road to paradise.

Acknowledgements

Working on this book, we received guidance, assistance, and help from many wonderful individuals from several different countries and fields of work. A special thanks goes to Vera Bondartsova, a graduate student at Michigan State University, who played a major role in the project as an organizer and researcher. We are indebted to Vivek Joshi and Chuck Petrin, whose computing talents greatly benefited the project. We would also like to extend our appreciation to the members of our research team, including the following students from MSU: Lin Wang, Paras Doshi, Anoop Namboodiri, Irfan Muzaffar, Devojyoti Bhattacharya, Marc Rathmann, Helga Rom, Sandra Fernandez, Tania Garcia, and Andrea Hamor. Former Vice President Charles Greenleaf and President Lou Anna Simon of MSU deserve our gratitude for their enthusiastic support of the project. We gratefully acknowledge the helpful advice of other colleagues from MSU: Bernard Finifter, Stan Kaplowitz, Tobias Ten Eyck, Christopher Oliver, Robert Solo, and Lawrence Busch as well as Scott Keeter (Pew Research Center for the People and the Press, Washington D.C.), David Levy (Pepperdine University, Los Angeles), Olga Makhovskaya (Russian Academy of Sciences, Moscow), Vlad Zubok (Temple University, Philadelphia), Sergei Tsytsarev (Hofstra University, New York). We acknowledge our gratitude to other unnamed friends and colleagues in London, Moscow, St. Petersburg, Vilnius, Prague, Los Angeles, New York, and other cities. These people have helped us with their ideas, polling data, insights, research publications, and personal observations.

In the United States, discussions with David Farber from Temple University in Philadelphia, Martina Klicperova from the Czech Academy of Sciences, and Mel Goodman, from the National Defense University in Washington, D.C. provided valuable ideas and gave interesting suggestions during different stages of our project.

We are also grateful for the support of James Goldgeier (Institute for Russian, European, and Eurasian Studies at George Washington University, Washington D.C.) and Robert Dudley (Department of Public and International Affairs at George Mason University, Fairfax, Virginia).

We express our appreciation to a wonderful publishing team at Ashgate including Kirstin Howgate, Carolyn Court, Halima Fradley, Sarah Horsley, Helen Harvey, Emily Poulton and Bibi Stoute. Thank you for your patience and help.

Introduction

After 9/11: Attitudes toward the United States

Vladimir Shlapentokh, Joshua Woods and Eric Shiraev

Few countries can compete with the United States in the amount of attention they command from the international community. It relates to the world through its foreign policies, military actions, cultural products, lifestyles, universities, foreign aid, corporations and non-governmental organizations. The country became an even more salient object of discussions after the events of September 11th, 2001. As Marta Lagos rightly suggested, regardless of where people lived or the language they spoke, everyone had an opinion about September 11th (Lagos, 2003).

The empirical basis for this book is the international research project, "World Attitude toward the United States After 9/11." Seven countries have been included in the project. Russia, India, and China are the three largest foreign countries that possess nuclear weapons and play important geopolitical roles. Germany and Lithuania represent Western and Eastern Europe respectively. Columbia was selected as the representative from Latin America, and Egypt represents the Muslim world. This book is also devoted to exploring the origins of America's image abroad, and explaining why this image has deteriorated in recent years. We will touch on several theories and examine a great variety of opinions on this subject.

Elites and the Media

While public opinion and the official policies are in the focus of our attention, the attitudes of domestic elites are our primary focus. The opportunity for most people, even in free nations, to shape their own image of foreign countries is quite limited. Elites, through a variety of means, and certainly through the media, form people's attitudes about distant countries (Belluci and Isernia, 2003; Shapiro *et al.*, 2000). Our definition of "elite" does not stray far from its elementary connotations. While some authors define elites according to their particular function in society (Keller, 1963), we define elites by their particular type of power. Elite individuals are those who, by virtue of their particular position, exercise power and influence on society.

In a project of this scope it was very difficult to operate with a representative sample of national elites. To simplify the task and assuming that the leaders of major political, cultural, and economic institutions have a crucial influence on the media and tend to express their views via electronic and printed sources, we chose to analyze the mainstream print media. In terms of foreign policy, the media are often more focused and united than in domestic issues, which are heavily influenced by domestic politics. It is also important to take into consideration that in democratic societies, media can be a source of opinion different from the mainstream elites' views. Therefore, certain small and marginal publications have been included in the analysis.

Nevertheless, even in the mainstream press different types of elites advance different, and at times, conflicting opinions. We expect, for instance, that reporters or columnists who regularly write for a national newspaper would frequently disagree with other correspondents or columnists. To address this potential obstacle, we were able in most cases to separate the media messages created by media professionals (editors, columnists and journalists) from the quotes and official statements made by other elites, such as politicians, religious leaders, entrepreneurs, and celebrities.

There is little debate over whose views appear in the media in non-democratic countries. The ruling government elite in authoritarian regimes, because of official censorship, influences the media's portrayal of almost all aspects of life. In history, the former Soviet Union or Nazi Germany represented such cases (Shlapentokh, 1986). In the current study, elites in some countries, such as China and Egypt, are less diverse than in other countries, such as Germany and India, where the elite's opinions are normally dispersed across a wider spectrum of political attitudes and beliefs.

Theoretical Background

Not many political aphorisms remain as famous as the ancient dictum: "My enemy's enemy is my friend." The underlying logic of this phrase can be detected in any number of creative works, from Greek mythology to Shakespeare's plays to several noted theories in the social sciences. This aphorism points to the important, if self-evident premise that people's attitudes about a person, group, nation, or object are influenced, randomly or systematically, by the views and behavior of other people. In particular, in this study, we were interested in detecting how the foreign elites' perceptions of the United States were impacted by their image of international terrorism.

The question of how people's perceptions are configured in the mind is one of the primary concerns of contemporary social psychology. Followers of the Gestalt tradition of psychology including Fritz Heider (1946, 1958) and his "balance theory," maintained that people desire balance in their attitudes toward sets of other people, objects, or issues. Applying this theory to the adage cited above, psychologists argue that a person's negative attitude toward an enemy predetermines this person's positive attitude about the enemy's enemy. Important for predictive purposes is the contention that a balanced structure tends to remain balanced, while imbalanced triads naturally move toward a state of internal congruence (Eagly and Chaiken, 1998). One of the problems of balance theory, however, is that it treats people's attitudes as simply positive or negative, and virtually disregards the magnitude of these feelings. Responding to this limitation, Theodore Newcomb (1968) created a model that takes the intensity of attitudes into account. Newcomb hypothesized that the tension produced by an imbalanced relationship (and the need for resolving this tension) increases as the extremity of the attitudes involved increases. Newcomb's theory illustrates how fluctuations in the perceived danger of a common enemy (in this case, the threat of international terrorism) would result in attitude change.

The ideas of Heider, Newcomb, and their followers can be used to explain the formation of group solidarity. Many authors have found strong empirical evidence that individuals join groups to compensate for feelings of personal insignificance, to validate their beliefs, to reduce uncertainty, or to bolster self-esteem (Abrams and Hogg, 1988). From this perspective, there is something inherently valuable in the process of *identifying* with a group. However, people are not only drawn to other people for the sake of social identification. There are also personal interests at stake, including a need to guard against dangerous "outsiders" such as minorities, foreigners, or people living in other countries. In fact, an "in-group" by definition requires an "out-group." This sort of "us" versus "them" distinction becomes more consequential to attitudes and behavior under competitive or hostile social conditions. In other words, the rise of a common enemy such as *international terrorists* or, on the other hand, *imperialist aggressors* may enhance the bonds of group membership, including groups and coalitions. Classic studies conducted in the 1960s have shown that people display more favorable attitudes toward "in-group" members and more unfavorable attitudes toward "out-groups" when placed in competitive or conflicting circumstances (Sherif, 1966).

Focusing on large social and ethnic groups and entire nations, political scientists, sociologists, specialists in international relations and social psychologists have applied the concept of balancing attitudes and the common-enemy rationale to the study of international relations and various developments including negotiations, conflict resolution, development of prejudice, patriotism, and nationalism. The impact of mutual perceptions on politics and the emergence of a "common enemy" on ideology and mass psychology have become a leitmotif in the literature published in the United States, Great Britain, other nations, and across several academic disciplines. Several recent works published by Ashgate including the series, U.S. Foreign Policy and Conflict in the Islamic World, incorporate the ideas related to the "common enemy" image and consolidation of political forces *vis-à-vis* a perceived enemy or adversity. The richness of this idea lies in its consideration of "third parties" in the creation and development of people's attitudes and beliefs.

A Historical Outline: Common Enemies in the Twentieth Century

Over the past century, the friendliness of nations toward each other and the United States in particular has derived in part from a mutual identification of major regional and international threats. Twice in the twentieth century, the mutual fear of Germany has unified many European countries. The reality of the threat posed by the Central Powers during World War I (1914–1919), and the Axis Powers during World War II (1939–1945), generated a mutual understanding, group identification, a spirit of cooperation, and positive interaction between Britain, Russia (the U.S.S.R. during World War II), France, and the United States. Though only considered an associated power (not an allied power) during WWI, after its entry into this conflict on April 6, 1917, the United States enjoyed a more favorable image among the Allies (Lacorne and Rupnik, 1990). Gratitude and respect for the U.S. contribution to the war, as well as its subsequent aid to Europe and Russia in the aftermath of the war, lingered in Europe for a few years before anti-American attitudes took hold in the 1930s, particularly in France and the Soviet Union.

With the start of WWII, however, the Western powers including the Soviet Union have recognized the U.S. as a leading partner in the anti-Hitler coalition. The radically improved image of America among the Soviet elites and people in the 1940s demonstrates how a commonly perceived danger could change negative attitudes and stereotypes. During WWII, there was an intensive cultural exchange between the United States and the Soviet Union. American movies were played in Soviet theaters and the Soviet press regularly quoted American radio and other news sources. In his analysis of the Soviet press from those days, Jeffery Brooks (2000) explains that during the war the British and American allies had been a faint but real presence in the press, and that the editors who printed such coverage allowed foreigners a legitimacy and authority that contrasted with the xenophobia of the 1930s.

For five decades after WWII, while animosity toward the United States in the Soviet Union rose to Herculean levels, the Western governing powers in Europe remained benign, if not favorable in their attitudes toward America. According to a study on national stereotypes conducted in 1948–1949, the four adjectives most frequently used by the French, British, Australians, West Germans, Italians, Dutch, and Norwegians to describe Americans were: "progressive, generous, practical, and hardworking" (Buchanan and Cantril 1953). In contrast, the four adjectives the group used most frequently to describe Russians were: "domineering, backward, cruel, and hardworking." These stereotypes, as the authors suggested, were partially caused by tension, threats of war, and territorial insecurity.

According to dozens of cross-national surveys, West European opinion of the U.S. was generally favorable during the entire Cold War period, from 1954 to 1991 (Smith and Wertman, 1992). Even in the late 1960s, when mass protests against U.S. policies in Vietnam reached a crescendo, the proportion and intensity of the European opposition never came close to the level of resistance to the war in Iraq of 2003 and its consequences. There were several factors that bolstered the positive views of America in Western countries during the post-war period—not the least of which were the formation of the United Nations, the North Atlantic Treaty Organization (NATO), and the contribution of vast amounts of U.S. financial aid to foreign countries under the Bretton Woods system and the Marshall Plan. In addition, the most important factors influencing perceptions were the dangers posed by the Soviet Union, and the role of the United States as a counterbalance to this threat. As U.S. political analyst Fareed Zakaria suggested in 2003, despite the fact that 1968 was a "bad" year for America's image abroad in light of the developments in Vietnam, it was also the year of the Soviet invasion of Czechoslovakia. During the Cold War, the Europeans' critical views of America were always balanced by the wariness of the Soviet and communist threats (Zakaria, 2003). As the New York Times columnist Thomas Friedman (2002) wrote about German-American relations, since World War II, America and Germany have had many quarrels, but always limited ones, because both sides had a dangerous opponent. Both Bonn and Washington realized they needed to fight together.

Each of the major conflicts of the twentieth century spawned international alliances, and increased the good will felt between the allies (to a greater or lesser degree depending on the country). WWI led to the League of Nations, and the tempering of the Central Powers. WWII gave rise to the United Nations, NATO, and heightened transatlantic interaction. The Cold War led to the East-West balance of power that functioned as the cornerstone of strategic cooperation between the U.S., Western Europe, and several other countries. Most importantly, this political nexus between nations translated into a popular accord between peoples.

However, with the collapse of the Soviet Union in 1991, the need for a counterbalancing threat disappeared. The former Allied Powers and their friends could discard the Cold War "security blanket." Although the decline of America's image in Western Europe was not immediate, the demise of the bipolar world created a new international context in which serious political, economic, and cultural differences could be felt more readily on both sides of the Atlantic (Owen, 2002). Dozens of scholars and journalists—from Robert Kagan to Jose Joffe—have cited the new geopolitical circumstances of the post-Cold War period as a major potential source of friction and animosity between the U.S. and its old allies (Kagan, 2003). The appreciation of the U.S. for its actions during the Cold War including the liberation of East Germany from the Soviet occupation, or the protection of Japan under its nuclear umbrella did not last long after the Soviet collapse. Perhaps nowhere else has this point become more obvious than in South Korea. At the cost of tens of thousands of soldiers, the U.S. saved South Korea from subjugation in 1950–1953, and then protected this country for decades thereafter. During this period, attitudes toward the U.S. were indeed friendly and stable. Nonetheless, America's image deteriorated in South Korea after 1991. Moreover, there have been opinions expressed among some people and politicians that the U.S. was obstructing reunification with North Korea (Yi, 2003). While the Soviet collapse marked the decline of America's image in much of the world, it had the opposite effect in Russia. In the early 1990s, concern about the American threat was at its lowest point in decades, and the ruling elites were genuinely interested in democratic ideals. Indeed, Russian attitudes toward the U.S. were favorable in comparison to the atmosphere of suspicion and hostility of the past (Shlapentokh, 1998; Shiraev and Zubok, 2000).

On September 11, 2001, the world changed dramatically. No terrorist attack before 9/11 had ever centered the world's attention to the problem of terrorism. Despite the worldwide interest in the 9/11 attacks, there was not a universal understanding of what they meant, or what the response should or would be. With the United States in the international spotlight, the debate over the determinants of pro-American and anti-American sentiments gained momentum. Anti-Americanism has become a popular topic.

Why Anti-Americanism? External and Internal Causes

Most discussions of anti-Americanism focus on two main topics: either the "nature" of the United States and its policies or on the particular political and cultural aspects of other nations. Authors who refer to the United States suggest that the causes of anti-Americanism are external and brought by America itself. The authors highlight the deleterious effects of the U.S. foreign policy, military actions, and cultural expansion. In a book titled, *Why Do People Hate America?*, the authors' underlying message is that hatred of America is a reflection of people's real-life experiences with its policies (Sardar and Davies, 2003). Midway through the text, the authors include an extensive list of every American military intervention in the last century, from Wounded Knee (a massacre of Native Americans in the 1890s) to the war in Afghanistan in 2002. The list, which spans ten pages, is intended to speak for itself as clear evidence of America's zest for violence. The emphasis on U.S. foreign policies and actions can be found in several other books, such as a collection of essays by Gore Vidal (2002a, 2002b), or Noam Chomsky's book titled, *9–11*, in which he declared the United States a leading terrorist state (Chomsky, 2001). Chomsky also includes a long list of nations where U.S. military actions led to civilian killings, including in Vietnam, Laos, Cambodia, Nicaragua, El Salvador, Guatemala, East Timor, Sudan, Iraq, Yugoslavia, and Afghanistan. Other external factors such as the role of the United States in globalization and the expansion of capitalism have also been cited as a basis or root of anti-Americanism. The U.S. has been characterized as the global harbinger of "arrogant secularist materialism," the destroyer of indigenous cultural traditions, a unilateral bully in international economic affairs, a pusher of unsafe modified foods, and an ominous threat to the environment, human rights, and worker protection. For those who emphasize external factors, whether it is the abandonment of the Kyoto accord, the steel tariffs, the insolence of multinationals, or the bombing of Baghdad, America's negative image is an inevitable product of its own actions.

On the other side of the debate, many authors stress the internal, domestic factors underpinning attitudes toward the United States. In general, the strength of anti-Americanism depends less on U.S. actions than on the particular internal features of foreign countries. Three types of internal factors, namely, political, psychological, and cultural, are prominent in the debates. Addressing psychological reasons, some authors insist that certain critiques of the U.S. are irrational and even pathological. Paul Hollander's *Anti-Americanism*, for instance, highlights the issue of irrationality. To Hollander, anti-Americanism is "less than fully rational ... a free floating hostility or aversion that feeds on many sources besides the discernible shortcomings of the United States" (Hollander, 1992). This position is not new and a somewhat similar stance is found in an earlier collection of articles on anti-Americanism in which attitudes toward the United States were said to be based more on imagination and perception than on the actual experiences of most people (Zeldin, 1990). "Envy" has also been frequently linked to unfavorable foreign attitudes toward the United States (Joffe, 2002). In a 2003 issue of *Policy Review*, an author derided anti-Americanism as "irrational" and "a fantasy ideology dressed up to look like Marxism" (Harris, 2003).

Many critics have also pointed to the cultural differences between the U.S. and foreign countries. In the wake of 9/11, Samuel Huntington's "clash of civilizations" hypothesis, which identifies differences in culture as the fundamental source of conflict in the world (Huntington, 1993), was cited by hundreds of journalists and experts around the globe. While most of these authors contrasted the Islamic World to the United States, the cultural factor has also been said to influence how Europeans, particularly the French and the Russians, regarded various aspects of America in the past (Shlapentokh, 1988) and continue to regard today. In the opinion of these analysts, negative attitudes about the U.S. have also come to fruition through domestic political forces. Anti-Americanism itself can be seen as a negative ideology, a "scapegoating" mechanism used by ruling political and religious elites to find excuses for massive domestic failures regarding social and economic issues. The opposition can use negative images of other countries as a means to struggle for political power. Bolstering anti-American sentiments or manipulating already existing mistrust toward the United States, religious leaders commonly attack modernization (often labeled as Americanization) or the free market (labeled as consumerism). America is criticized from the "right" for being too liberal. On the other hand, America is portrayed as the enemy of the "left," the main obstacle to radical revolutionary changes. Anti-establishment groups evoke anti-Americanism too. For example, historian Francoise Thom has stressed the importance of anti-Americanism as an idea important in the internal political and ideological struggle in France. She insists that French anti-Americanism has favored the coalescence of various destructive forces in France, including virulent Trotskyists, Islamic extremists, and the radicals of the anti-globalization movement. Thom contends that Chirac's anti-Americanism is a "preventive capitulation" before "the wild youth which France failed to civilize" (Thom, 2003).

Most of the criticisms against the United States are viable. Nevertheless, any criticism gets strength if it is clothed in an ideological or political outfit. To a certain degree, the emphasis placed on ideology explains why such an important issue as the concern about the threat of international terrorism has not played a major role in the debate of America's critics.

Hypotheses

Drawing on the logic of the "common enemy" rationale, we hypothesized that a greater degree of concern about international terrorism would be positively associated with a more favorable attitude toward the United States. In other words, the countries that are more concerned about international terrorism tend to have more positive attitudes about the United States than the countries that are less concerned. Our second hypothesis considered the emotional character of the world's response to the events of 9/11, which caused an enormous loss of life and property. The images of airliners smashing into the Twin Towers, bodies tumbling through the air, a gaping hole in the Pentagon, and the crash site in Pennsylvania were televised around the globe, and continue to appear in the media. In the first days after the terrorist strikes, the United States faced the world not as an aggressor or opponent, but as the victim of what most people perceived as a heinous attack. At the same time, majorities of the population of several of the countries studied in this project held unfavorable attitudes toward the United States (particularly its foreign policies) prior to 2001. Considering both the expected emotional response to 9/11 as well as the negative preexisting attitudes toward the U.S., we hypothesized that the attacks would result in an outpouring of condemnation of the terrorists, but considerably less identification with the United States and its plans to respond to the attacks. One of the defining characteristics of the international press coverage of the events of 9/11 and immediately after was a mix of both sympathy and criticism for the United States. This reaction, which may seem contradictory, demonstrates the cognitive and affective processes at work during this pivotal moment in world history.

We will also explore the hypothesis rooted in preliminary observations that the masses in most nations are generally more benign toward the U.S. than the elites. In general, ordinary people are absorbed in their everyday lives, and less focused on foreign affairs than most elites. Moreover, unlike the elites, the masses rarely compare themselves and their social status to foreigners. The elites, on the other hand, are more directly affected by the political, economic, and cultural influences of the United States. In some cases, their interaction with America and American people (business, travel, diplomacy, etc.) leads to heightened attachment and affection toward the country. In many other cases, however, America's influence in the world is perceived as a serious threat, in which case the national elites' greater degree of interaction and psychological involvement generates more acerbic attitudes toward the United States (Shlapentokh and Woods, 2002). Whenever possible, we will compare our data from the content analysis to the statistics collected by various international public opinion firms.

The Research Design and Methodology

To measure a country's level of identification with America we first needed to clarify the concept of "identification." We defined this concept as the agreement versus disagreement with the official American position, as described by George W. Bush, on all the pertinent issues surrounding 9/11: we analyzed the content of 46 public speeches and statements made by President Bush on September 11–25, and October 7–21, 2001. We should point out that in the wake of 9/11 a majority of the American people strongly supported the official position. In other words, we applied the self-perceptions of most Americans as a reference point for measuring a foreign country's degree of identification with the United States.

The main method of this study was content analysis of publications. All members of the research team, or "coders," were native speakers of the country selected for them with near-native proficiency in English. For India, we needed five coders to handle the five different languages, besides English, that were used in the ten largest Indian newspapers (Hindi, Gujarati, Malayalam, Urdu, and Bengali). The codebook consisted of six major issues, which may be thought of as survey questions, related to various aspects of America and 9/11. These issues, selected on the basis of a pilot study of more than 200 articles from around the globe, represent the most popular international news items published in the first four days after the attacks. They included: *1) What words or phrases should be used to describe 9/11, or its perpetrators? 2) Who were the possible perpetrators of 9/11? 3) What were the root causes of 9/11? 4) How should America react to 9/11? 5) How should "your country" react to 9/11? 6) What words or phrases should be used to describe America, its government or people?* For each of these questions, we compiled an extensive list of response options, referred to here as "codes." For instance, the question regarding the description of 9/11 contained twenty-four codes, ranging from "Horrible, Evil, and Cruel" to "Brave, Freedom fighters, and Moral."

In addition to the main codes, we included the option of choosing "Other" and "No response." The "Other" code allowed us to gauge how accurately our codebook corresponded to the press in the given country. Considering how frequently the

"Other" code was selected, we could assess how well the codes matched the given country's press. When a coder selected the "Other" code, he or she translated the word or phrase in question and entered it in our files as string data. The extra information generated by this procedure helped us gain insight on the specificity of particular subjects in the international press. Besides the six quantitative issues discussed earlier, the coders were asked to give their own qualitative assessment of each respondent in the sample. "Respondents" were either the byline author of an article, or someone quoted in an article. Answers ranged from 1 ("completely favorable toward the U.S.") to 5 ("completely unfavorable toward the U.S.").

We also asked our coders to translate at least one of the key statements in each article and record it as string data. By using this strategy, we hoped to improve the summarization of the content analysis, create a storehouse of quotes and anecdotes, and substantiate the data by placing our quantitative analysis closer to the actual context of the given print media. We used a multistage sampling procedure for collecting the units of analysis in this study. We first divided the total universe of international newspapers according to circulation size using a version of stratified sampling, and then selected the top ten largest newspapers in each country. In addition, one or two purposively selected publications from each country were included for the sake of comparison. From this "population" of newspapers, we selected articles according to the date of publication and whether it contained at least one statement that matched the codebook. In almost all cases, the articles sampled from each newspaper represented a census of all the related materials published during the project's targeted time frame.

To increase the size of our sample we elaborated a special procedure based on the assumption that many articles contained the views of more than one person. If this was the case, the article was broken into separate units. In this way, the basic unit of analysis was either the written material produced by the byline author of an article, or the quotes and paraphrases that the author attributed to other people. For this reason, our sample contains a total of 2,856 units of analysis, but only 2,369 articles. Sixty-four per cent of these units represented the views of "authors," and 36 per cent were "quotes."

The inter-coder reliability of our content analysis was tested using Cohen's kappa, which assesses inter-coder agreement beyond chance levels (Cohen, 1960). Reliability checks were conducted on four different coder pairs on an average of 8 per cent of the articles in the samples. The articles were selected randomly for the reliability checks. Each test was applied to a different language (Spanish, Chinese, German, and English) so that we could compare the reliability of the data across countries. According to Landis and Koch (1977, p. 165), the strength of our inter-coder agreement may be interpreted as "moderate to substantial."

Several national samples drew special attention. The sample of articles from Lithuania was drawn from only two major newspapers (*Lietuvas Rytas*, and *Respublika*) resulting in a reduced number of cases. Due to strict state censorship, the mainland Chinese print media remained silent, or ambiguous, on some of the more controversial issues surrounding the events of September 11th. For instance, none of the nine largest newspapers in China published an article about the "root causes of 9/11," a popular topic in other countries. One of the strategies we used to mitigate these limitations was to analyze the most widely circulated newspaper in Hong Kong

(*The Apple Daily*), which does not have political censorship of the press. In addition, we examined a popular internet chat room in China, the *Peoples Daily Online Forum*. Taken together, these two publications painted a somewhat different picture of America compared to the views published in the official mainland press (even if there are some limitations to the representativeness of this data). These differences will be outlined in detail in the individual chapter on China that appears later in this book.

We faced a similar problem with the Egyptian case, although, considering the results of the content analysis, the Egyptians appeared to be more free to discuss controversial topics and criticize America so long as they avoided severe critiques of the Egyptian government. At the same time, we discovered some evidence that the views in the press had been constrained, particularly in the government-run newspapers. Newspapers owned by the government were more benign toward the United States than the publications from the opposition and other sources. A content analysis of articles from the foreign (non-Egyptian) press about the attitudes of the Egyptians also showed some interesting differences. In the interviews of Egyptians conducted by Western journalists, the level of hostility toward the U.S. was higher than the portrayal of America in both the state-owed and opposition press in Egypt.

For a more detailed description of the methodology used for this book visit our website.

A Preview

Before the 2003 war in Iraq, and before the anti-war protests swept the globe, and before the flood of articles about "anti-Americanism" hit the headlines in 2002, most Americans believed that the world had responded to 9/11 in the right way by offering sympathy and solidarity. Early on, President Bush seemed confident in America's international alliances. He repeatedly discussed the broad support that had been offered by America's many "friends and allies." In his Presidential Address on October 7, 2001, he mentioned several countries as "staunch" or "close" friends, including Great Britain, Canada, Australia, Germany, and France. He also claimed that more than 40 countries had granted air transit or landing rights. Many more had shared intelligence. America believed it was supported by the collective will of the world. The American media also conveyed the impression that the international community had identified with the U.S. in its time of sorrow and great need. The American press was inundated with stories about candlelight vigils held at U.S. embassies, the material aid flowing in from various nations, and the strong voice of support in the official statements of foreign leaders. Even the international press offered several vivid examples of foreign authors, editors and other elites who seemed to identify with the U.S. as a collective "we" during the crisis. For instance, a French newspaper ran the now-famous headline, "We are all Americans." However, as our study showed, international responses tended to identify not with America, its values, or plans for countering terrorism, but with the denunciation of the terrorist attacks. However, even the level of condemnation of 9/11 varied across the seven countries studied in this project.

Right after September 11th, a majority of responses in the studied countries described the attacks against the United States using clearly negative terms, such as "horrible," "terrible," or "a killing of innocent people." There were very few articles (no more than 5 per cent) or comments defending the perpetrators of the attacks portrayed as "heroes" or "victims of oppression" who took up arms against the hegemonic power. Although the international press generally described 9/11 in negative terms, there were, however, some discernable differences in the proportion of condemnation. Lithuania's media were the most negative about the perpetrators of the attacks, while the Egyptian media were the least. The highest level of antipathy toward America was found among those who linked the event of 9/11 to the U.S. as the perpetrator of its own tragedy to gain political objectives. Media in Egypt and Russia stood out as "leaders" in making this suggestion.

None of the studied countries have demonstrated a particularly strong sense of identification with America after the tragedy. In the days immediately following the attacks, as you can read in this book, rather than blaming the terrorists, many people pointed at American foreign policies as the root cause of the disaster. Commentators in the Egyptian print media led the way in making this claim. The respondents advanced several different variants of this critique, ranging from specific to general targets of criticism. General references to "U.S. foreign policies" as the underlying cause of 9/11 prevailed in most of the countries. The most salient "specific" policy critiques were directed at America's Middle East policies, particularly in regard to the Israel/Palestine conflict.

In most of the studied countries there was an active debate over whether or not the events in America represented a "clash of civilizations." Some authors took an accusatory or conspiratorial tone suggesting that the United States has provoked the clash on purpose to increase its domination. Support for this idea around the world, however, was minimal. Germany and Lithuania, as a common trend, showed the most solidarity with the U.S. position. Reactions in Egypt followed a general pattern by showing little support for the U.S. stance. Not only was there a lack of support for a military response, but most foreign elites made open demands on the U.S. to avoid any future war.

The developments of 9/11 have aroused the debates on the status of the U.S. in the world. The elites around the world were generally more critical of America's foreign policies than the masses and people in foreign countries who were more supportive of a military response than the elites. There were common requests from prominent intellectuals in printed media demanding that their governments should refuse giving any type of military support to the United States. In their minds, the proper course of action involved political, or diplomatic engagements, but not military actions. One of the most apparent signs of the international elites' identification (or differentiation) with America was found in the words (labels, nouns, adjectives, or metaphors) used to describe the United States. For some period, the words were mostly positive but the image of America abroad, however, varied quite dramatically from one nation to the next. Among the 40 different images we considered, America's status as the "only superpower in the world" ranked overall as the most popular description of the United States. At the same time, the September 11th attacks provoked questions about America's status in the broader geopolitical context. There were a few comments that 9/11 marked the beginning of a major decline in American influence in the world. However, commentators in all studied countries focused on the current dominant status of the United States.

Two major findings appear evident in the analysis. First, according to the two quantitative indicators, there is a positive association between each country's degree of concern about the terrorist attacks, and its attitude toward the United States. In general, higher levels of denunciation of the terrorist actions of Osama bin Laden brought higher levels of sympathy and support for the U.S. and the war against international terrorism. These data present evidence of an association, but not necessarily causation. Although it was assumed that the large-scale attacks of September 11th would generate positive group identification and sympathy with the U.S., the inverse is also possible. That is, increased (or decreased) identification with the U.S. could cause greater (or lesser) levels of condemnation of 9/11 and its perpetrators. Second, while a majority of elites denounced the terrorist attacks of September 11th, far fewer elites identified with the U.S. on the major issues surrounding 9/11. In each of the seven studied countries, the proportion of respondents who "identified" with America was significantly smaller than the proportion of those who "condemned" 9/11-like terrorism. These differences can be attributed to several factors, not least of which is the emotional impact of the attacks. As the project results show, most foreign elites watched the shocking images of 9/11 and felt emotionally compelled to condemn these terrible acts and sympathize with its victims. However, this emotional salience weakened when elites speculated, on the rationalized level, about the U.S. response. What would, or what should happen next was an international concern that emerged immediately after the first plane hit the Twin Towers. This issue drew on the elites' previous attitudes and beliefs about the United States and its influence in foreign countries. This mix of emotion and cognition can explain some of the variance between each country's level of condemnation of 9/11 and identification with the United States.

If other countries' attitudes about the United States are linked to general perceptions of international terrorism, then these general perceptions become very important for understanding anti-Americanism. Although many factors determine how a foreign country perceives the threat of terrorism, one of its most direct components is the image of the enemy. If people do not understand or misunderstand the threat or its source, the support for any country defending itself from the threat is supposed to be insignificant. Support grows if the common threat is identified.

CASE 1
GERMANY

On the morning of September 11, 2001, when two airliners crashed into the Twin Towers of the World Trade Center and the collapsing skyscrapers buried nearly three thousand people under the rubble, reactions in Germany were similar to those in most nations of Europe. Politicians expressed horror and voiced their solidarity with the people and government of the United States. German Chancellor Gerhard Schröder spoke of a "declaration of war on the civilized world" and assured the United States of "any help it might wish for" (No Author, 2001). Friedrich Merz, leader of the conservative CDU party in the German parliament, declared: "We stand on America's side." The cry, "We are all Americans" echoed throughout Europe. Intellectuals of varying political shades proclaimed their unity with the citizens of New York. Lead articles and letters to the editor showed that the events of September 11 had generated in the German population a vague fear that the values their civilization was built upon might now come under threat. However, the Germans' sympathy and support for the United States waned in the coming months as the country came to be seen less as a victim than as an aggressor who would use military force to answer the terrorist attacks.

Chapter 1

The Historical Context of the German Reaction to 9/11

Alexander Stephan

Like most Americans, I just cannot believe it, because I know how good we are.
George W. Bush, *A Prime Time News Conference, October 11, 2001*

Washington must ask itself the reasons for this hatred.
Süddeutsche Zeitung, *September 13, 2001*

Historical Causes of German Attitudes about the United States

Almost three months after 9/11, by December 2001, the mood in Germany appeared to have changed, as it had in much of the world. While Americans were enthusiastically celebrating the victory over Afghanistan as a mortal blow to international terrorism, people in Berlin, Frankfurt and Munich felt a growing concern that the United States, on the hunt for Arab fundamentalists, could attack other nations on its list of rogue states—a concern that has since been confirmed by the war against Iraq, which substantially widened the gulf between America and Germany. In short, the nearly 100 per cent solidarity with the United States in the days following September 11—solidarity which is documented in the present volume—gave way, within a few weeks, to a deep distrust of the American administration and its policies. This suspicion cut across all political camps and all age groups and sectors of the German population.

What had happened? Two closely related explanations can be offered for the mood shift in Germany after the events of 9/11. The first, more obvious but ultimately less adequate explanation reflects Germany's specific historical experiences with the United States, among which are a deep-rooted suspicion of the American culture and way of life and the memory of two lost wars in which the United States played a decisive role.

The second group of causes is harder to pin down. Long present in a latent form, they did not surface until the end of the Cold War and the removal of the Soviet Union as the common enemy of both Europe and America. Central to the ensuing clash of civilizations, which has intensified further since autumn 2001, are fundamental differences in the thought and behavior patterns of Americans and Europeans, differences that are largely independent of current policy and the decisions of any particular administration, and that in recent times have led Europeans to attempt to define a specifically European identity.

15

Between the World Wars

A brief review of the positive and negative images of America which Germans have
held since the United States was founded makes clear that the concepts of
Americanization and anti-Americanism have been shaped by a small number of more
or less constant factors, and are similar to those formed by other Europeans. Already
in the nineteenth century, we see the contrast between positive and negative views of
the United States, as the reports that German émigrés send back about a youthful,
dynamic and open land of opportunity, clash with the admonitions of intellectuals
who stayed at home warning against the New World's aspiration for material gain
(Hegel) and its "odd mindlessness" and "crude obviousness" (Nietzsche, 2001,
183–4). The famous verse lines from Goethe, "America, you're better off than/Our
continent, the old" (1948, 655) were balanced by Heinrich Heine's critical portrait of
a country "where the most repulsive of all tyrants, the populace, holds vulgar sway"
(1985, 263). And while citizens of German cities around 1900 were entertained by
traveling wild-west shows and danced to American music in the dance halls,
conservative cultural critics saw in America's mass society a burgeoning cult of
hedonism, powered by commercial attitudes, which undermined the traditional
values of German high culture.

This culture clash, which reaches far back into the past, was underpinned by a
political power struggle between Germany and the United States that turned into a
shooting war in World War I and was reactivated from 1933 to 1945. When
Washington entered the war on the side of France and Britain in 1917, it made
clear that it was willing, so to speak, to expand the Monroe Doctrine by using
military means to oppose the establishment of a German hegemony in Europe and
an expansion of German power, which could compete with America's expanding
global interests. When, a short time later, the United States withdrew from Europe
during the negotiations over the Versailles Treaty despite Woodrow Wilson's
promise to "make the world safe for democracy," reactionary circles in Germany
viewed this as a "betrayal" on a par with the "stab in the back" from the
revolutionary German left who overthrew the Kaiser and set up a social-
democratic state in the wake of Germany's retreating troops. And the old-
established system of the so-called Rhineland industry, weakened by postwar
inflation and reparations, had a struggle to survive when the United States
swamped the new Weimar Republic with investments, production methods
developed by Henry Ford and Frederick Winslow Taylor, and theories of economic
growth based on the manufacture of cheap consumer goods, that ran counter to the
deeply-rooted German ethic of quality over quantity. Moreover, even in the field of
arts and culture the German elites felt under pressure during the so-called Golden
Twenties when they were forced to confront an onslaught of popular culture from
the United States.

Debate soon focused on Germany's explosion of technology and rapid
development of a mass society, which were misunderstood as American made.
German conservatives vehemently criticized these trends for their
"monotonization of the world," for promoting the "extinction of the individual in
favor of the type," and for spreading "American tedium" (Zweig, 1994, 268, 270).
Hermann Hesse, in his 1927 novel *Steppenwolf*, contrasted Mozart and Goethe

with jazz, the shimmy and free love. Other German writers and dramatists developed an ambivalent fascination with the power of the masses, who, in the writings of Ernst Jünger, died senseless but heroic deaths on world-war battlefields, while in Georg Kaiser's drama *Gas* we see them in the form of nameless yellow- and blue-uniformed troops who usher in the destruction of the world. Alfred Döblin created a German version of John Dos Passos's *Manhattan Transfer* when, in his novel *Berlin Alexanderplatz*, he linked the dynamic energy of high-tech, but anonymous city life to images of the Whore of Babylon and the Christian Hell. Notions like "speed," "sport" and "speculation" dominated both the new entertainment culture and the precarious transactions on the stock exchange. Hollywood began to flood the German market with films and the cult of stardom, when, in the mid-twenties the German film company UFA financially overextended itself by making the Fritz Lang film *Metropolis*, which, ironically, many Germans regarded as a representation of American Fordism and megacapitalism. And when the American advertising industry exported to Germany the so-called "girl culture" and the cult of "women as shoppers," thus helping to promote the Americanization of Germany during the Golden Twenties, right-wing cultural critics warned of a feminization and commercialization of German society.

The attitude about the United States among Germany's left-wing groups during the period between the two world wars is even more complex, given the ideological ties of many to the Soviet Union. The communists, social democrats, and trade unionists initially felt admiration for America's technological advancement and efficient provision of industrial goods to the masses. This admiration, however, was mixed with rapidly growing criticism of the exploitation of workers by capitalist robber barons—a criticism that was confirmed by the collapse of the United States financial system when the stock market crashed on Black Friday, 1929, and today is experiencing a resurrection in Europe following the "shareholder value" frauds, the Enron affair, and the illegal business practices on Wall Street. Bertolt Brecht, the renowned poet and playwright, in his poems and plays, initially described Chicago and Las Vegas as strongholds of dynamism, energy and modernity, but soon after, he portrayed them as the breeding grounds for violence and treachery, and for the gangsters on whom he modeled a drama-parable about Adolf Hitler. Brecht's friend Walter Benjamin, in his 1936 essay "Das Kunstwerk im Zeitalter seiner technischen Reproduzierbarkeit" (The Work of Art in the Age of Mechanical Reproduction), was among the first to reflect about the potential benefits and risks that modern technology brought to the production and distribution of art. Also, the Bauhaus school of design, whose members came together out of Germany's November Revolution of 1918 and were later driven from the country by the Nazis, first supplied America with a stable of celebrity architects, and then more or less Americanized, after World War II traveled back across the Atlantic to Germany, where it left a strong mark on the reconstruction of cities devastated by Allied bombing.

However, criticism of the United States, "counter-Americanism" (Ermarth, 2004) and anti-Americanism were not just a feature of the right-versus-left conflict in the Germany of the twenties. As in other countries of Europe, they also reflected a universal, often subconscious fear of modernism, which people felt was causing drastic changes in social and cultural life, challenging the traditional values and structures of religion, morality and the family, promoting the transfer of populations from the countryside into cities that grew ever larger and more anonymous, facilitating assembly-line labor, a soulless technology, and mass deaths in a senseless world war, leading to the dissolution of artistic forms, and leveling the distinctions between high and popular culture.

The National Socialists skillfully exploited these rather vague fears after 1933. Using Germany's position as the European *hegemon*, they applied brute force to reverse cultural modernism and spread their own ideology by both political and military means. And for the second time in half a century, Germany entered a violent conflict with the United States. However, a new feature compared to World War I was that, although the Nazis immediately and radically halted the Americanization of German culture, at the same time, like the Soviets, they deliberately and successfully imitated the efficiency and production methods of the American economy. Government-run projects such as the Arbeitsdienst (Reich Labor Service) and the construction of the autobahns mirrored concepts of the New Deal. The Nazi motto "Strength through Joy" and the projected mass production of Volkswagen automobiles were designed to satisfy consumer needs using methods similar to those employed by Henry Ford. And the rapid buildup of the German military machine based on technology and speed ("blitzkrieg") would no doubt have been impossible without modern organization methods.

But Nazi Germany's special approach to progressive methods, which was later described as "reactionary modernism," did not lead it to closer relations with the United States. Instead, the geopolitical strategists of the Third Reich correctly viewed America as a rival to German claims to hegemony, a rival as dangerous as the Soviet Union. Similarly, but with a reverse set of values, enemy-images were merged in Washington during the thirties when Germany and Russia were blended together in a theory of totalitarianism that equated communists with Nazis and made so-called "Communazis" the targets of a world-wide crusade for the American Way of Life and its ideals of "freedom," "equality of opportunity," "self-reliance," "justice," "truth" and "charity" (Luce, 1999, 28).

Post WWII Developments

The negative outcome for Germany from this political, economic, military, ideological and cultural power struggle at the end of World War II created a fundamentally new situation for German-American relations and for the role of the United States in the world. In 1945, Germany had to swallow not only its final military defeat and its consequent departure from the global political stage, but also the victory of the American economic and social system (in East Germany this was paralleled by the victory of the Soviet system) and the closely related triumph of American culture over German traditions last promoted with violence, pomp and propaganda by the Nazis. At the same time, the United States, having eliminated its strongest competitors in Europe and Asia, emerged from World War II as the leading economic superpower, if not yet the sole ideological and military power, while for decades to come Germany played no role on the international scene and the rest of

Europe a relatively small one. Contrary to all expectations on both sides of the Atlantic, the United States maintained a political and military presence in Germany and Europe for almost half a century. And surely no one guessed in 1945 that when the United States completed its evolution into the world's only hegemon almost fifty years later, it would happen, once again, on German soil, as the Berlin Wall came down, sealing the collapse of the Soviet empire.

Among the most important results of America's political and military presence in West Germany still evident today, is that the Federal Republic became politically, economically and culturally a special case of Americanization and anti-Americanism in Europe. The reasons for this are obvious. Germany lost its sovereignty with its unconditional surrender, and like Japan was dependent on the United States far longer and more completely than Italy or Austria. The disparity in power was intensified because the partitioned and largely demilitarized Germany remained on the front lines of the Cold War until 1990 and had to rely on the military protection of the United States. The economic reconstruction of West Germany, largely destroyed by the war, divided into zones of occupation and destabilized by millions of refugees, required United States support, at least in the beginning. No other people in Europe had so desperate a need to replace their lost national identity, their discredited history, their damaged culture and their polluted language. Few Germans in this morally disoriented country had the strength or courage to evolve their own alternatives to the ideals that had been lost. Phrases such as "Zero Hour" (Nullpunkt) and "clear-cutting" (Kahlschlag) showed that they felt they were starting over from scratch, insecure but also hopeful for a new beginning.

Accordingly, the first contacts between Germans and American GIs in the chaos of the weeks and months after the war were generally positive. Soldiers of the *Wehrmacht* tried desperately to be captured by Western forces because they feared the vengeance and brutality of the Red Army. Civilians, threatened with looting and rape in the east of the country, associated the arrival of the Americans in West Germany with liberation, chewing gum, Lucky Strike cigarettes and chocolate bars. Also, it quickly became clear to confirmed Nazis that the Americans intended to punish only the very top of the Nazi leadership while recruiting, after a brief spell of reeducation, the lower ranks for the Cold War against communism.

But the honeymoon between the occupiers and the occupied would not last long. The conservative elites surrounding the Adenauer government, who readily supported the Americans in their containment policy toward the Soviet Union, put up a fierce and initially successful resistance to any modernization of the German educational system and to the Americanization of German culture. Leftwing intellectuals in turn deplored the lax denazification in the western occupation zones, and the ideologically motivated cultural policy of the occupation authorities, who not only destroyed Nazi writings en masse, but also removed from the libraries of the America Houses books of social criticism by so-called liberal writers like John Dos Passos, Thomas Mann and Frank Lloyd Wright, an action which reminded many of the Nazi book burnings of 1933. Germans who had never been Nazis or Nazi collaborators could not help pointing out that it was, after all, a military occupation force that was trying to teach them basic concepts of democracy such as freedom, equality and justice. Others wanted Germany to follow a neutral "third way" and complained that the United States was making no moves to pull out of Europe and had permitted the Cold War partition of Germany and the building of the Berlin wall. Educated Germans eagerly studied the wide selection of materials made available to them in the America Houses and American reading rooms that were rapidly set up in the Western zones, but at the same time they shook their heads when United States cultural officers thought they could spread American high culture by sending symphony orchestras from Boston and New York to tour Germany playing works by Mozart or Beethoven. Less-educated Germans pieced together their own brand of anti-Americanism out of rage at the arrogant triumphalism of the victors, envy at their open display of wealth, and gloating at the racism within the American military. German women who, from loneliness or simply for financial reasons, fraternized with the foreign soldiers after their husbands and sweethearts had been killed in the war, were called "Ami whores." In short, in the first decades after the war Germans showed no enthusiasm for the Americanization of their society, but neither was anti-Americanism a "key force in the political culture" (Gassert, 2001, 944).

The Cold War

All this would change gradually once life in West Germany and in Europe started to stabilize and became more normal during the fifties. When Washington promoted German rearmament during the Cold War, German activists wrote antiwar tracts criticizing what they viewed as American imperialism, paving the way for later protests against the Vietnam War, the deployment of American Pershing missiles in Germany, and ultimately, against the American attacks on Iraq and Afghanistan. In 1957 the German-Swiss writer Max Frisch published a novel expressively titled *Homo Faber*, which rekindled old resentments of an America that worshipped technology at the expense of history and culture and prefigured similar criticisms, which were to resurface decades later among Greens on the left as well as among far-right opponents of modernism. When German youth in the mid-fifties used American culture to liberate themselves from the narrow confines of their parental homes and schools, American culture was criticized for its vulgarity and mediocrity.

German conservatives, who were quickly integrated into the Cold War on the American side and thus emerged from the Third Reich more powerful than before, believed then, as they do now, that American culture was soulless and lacking in myth because Americans lacked the will to endure pain and loss. They also felt that the American emphasis on mass marketing reduced everything to the lowest common denominator and led to a loss of quality for the sake of quantity. What on the surface looked like a democratization of culture, for them was in fact a standardization powered by pragmatism and the profit motive that produced total monotony. In the conservative view, imports from America like jazz, rock music, Hollywood films, and, from the mid-fifties onward, American television programs, were undermining customs and morals, coarsening the character of German youth, leading to habits of passive reception, and ultimately causing the creeping death of traditional German high culture.

In contrast, Germans on the left, who in the twenties had been among the most vocal critics of the United States, remained comparatively silent during the fifties, although in postwar France, Italy and other European countries the left campaigned actively against America's political and economic imperialism and the resultant commercialization of their own societies. German communists who managed to flee the Nazis in the thirties, in view of Stalinist oppression either ended up as renegades or lost their credibility as artists by supporting Socialist Realism. Others, who remained in East Germany, found themselves sitting on the wrong side of the Iron Curtain. Liberal intellectuals like Hans Werner Richter, who campaigned for a European socialism in his magazine *Der Ruf*, were caught in the machinations of the Cold War, co-opted by America's Congress for Cultural Freedom, which was financed and controlled by the CIA, or suffocated in the materialism of West Germany's "economic miracle." And in the chaos of the postwar period, the young generation, who had barely survived war and captivity, lacked the strength and ideas to resist plans of the occupying power, or to redesign German culture along different lines.

The left-wing critique of America gained strength only in the sixties, after the end of the Konrad Adenauer era, the first economic crisis, the clear shift of the Social Democrats toward America, and the victory of American-style consensus liberalism in the Great Coalition between the Conservatives and the Social Democrats. The left's confrontation with the United States and its presence in Europe—a confrontation which at times took a radical or, in the case of the Baader-Meinhof Gang, even a terrorist form—was led by student youth. They merged their protest against the Vietnam War with a fundamental criticism of American society, which they viewed as aggressively capitalist, and with a critique of German materialism and of Germany's failure to deal adequately with its Nazi past.

Attempts to dismiss such criticisms of America as a German maneuver to avoid confronting the Holocaust and the atrocities committed by the Third Reich are not convincing: first, because young Germans were at least as harsh in their criticism of their parents and teachers' generation as they were of the United States superpower; second, because almost all leading German intellectuals linked their critique of capitalism directly with efforts to analyze the bases of National Socialism; and third, because European countries that did not have a fascist past offered the same criticisms of America as Germany did.

Also, German students who opposed the so-called military-industrial complex had no wish to attack American popular culture along with it. On the contrary, they viewed many Americans as their allies, because unlike today in the wars on Afghanistan and Iraq, American intellectuals and artists and a good part of the media were on the same side as the Europeans. Students of the so-called generation of '68 looked to the American civil rights movement as a model for their own struggles against what they saw as aggressive policies by a militarily and economically overweening superpower. Forms of civil disobedience such as sit-ins and teach-ins traveled across the Atlantic. "We shall overcome" was sung on university campuses in Berlin and Frankfurt.

But the two-way approach to the United States—attacking its prominent flaws while at the same time drawing inspiration from America for both the form and content of the criticisms—was relatively short-lived. The American antiwar movement, always less ideologically based than its European counterparts, lost strength at the end of the Vietnam War as fear of the draft ebbed away, and large segments of the public on both sides of the Atlantic became preoccupied with their anxieties over the oil crisis and the economy. Whereas the Germans of '68 as they grew older joined with young Greens, moved on to new missions such as the protection of the environment, or started their long march through the political institutions to reach Parliament and, more recently, form a new government, in America the me-generation stood by passively as Ronald Reagan resurrected power politics, George Bush practised it and, following September 11, his son turned it into an official doctrine. While German writers and artists who protested against the deployment of American Pershing and Soviet SS-20 missiles and opposed the Reagan administration's Star Wars program in the 1980s went on to criticize America's first war on Iraq in the nineties, their colleagues on the other side of the Atlantic seemed comparatively uninterested in opposing United States policies. Following 9/11, open conflict broke out between German and American intellectuals when the latter spoke in support of preventive strikes and just wars against so-called rogue states. Germans responded with ill-concealed irony to American writers who, in an anthology commissioned by the Bush administration in 2002, lavished praise on "American values" and boasted that America has a "powerful sense for the universal" which directly links Americans to "all humankind" (Clack, 2003). Greens, who are not only antiwar and anti-capitalist but are concerned about the world's ecological future and the disparity in wealth between north and south, have seen themselves under attack from the American right and abandoned by those such as Bill Clinton whom they had looked upon as allies. And since the United States rose to become the world's only superpower, many Germans suspect that Washington is no longer willing to solve conflicts at the negotiating table, and thus is furnishing to other countries less experienced in democracy justification for using violence to solve their own regional conflicts.

The Old vs. New Worlds?

The foregoing is one explanation, the more obvious one, for the mood shift of Germans toward the United States since 9/11. But there seems to be a second and more significant conflict between the Old and the New World, which has long smoldered under the surface and has become increasingly evident since the end of the Cold War: the fundamentally different historical perspectives between the United States on one hand, and Germany, and indeed much of Europe, on the other, resulting from their different historical backgrounds. Since 1990 these differences have evolved into a system conflict, a clash of civilizations or cultures, which has begun to challenge the basic values of the "transatlantic community" that have long been regarded as unshakeable. The traditional anti-Americanism outlined earlier may in this case be giving way to a contrast between a more or less clearly defined American Way of Life on one side and, on the other side, a European identity which is still in the process of being formed. In other words, the familiar America-criticism, counter-Americanism, anti-Americanism, and "Europe bashing" could be replaced by a competition between the systems which could have disastrous consequences or which may, if handled properly by both sides, prove beneficial to Europe, the United States and the rest of the world.

Among the few politicians and scholars who foresaw this clash of civilizations long before September 11 is Georgy Arbatov (1987), who, in his role as director of the Institute of the United States and Canada in the Soviet Academy of Sciences, shortly before the collapse of the Soviet Union, wrote a commentary on the policy of the Gorbachev government for the *New York Times* in which he offered the following warning to his American readers: One day you will all miss the Soviet Union, because it has been the glue that held the transatlantic alliance together for more than half a century.

In the 2000s, it looks as if Arbatov's prediction may come true. United States wars, police actions and sanctions against Iraq, Serbia, the Sudan and Afghanistan since 1990 have made clear that military conflicts, pacifism and international law do not have the same value in the Old and in the New World. A militarily irrelevant and politically increasingly marginalized Europe urges the strengthening of organizations such as the United Nations and the International Criminal Court, a ban on nuclear tests and a moratorium on development of new nuclear weapons, while the majority of Americans regard these initiatives with distrust because they limit American sovereignty. Since 1990 the United States has stepped up the pace of withdrawal from international treaties and agreements that are important to Europeans, including the Kyoto accords, the ban on landmines, and elimination of stores of long-range missiles. After the post-9/11 wave of sympathy with the United States had waned and Washington had issued its worldwide declaration of war against terrorism, a debate broke out between American, European and Arab intellectuals over the ideas of "just war" and "preventive" or "preemptive strikes." Polar oppositions which are important to Washington's neoconservatives trying to found a "second American Century"— European paradise versus American power, Jihad versus McWorld, evil versus good, Venus versus Mars, the West against the rest—awaken in the Old World unpleasant memories of the centuries-old spiral of violence which had just been laid to rest, with America's help and as a result of the Cold War. Politicians and intellectuals as well as the wider public in Europe are concerned by the "go it alone" policy of the United States, which now seems less hesitant than ever to apply concepts such as "new world order," "empire" and "American exceptionalism." Germany and many other countries complain that Washington has set the United States outside international law by allowing America privileges that are not granted to other states.

At the same time, Americans reproach Europe with constructing a postmodern Eden while living under American military protection since 1945, and with failing to respond to crises such as those in the Balkans, not to mention what Washington calls "international terrorism." Europeans who hoped for a peace dividend after the opening of the Iron Curtain, are, according to the United States, unwilling to make sacrifices for freedom, democracy and globalization of the economy, and do not care to defend these values with force of arms throughout the world. Because in the economic sphere America swears by growth, "deregulation" and free trade zones, it resents Europe's greater reliance on the regulatory powers of the state, its socialized market economy and its pursuit of a capitalism with a "humane face." As for Europe's active role in international organizations, its preference for negotiation over military operations, and commitment to ecology, humanitarian issues and development aid, American analysts often attribute these to Europe's loss since World War II of the ability to engage in power politics.

In short, the relationship between the United States and Europe since the elimination of their common enemy the Soviet Union, appear to have deteriorated beyond the predictions of Georgi Arbatov. Many elements in the seemingly solid canon of shared Western values have come unstuck since 1990 and, more so, since 2001. Terms such as "hegemony," "geopolitics" and "Eurotrash" are now in circulation, and the law of strength threatens to crowd out the strength of law. *Egalité* and *fraternité*, it appears, are not identical with the inalienable right to the "pursuit of happiness." The international law born out of the wars of religion in the sixteenth and seventeenth centuries and out of the Treaty of Westphalia, is not consistent with George W. Bush's proclamation: "May God continue to bless the United States of America" (Bush, 2003). And even a basic concept such as "freedom" is interpreted differently in the United States than in Europe, not to mention other parts of the world.

This continental drift that is pulling apart the United States and Europe has relatively little in common with the traditional forms of anti-Americanism or America-criticism on one hand and "Europe bashing" on the other, even though both sides, in the wake of September 11, are trotting out the familiar clichés about an ungrateful Europe and an uncivilized and trigger-happy America. Rather, the current discord between the Old and New Worlds seems the manifestation of a conflict between rival systems, a "clash of civilizations" grounded in fundamental differences in politics and economics, social organization and the conduct of everyday life, human relations and the function of culture. The term "anti-Americanism," defined as an emotion-based rejection of the American lifestyle, is clearly outdated, but even the more politically correct phrase "America-criticism," meaning disquiet at specific decisions by a current United States' administration, inadequately reflects the differences in intellectual traditions which have shaped the United States and Europe and which have become more prominent since the end of the Soviet Union. Values of the "transatlantic community" that seemed fixed for more than half a century seem to be undergoing a change, and are being replaced by a competition between systems that requires both sides to redefine their positions. The United States has pulled away from "old Europe," partly because of the changed strategic situation in which the Old World lost its privileged position on the front lines of the Cold War, but also, it appears, because America has made a cultural break from Europe. Theories that European thinkers helped to draft in 2002—including the somewhat abstract notions of an end of ideology or the end of history—were actually put into practice in the *National Security Strategy of the United States of America* and the policies of the George W. Bush administration.

While back in 1941 the idea of an "American Century" was born from a single mind, that of Henry Luce, the publisher of *Life* magazine, today the government in Washington collaborates with well-endowed think tanks on the project of a "second American century." Concepts like "manifest destiny," "city upon a hill," and "entangling alliances," which belonged to the foundation myths of the United States, are being resurrected as if the world has not changed since the Puritans landed in New England. Instead of reflecting cautiously on the theme of "Our Country and Our Culture" as was done in the early fifties (No Author, 1952), both conservative and liberal intellectuals from New York to Los Angeles are demanding the right to a military first strike, and thus cross over the fine line from "unilateralism" to "exceptionalism." The United States, with its postmodern ideology and a democratic mass culture that almost totally dominates the society, is exporting to the world cultural models that claim to realize the unfulfilled dreams of the European Enlightenment and of European modernism. And while European culture, unable to screen out American imports, is forced to remain adaptable and to learn new things, American culture, which is shaped by the American internal market and, at the same time, by its mission as the leading global culture, has, despite occasional politically correct debates about the rights and wrongs of a cultural canon, less and less reason to open itself up to the classical cultural tradition or to ideas from other parts of the world.

Europe, meanwhile, seems to have developed a new self-confidence since the fall of the Berlin Wall and is operating with categories that often blend its own historical memories with past influences from the United States. At least for the moment, its experiences in the twentieth century have left Europe less interested in armaments and preventive wars than in using multilateral agreements to make the world safe for democracy. Memories of the negative consequences of "imperialism" and "colonial overstretch" are still fresh in France, Britain, Germany, and somewhat older in Portugal and Spain, making global military operations less appealing than "soft globalization" through development aid, the promotion of human rights, and the extension of international aid organizations. Europe believes that it offers an alternative model to the social and cultural overstretch of American postmodernism, and can create a hybrid cultural landscape where regionalism remains free of fundamentalism. Instead of the American reliance on a popular culture regulated by supply and demand, Europe pursues its own multilateral blend of entertainment and publicly subsidized high culture.

Two concrete examples from the period after September 11 may clarify the way in which concepts like Americanization, anti-Americanism and "Europe bashing" have become outdated since the end of the Cold War and are beginning to give way to a deeper, ongoing and probably more consequential discussion of values between the Old and New Worlds.

Robert Kagan in his book *Of Paradise and Power* theorized that Americans are from Mars and Europeans from Venus (2003, 3). Kagan's comparison might be somewhat facetious, but it is, nevertheless, fairly accurate when it comes to describing the 2002 debate between American and German intellectuals on a theory and practice of "just war", which is offered in this chapter as the first example of the clash of systems between the United States and Europe. This exchange of ideas is especially interesting for two reasons: First because, unlike protests against the Vietnam War in the sixties, it reflects the positions of the political classes and of the majority of the populations on both sides of the Atlantic. And second, because the transatlantic conflict over war and peace makes clear how difficult it is— independently of any specific cause such as the United States attack on Afghanistan—for the two sides to understand each other's starting positions, vocabulary and goals. Thus the premise of American intellectuals, seamlessly derived from their own history, that terms such as "freedom," "government" and "religion" represent "universal principles" (No Author, 2003), which have the same meaning to all people, was interpreted by Germans as a "hegemonic position" and a claim by the last remaining superpower "to decide the fate of peoples largely on its own authority" (No Author, 2003a). While David Blankenhorn, Francis Fukuyama, Samuel Huntington, David Patrick Moynihan and Michael Walzer, all of whom signed the American proclamation "What We're Fighting For," saw it as the mission of their government to stop "global evil" and defend "opportunities for a good life" (No Author, 2003), Germans Hans-Peter Dürr, Carl Amery, Christoph Hein and Peter Rühmkorf were suspicious of the division of the world into "good" and "evil" and pointed out that "globalization" creates "social inequality" and destroys "cultural differentiation" (No Author, 2003a). "War" (No Author, 2003) on one side stood in contrast to "conflict management" (No Author, 2003b) on the other, while the acceptance of "unintended civilian casualties" (No Author, 2003c) was countered with the "inviolability of human dignity" (No Author, 2003a). And while the Americans voiced concern that international terrorism not only was attacking the policies of the current administration but also showed contempt for "consumerism as a way of life" and the individual as "self-made and utterly sovereign" (No Author, 2003), the Germans made reference to international, "universally valid … law" as "one of the great cultural achievements of the twentieth century" and to the United Nations and the International Criminal Court as guarantors in the definition of "justice" and "universal moral criteria" (No Author, 2003b).

The transatlantic debate of intellectuals about "just war" has continued to reflect some of the themes and forms of traditional anti-Americanism on one side, and of "Europe bashing" on the other. However, a second pair of examples may illustrate that the conflict between the United States and Europe may indeed be moving onto yet another plane: the public statements by a group of Western European intellectuals led by Jürgen Habermas and Jacques Derrida on the theme of "the rebirth of Europe," which have been published in a number of European newspapers since May 2003, and, on the American side, the *National Security Strategy of the United States of America* formulated by the Bush administration in September 2002. In both instances, emphasis has been placed on defining the current positions of one's own side rather than on criticizing the principles or present policy of the opponent, a pattern which can be seen as well in recent works like Robert Kagan's 2003 volume *Of Paradise and Power*, Ernst-Otto Czempiel's *Weltpolitik im Umbruch* (2003), Gret Haller's *Die Grenzen der Solidarität* (2002), and, somewhat earlier, Werner Weidenfeld's work *America and Europe: Is the Break Inevitable?* (1996).

There is a clear advantage to this approach. Unproductive and emotional pro- or anti-American outbursts of the kind issued in Germany by Henryk Broder, Dan Diner, Richard Herzinger, Gustav Sichelschmidt, Rolf Winter and others, can be replaced by a relatively objective method that derives national idiosyncrasies, processes of political decision-making and cultural thought-patterns from the specific historical experience of a country or region. The disadvantage of such an approach is that the transatlantic community, which was scarcely questioned before 1990, could quickly be revealed as a marriage of convenience that has lost its meaning in the New World Order of the twenty-first century.

Habermas and his allies, for instance, do not hesitate to postulate a "European identity" based on "historical experiences, traditions and achievements" which "establishes for European citizens the sense of a political fate suffered in common and shaped by a collective effort." The "populations" of Europe must learn to expand their national identities to a "European dimension." "Government beyond the nation state" is one aspect of Europe today, as is defense of "measures promoting solidarity" and "security guarantees for the welfare state … to protect it from the depredations of market-based productivity." And Habermas and Derrida link the "desire for a multilateral international order under the rule of law" with the "hope for an effective worldwide domestic policy within the framework of a reformed United Nations" (Habermas, 2003).

Similarly, the Bush doctrine, composed after September 11, based in the American tradition, and modeled on the nineteenth-century theory of the sovereign nation state and thinking patterns from the period of the wars of religion before the 1648 Treaty of Westphalia, is oriented toward the future, although in other respects it differs completely from the European declaration. The victory of the "forces of freedom" over Soviet-style totalitarianism has left the world with only one "sustainable model for national success" (No Author, 2002, preamble), states the Bush administration document. Central to this model are "free trade" and "free markets" (Ibid., 17), which are the guarantors of "real freedom" and are "the best way to promote prosperity and reduce poverty" (Ibid., 17–18). "All nations and all societies can choose for themselves" whether or not to accept this model. Either way, the United States will use its "unparalleled military strength" (Ibid., preamble) not only to defend its own form of society but to "dissuade potential adversaries from pursuing a military build-up in hopes of surpassing, or equaling, the power of the United States" (Ibid., 30). To bring peace and free trade to the world—so states the Preamble to the National Security Strategy paper—the United States "will use this moment of opportunity to extend the benefits of freedom across the globe. We will actively work to bring the hope of democracy, development, free markets, and free trade to every corner of the world. The United States welcomes our responsibility to lead in this great mission" (Ibid., preamble).

In February 2003 the magazine *The Nation* carried a lead article on "How Europeans See America" and headlined it "USA Oui! Bush Non!" (Alterman, 2003). These sorts of simple distinctions are no longer adequate in the wake of the Cold War and September 11. Instead, indications are that in the future there needs to be reflection on both sides of the Atlantic about the fundamental differences between the United States and Europe, or, should this "Europe" not yet exist, between the United States and Germany, France, England, Italy and other countries. Such reflection would go beyond anti-Americanism, "Europe bashing" or criticism of the policies of this or that particular government by examining disparities between the Old and the New World over such basics as freedom and democracy, the relations between the state and the individual, the place of religion, the organization of society and the role of culture. It would be useful for both sides and for the rest of the world if this currently still rather unproductive clash of cultures or civilizations, which might well be here to stay, would develop into a healthy transatlantic competition from which *both* Americans and Europeans are capable of learning.

Or could such ideas represent a suppressed and particularly insidious variation of anti-Americanism? An article with the title "A Genealogy of Anti-Americanism" published in the most recent issue of the magazine *The Political Interest* (Ceaser, 2003) seems to hold this view: "Not only does anti-Americanism make rational discussion impossible ... it threatens the idea of a community of interests between Europe and America. Indeed, it threatens the idea of the West itself. According to the most developed views of anti-Americanism, there is no community of interests between the two sides of the Atlantic because America is a different and alien place."

Chapter 2

The German Perception of the United States Since September 11

Russell A. Berman

These attacks were a declaration of war, not only on the United States, but on everyone who dreams of a peaceful world without borders.
Uwe Knuepfer, *Editorial in* Westdeutsche Allgemeine Zeitung, *September 12, 2001*

The victims and their families deserve our help, support and solidarity ... but I do not want to be an American. I don't approve of pure capitalism, such as the one pursued by the United States. I favor the socially responsible variation.
Juergen Sabarz, *Letter to the Editor*, Westdeutsche Allgemeine Zeitung, *September 15, 2001*

When George W. Bush visited Berlin in May 2002, he was greeted by large, hostile demonstrations. The ongoing war in Afghanistan had been very unpopular in Germany, amplifying a diffuse anti-Americanism associated with various policy decisions: the United States rejection of the Kyoto Treaty, the opposition to the International Criminal Court, and other aspects of United States foreign policy, especially support for Israel. Yet when Bush visited several formerly Communist countries in Central and Eastern Europe during the subsequent fall, his visit elicited friendly, pro-American crowds, especially in Vilnius and Bucharest. It would be very difficult to argue that American policies had changed in the interim between the two visits in a way that could explain a shift in the foreign perception of the United States. On the contrary, what is clearly at stake is the phenomenon of how the United States is viewed differently in different countries. In other words, the perception of the United States is not, or not only a function of the "external" factor of the character of American policy. Rather, the perception of the United States in a particular country is very much framed by "internal" factors, sets of local circumstances, cultural legacies, and political habits. It is therefore quite plausible to surmise that the warm reception accorded Bush in the formerly Communist capitals reflected the local memories of the productive leadership role the United States had played in opposing Russian domination during the Cold War, leading up to the turning point of 1989. To be sure, there may well be many nuances in the individual Eastern European countries, despite the common denominator of viewing America through the lens of anti-Communism. In this chapter, however, the other side of the comparison is at stake: the internal factors that determine the German perception of the United States, especially the attitudes toward America since September 11.

Contemporary Events

There is one important dimension of the German situation that intrudes on current perceptions of the United States: the process of European unification. An aspiration to develop a unified continental political system has deep historical roots. In its current form, it commenced after the Second World War as a project for a common economic market in Western Europe. European institutions have gradually grown more political, i.e., not solely economic, and more regulatory. Some political prerogatives of national governments have been transferred to European institutions, including the maintenance of a currency: the Euro is now the coin of the realm through much of Europe, and monetary policy has ceased to be a national prerogative. In addition, Europe has expanded its membership considerably, largely due to the fall of the Iron Curtain and the ability to include central and eastern European states. Although the United States generally has supported the process of European unification, a subtle shift has taken place, particularly after 1989. While European unification once represented part of the bulwark that the West presented against Soviet expansionism, after the collapse of Russian hegemony, European unification began to define itself in relation to the United States, i.e., as an alternative to the United States in a multi-polar world. Anti-American sentiment has become the vehicle for the expression of this new European identity.

Meanwhile, for various reasons, the European Union suffers from a so-called democracy deficit: political powers have been shifted to a bureaucracy largely shielded from public scrutiny and electoral control. This bureaucratization of Europe means that the process of unification has little capacity to appeal to the ideals or loyalty of a pan-European citizenry; so far, individuals typically remain loyal to their respective nation states rather than to the abstract super-state. Germans, however, given their troubled national past, have been among the strongest supporters of the European unification process: becoming European is a way to be less German. The central lesson on which this unification process has been based involves the presumed urgency to overcome the egoism of individual nations and replace it with multilateral cooperation. This multilateralism ultimately entails a renunciation of elements of national sovereignty in the name of greater cooperation among nation states. While many of the continental European states are prepared to take this step, some are reluctant to do so (the United Kingdom), and in any case, the United States has shown little interest in subjecting itself to international governance structures. Hence the debate over multilateralism and unilateralism that erupted in the context of the Iraq War. This material often colors German views of the United States. As deep as the alliance has been between the United States and West Germany, the West German political cultural legacy for unified Germany involves a willingness to renounce aspects of national independence and an inability to understand why the United States might be less prepared to do so. In this case, it is not, strictly speaking, an "internal" factor that shapes the perception of the United States, but a regional process, the relationship of Europe, of which Germany is a key component, to the United States.

Representation of the United States in German Print Media

Several surveys of representations of the United States and of public opinion regarding foreign policy matters can help shed light on these matters. The study of

"World Attitudes Toward America After 9/11" provides data concerning the representation of the September 11 attacks and related issues during the autumn of 2001. To be sure, one should be cautious not to overstate the significance of this data. While it surveys several key organs of the German print media, both daily newspapers and weekly news magazines, it does not include electronic media, through which large sectors of the public receives its news information. Moreover, the data is not corrected for circulation size. Hits from newspapers with largely local or regional readership (e.g., *Augsburger Allgemeine, Südwest Presse*) are put on the same level as the large circulation *de facto* national newspapers (e.g., *Frankfurter Allgemeine, Süddeutsche Zeitung*) as they are with influential weekly publications (*Der Spiegel, Die Zeit*). To begin to presume to extrapolate from representations in the various press organs to public opinion in general, one would surely have to reflect on these various circulation profiles and their implications for readership influence. Germany has a variegated media environment, and it is not uncommon for readers to draw on combinations of these publications, at least in the educated strata. At the other end of the literacy spectrum, however, significant strata of the publication may only read mass distribution "boulevard press," such as *die Bildzeitung*.

Although the data collected cannot be directly mapped onto public opinion, it does at least present an initial rough cut of the representation of the United States under the impact of September 11, and as such it does provide some important insights into German political culture. A particularly dramatic result is displayed in the data collected regarding the issue 11: "How should America respond to the September 11 events?" The aggregate results display a profile polarized around diametrically opposed positions, with 23 per cent of the comments (or "hits," to use the project's terminology) attributed to the negative "Do not use military tactics or force. Do not declare a war against terrorism or those deemed responsible for it," while more than 37 per cent are counted for "Use military force or bombings against the governments, states, or groups that harbor or support those responsible for the 9/11 attacks. Make no compromises with these governments." The policy at stake, obviously, involved the pursuit of a war against terrorism in the form of the campaign against the Taliban regime of Afghanistan. German press representations appear, on first glance, to tilt considerably toward the pro-military and, in this historical context, pro-American option.

However, the ratio of 37:23 is to some extent an arbitrary result of the structure of the content analysis. If one takes into account the numerous other responses, none of which on its own gets above 8 per cent, and attributes them reasonably to the two camps, the overall polarization becomes even starker. Thus one can attribute proposals to alleviate poverty, change foreign policy, "pause and reflect soberly," and work with the United Nations, to the anti-military camp. Alternatively, calls to improve intelligence, gather credible evidence, work with the entire world, and attack (only) terrorist camps might be counted on the military side of the ledger (arguably, some of these items belong to the anti-military camp, but that would only amplify the results of this exercise). Making these assumptions, one finds a split of more than 45 per cent against the use of force, and almost 50 per cent supporting it.

This structural polarization is corroborated by an accompanying tendency. The data display an increased polarization in October, as measured against September. In other words, after the initial shock of 9/11 and as a public debate unfolded, positions tended to harden into two opposing camps. Thus (looking now only at the major categories and bracketing the smaller, peripheral ones), opposition to American use of military force rose from 18 per cent in September to 30 per cent in October, while support for military force grew from 26 per cent to nearly 50 per cent. In fact, support grows to 75 per cent in December, although this number is based on a much smaller number of hits and, in any case, the Afghanistan campaign had largely come to an end at this point. (It therefore made little sense to oppose the use of force any longer, so that a reasonable comparison with the data from previous months becomes difficult).

Thus the data from issue 11 alone suggests a complex representational process in the German print media. In the aftermath of September 11, it is clear that there was considerable support for the American use of force as a proper response, and not limited specifically to terrorist camps. Nonetheless, there is also evidence of considerable dispute and polarization. The treatment of the issue in the press appears to have been split nearly equally. Even in the context of the war against the Taliban—where the case for a connection to September 11 was always much stronger and clearer than later with regard to the highly contested war policy in Iraq—nearly half of the press treatment opposed the unlimited military solution. To be sure, there is evidence of a pro-American predisposition, and the anti-war opposition represented a (slight) minority of items in the content analyses. Still this minority indicated a considerable anti-war potential: precisely the potential that turned into the crowds at the anti-Bush demonstrations in the subsequent May and on which Chancellor Schröder made his electoral calculation a year later, when he chose to oppose the intervention in Iraq.

The results for other aspects of the content analysis add interesting detail to this hypothesis of a German press, prepared to tilt toward the United States in a post-September 11 solidarity effect but already displaying signs of reluctance or even resistance. Thus with regard to the question of how Germany should respond to September 11 (what the project termed "issue 12"), a clear majority of the hits (51 per cent) indicate support for working with the United States, even in military responses. There is, curiously perhaps, more support for Germany to cooperate with the United States, even in military steps, than there is for the United States to pursue such military steps. One can surmise that for the German public sphere, the need for identification with the United States appears to have been even stronger than a judgment on the particular political means (i.e., some of the reluctance to support military initiatives could be set aside in order to maintain a loyal relationship to the United States). This too could be taken to be indicative of the post-September 11 solidarity effect. If one counts calls for cooperation with the United States in restricted military responses (terrorist camps only) or non-military responses, then the hypothetically pro-American count comes close to 84 per cent. However, it is perhaps more reasonable to assume that these variants—restricted military and non-military responses—in the context of the German debate on the Afghan war in effect represented positions defined as oppositional to United States government policy. If one combines their counts (10 per cent and 8 per cent) with a marginal call for an independent German strategy (1 per cent) and other opposition to support for the United States in general (1 per cent) then one discovers a "rejectionist" field totaling a not at all insignificant 19 per cent. This, it would seem, clearly suggests that the notion of universal solidarity with the United States in the immediate aftermath of

September 11 is not tenable. From the very start, there was a non-trivial minority that staked out several positions in precise opposition to the policy pursued by the American government, i.e., the attack on the Taliban regime in Afghanistan. It is fair to speculate that if nearly one fifth of the German press representation of the issue in the context of the Afghanistan War (where the case was both clearest and most temporally closest to the September 11 attacks) implied an adversarial attitude toward the United States, then it was quite plausible to predict that a much greater hesitation would emerge regarding American-led military solutions in the less obvious case of Iraq.

Other aspects of German public culture are apparent in the data. Issue 13 ("Who carried out 9/11?") demonstrates the significance of moderate centrist views, with more than 87 per cent regarding Osama bin Laden or Islamic fundamentalists as the perpetrators. This is clear evidence of the reasonable, democratic character of German public life. Nonetheless, the fringe position that attributes the September 11 attacks to Israeli special forces is represented minimally, but equally on the left (*die Tageszeitung*) and the right (*Bildzeitung*). The convergence of left anti-Zionism and traditional right anti-Semitism is certainly not a solely German phenomenon, but it takes place closer to the center of public debate in Germany than it does elsewhere. While these two newspapers can be taken to represent the respective ends of the political spectrum under discussion, they are surely not in any sense part of extremist subcultures.

Issue 15 ("root causes of September 11") attributes 12 per cent to religious fanaticism and 18 per cent to Islamic fundamentalism, making a total of more than 30 per cent. Moreover, this interpretation increases from September to October, presumably an effect of the case against the Taliban being made with increasing clarity. Nonetheless, in September nearly 30 per cent of the hits account for the September 11 attacks with reference to United States policies—be it a matter of support for Israel or the earlier support for the mojahedins against the Soviets in Afghanistan. In other words, the significant support for the United States in the German public sphere is again accompanied by varying degrees of reluctance, rejection, or opposition, even immediately after 9/11. Despite the 58 per cent describing September 11 as "an attack against freedom, democracy, humanity, or the civilized world" (issue 16), there is remarkable balance between assertions of a conflict of civilizations (10 per cent) and denials of the civilization conflict paradigm (11 per cent). Underneath a presumably pro-American consensus, there is evidence of an unstable and unsettled public opinion. In the same vein, one can contrast the strong 61 per cent that attributes the United States motivation to a goal of stopping terrorism (rather than some less than ideal ulterior motive) with four out of ten people who provide a negative assessment of the American war in Afghanistan, describing United States humanitarian aid as "useless, hypocritical or insincere." In sum, the German press accounts of America in the context of September 11 reflect both a predisposition to support the American initiative in the war against terrorism, while also giving evidence of considerable hesitation just below the surface.

The final pertinent data from this study, issue 19, involves descriptions of the United States. Initially the results seem unexciting: the only term that gets a significant percentage of hits is the obvious designation of the United States as "the only superpower" at 20 per cent. Nearly all other terms get quite low ratings.

Nonetheless, explicitly negative characterizations do total to 13 per cent, hardly insignificant. These terms include designations such as indifferent, stupid, exploitable, naïve, money-hungry, "capitalism in a negative sense," warlike, and terrorists. This item too corroborates the overall profile presented by the content analysis data. The hypothesis of universal solidarity with the United States in the months immediately following the September 11 attack is not borne out by the evidence. While press representations of the United States in this period are largely positive or pro-American, there are indications of instability in the structure of public opinion and, depending on the particular question, considerable hostility as well. This negative potential, recorded here in the contents of the print media, would come to play a larger role during the following eighteen months, as the German political leadership positioned itself against the United States, and the United States proceeded from pursuing the war on terrorism in Afghanistan to the less obvious and more consequential case of regime change in Iraq.

2002 Public Opinion

The textured account of the German press representations of the United States in the fall of 2001 is corroborated in various ways by the results of the public opinion survey sponsored by the Chicago Council of Foreign Affairs and the German Marshal Fund in June of 2002 (*Worldviews 2002: Comparing American and European Public Opinion on Foreign Policy*, Chicago Council on Foreign Relations). A pro-American predisposition and sets of shared values coexist with hesitation, opposition, and elements of anti-Americanism.

It is certainly true that with regard to many issues, the public opinions in Germany and the United States are very similar. This is hardly surprising: both countries are advanced industrial societies with stable democratic regimes, similarities which only amplify long histories of cultural interaction, from extensive German emigration to the United States in the nineteenth century to the American occupation experience in West Germany after the Second World War. Despite the hostile war experiences themselves, extensive exchange and positive interaction has also characterized the German-American relationship. Indeed in the early 1990s it seemed that Germany might even become the primary anchor of the trans-Atlantic relationship, possibly even displacing the "special relationship" between the United States and the United Kingdom. The precipitous deterioration of U.S.-German relations since September 11 is all the more remarkable against the background of exceptionally strong German-American relations not that long ago.

The proof of shared values in Germany and the United States—like the evidence of extensive support for the United States in the German press after 9/11—is quite pronounced. Expanded spending on education is supported by 73 per cent of Germans and 75 per cent of Americans. Similarly, 67 per cent of Germans support greater programs to combat violence and crime, as compared to 70 per cent of Americans. In both cases, the differences are negligible; it would appear that public values are quite similar in the two countries. There is also considerable overlap in the estimation of world problems. Fifty-five per cent of Germans see Islamic fundamentalism as a possible threat to their vital national interests, as compared to

61 per cent of Americans. Forty-seven per cent of Germans view global warming as extremely important, effectively identical with 46 per cent of Americans.

This sort of evidence can be cited to show the ongoing vitality of a community of values, the shared perspectives in Germany and the United States, which then could be taken as demonstration of the fundamental solidity of the relationship between the two countries. Yet this sort of reassuring conclusion would not only be ignoring the real character of German-United States relations between September 11 and the Iraq War, it would also ignore the public opinion data that demonstrates the basis for the tensions. As will be seen in a moment, there are plenty of policy points where Germans and Americans do not at all see eye to eye. In other words, the conflict between Germany and the United States cannot be attributed only to diplomatic failures or deleterious personal interactions between the respective political leaders. Rather the *Worldview 2002* survey, examined closely, yields evidence of anti-American potential in German public opinion, which in fact was foreshadowed in the content analysis of the German print media after September 11.

A crucial issue involves attitudes toward future defense spending. In both Germany and the United States 38 per cent of those surveyed believe that defense spending should not change, but that is as far as the similarity goes on this point. Otherwise the data are diametrically opposed. In the United States, 44 per cent support expanded defense spending, while 15 per cent call for cutbacks; in Germany, 45 per cent urge cutbacks, while only 14 per cent argue for expanding the defense budget. The distinctiveness of the German position can be better understood if it is compared to the aggregate European result as well as those of particular other European countries. For Europe in general, there is 22 per cent support for expanded defense spending and 33 per cent support for less, i.e., German public opinion is not only less supportive of defense spending than are Americans, but it is less supportive of defense spending than Europe as a whole. Only the Netherlands (6 per cent) and Italy (12 per cent) have lower rates for supporting increased defense spending.

The pronounced anti-military sentiment in Germany is an effect of German national history, the defeats in two world wars, and the extraordinary devastation—both physical and moral—in the wake of the Second World War and, perhaps less admirably, the habit acquired during the Cold War of relying ultimately on American military protection. That national history structures public opinion on this point is confirmed by the results of other European countries. The German data for expanding and cutting back defense spending 14:45 are closest to the Italian results of 12:52. (The results for the Netherlands are anomalous because of a curiously high rate for making no change and keeping defense spending at the same level.) In contrast, the two American allies in the world wars display slight majorities for increased spending: in the United Kingdom 24 per cent for expanded spending and 21 per cent for cutbacks, as compared to France with 28 per cent for expansion and 23 per cent for reduction. The results for Poland are particularly noteworthy with percentages nearly identical with the results for the United States: 45 per cent for expanded spending and 14 per cent for cutting back (indeed, if only by a 1 per cent difference, Poland supports increased defense spending more adamantly than does the American public opinion). It is worthwhile to note that these results predate the "old Europe vs. new Europe" controversy, but they lend considerable credence to the hypothesis. The German public views defense spending in the light of a catastrophic militaristic history; Polish public opinion addressed the question in light of a long history of threatened independence and recognition of a need to be able to defend its territorial integrity and sovereignty.

When asked to comment on whether the United States should exert strong leadership in world affairs, the aggregate results for Europe show 31 per cent viewing such an outcome as undesirable (22 per cent as somewhat undesirable and 9 per cent as very undesirable). The German total is 27 per cent, i.e., a somewhat less negative view of American leadership than in Europe as a whole, although considerably above the American response at 14 per cent. The combined negative results for France total 48 per cent. With regard to hostility to American leadership in world affairs, there is therefore a significant anti-American minority in Germany, but it is less significant in scope than in Europe as a whole and considerably smaller than in France.

German attitudes to the United States, however, are not only a function of direct estimations of United States policy, past or future. They are also consequences of how Germans evaluate the European Union and their own role in world affairs. Question 7 of the *Worldview 2002* survey asks whether it is desirable for the European Union to exert strong leadership. Twenty-seven per cent of Germans saw a leadership role for the EU as very desirable. Interestingly this is the lowest rate for any European country (except Poland, at 16 per cent, which, at that point in time, was not in the EU). Even in the United States, more Americans saw a leadership role for the EU (31 per cent) as desirable than did Germans. The results were 32 per cent in the United Kingdom, 40 per cent in France, 42 per cent in the Netherlands, and 53 per cent in Italy. The Germans appear to be the least supportive of EU leadership. Yet Question 9, asking whether one's own country should play an active role in world affairs, again found Germans least willing to be engaged. While it is true that a considerable majority of 65 per cent estimated that Germany should be active in world matters, that is a rate far below the aggregate European results of 78 per cent and positively overshadowed by 82 per cent in the United Kingdom, 86 per cent in France, and even 90 per cent in Italy. In both cases, the German results indicate a greater hesitation, either on the European or national level, to take on prominent responsibilities in world affairs. It is plausible to argue that, as with the case of defense spending, it is the German national past that restrains the German public from envisioning an aspiration for a leadership role in international matters.

This result is confirmed by another German anomaly. Sixty-five per cent of Europeans support the notion that the EU should become a superpower like the United States. In Italy the rate soars to 76 per cent and in France to 91 per cent. The result for Germany is a humble 48 per cent, the only European country with results below 50 per cent. As in the above examples, Germans display a predisposition to avoid prominence in world affairs. Yet among those Europeans who do support superpower status for the EU, there is considerable variation in their vision for the future relationship with the United States. While most respondents in all countries favor cooperation with the United States over competition, the results for Germany indicate a significantly more competitive, and therefore less cooperative relationship with the United States than is expressed by the public elsewhere in Europe. Eleven per cent of Europeans favor a competitive relationship with the United States: the figure for Germany is 22 per cent, as compared to France at 9 per cent, United Kingdom at 7 per cent, and Italy at 5 per cent. Meanwhile cooperation is favored by 84 per cent of Europeans in general, 87 per cent of the French, 89 per cent of the

British, 92 per cent of the Italians, but only 70 per cent of the Germans. Clearly, even in Germany, proponents of cooperation are much greater than the advocates of competition. Nonetheless, Germany tilts toward a more aggressive posture with regard to the United States in a way that distinguishes it considerably from its European neighbors. This result confirms the observation in the print media content analyses of a significant minority predisposition toward anti-American positions.

Still, these data yield a seemingly paradoxical result: a German public opinion that, in response to several questions, displayed a greater hesitation toward world affairs than was characteristic of other European nations, yet at the same time evidence of a possibly greater adversarial stance toward the United States than elsewhere in Europe. Both attitudes can, of course, be explained with regard to the "internal" factors of German national history: the scars of earlier German international ambitions, on one hand, and, on the other, certain resentments against the United States. This profile does in fact map onto the cultural-historical model of a romantic "German interiority": an inward-turning rejection of the world, coupled with an imperious external projection. As tempting as the thesis might be, however, the data at hand are insufficient to prove it. The two positions at stake—international hesitation and competition with the United States—are not conclusively linked, i.e., the results may well derive from separate sectors of the public. One might conjecture, for example, that the greater reluctance to engage in international matters, reflecting the German past, might be associated with older generations, while the adversarial relationship to the United States might plausibly derive from the ideological background of the populations in the "new states," i.e. the formerly Communist East Germany. More differentiated data would be needed to explore these hypotheses.

Views of a Changing World

While a specific "German interiority" hypothesis is not conclusively supported by the data, nothing disproves it. Greater demographic differentiation of the data would be helpful, for example in order to distinguish among the attitudes of various population sectors. Nonetheless certain conclusions are possible. The content analysis identified a preponderance of pro-American descriptors in the immediate aftermath of September 11; part of that support may represent a "September 11 solidarity effect," but surely some is indicative of older pro-American sympathies in parts of the German public. Yet any solidarity effect related to the September 11 attacks was, we have seen, clearly not universal. Therefore it appears that the later deterioration of German-American relations cannot be attributed to some failure to make the American case in the German press. On the contrary, that case was being made from September on. The point is rather that support for the United States was not universal. Other political positions were also present in the public debate and this debate reflected deeper fissures in German attitudes regarding world affairs. In other words, internal factors—German history, cultural values, and the structure of public debate —have evidently played crucial roles in formulating German attitudes toward the United States, including anti-American sentiments.

The Pew Global Attitudes Project survey, *Views of a Changing World, June 2003*, provides insights that allow us to trace the problem of Germany and the United States out another year. The image of the United States throughout Europe dipped in the course of the Afghan and Iraqi wars, but by June of 2003 it rebounded, although not to the levels of 1999/2000. Nowhere has this trajectory been as precipitous as in Germany: from a 78 per cent favorable image of the United States in 1999/2000 to 61 per cent in the summer of 2002 (Schröder election campaign) to 25 per cent in March of 2003 (Iraq War), and then to 45 per cent in June. The difference between the extensive support for the United States at the outset to the current 45 per cent—in other words, less than half of Germans have a positive image of the United States— is a measure of the decline in German-American relations. This data also sheds interesting light on the question of the internal/external formulation of attitudes toward the United States. The fact that similarly curved trajectories are observable in other European countries indicates that any adequate explanation cannot be restricted to endogenous German circumstances alone, i.e., external factors are clearly at stake: the character of United States' policy and the European (rather than merely German) perspective. Yet the fact that the German curve is so extreme is a result of internal, German cultural factors: the pro-American legacy of Cold-War era relations, on one hand, and, on the other, the devastating judgment on the American wars as viewed through the historically over-determined German pacifism. The positive approval rate for the United States in Germany has dropped by a remarkable 33 percentage points, more than anywhere else. (The rate in France has gone from 62 per cent to 43 per cent, a loss of only 19 points; in Italy from 76 per cent to 60 per cent, a loss of 16 points; and in Russia from 37 per cent to 36 per cent, a loss of only 1 point.) (*Views of a Changing World*, June 2003, 19.)

It is not unreasonable to assume that estimations of another country will be based partially on perceptions of value systems: shared values may support a positive estimation, while conflicting values may lead to negative judgments. In this case, it is worthwhile to differentiate among various constellations: German congruence with American values, because of a shared "western" paradigm; differences between America and Europe, including Germany; differences within Europe, and so forth. The Pew Study provides examples of some of the possible permutations. Evaluating the statement "Most people are better in a free market economy, even though some people are rich and some are poor," 72 per cent of Americans said they would completely agree or mostly agree. The result for Germany is 69 per cent, although in West Germany the result is identical with the United States, at 72 per cent. Results in other Western European countries vary minimally: United Kingdom 66 per cent; France 61 per cent; Italy 71 per cent. Interestingly the free market finds considerably less approval in Eastern Europe: Poland at 44 per cent; Russia at 45 per cent; and Bulgaria at 31 per cent. (The most westernized part of the East, the Czech Republic, shows 62 per cent support for the free market, higher than in France.) In general, then, Western Europe appears closer to the United States on the question of the free market than does Eastern Europe, and Germany is the country most like the United States (Ibid., T-6).

Yet when the statement is changed to one regarding individual freedom and the force of social conditions, the results change significantly. Evaluating the statement, "Success in life is pretty much determined by forces outside our control," 32 per cent of Americans completely or mostly agreed. The German result is quite different, with 68 per cent asserting the power of uncontrollable social forces, i.e., the opposite of individual initiative. This result is at the high end of comparable Western European results: United Kingdom at 58 per cent; France at 54 per cent; and Italy at 66 per cent. Several of the Eastern European results are surprisingly lower than those from Western Europe, i.e., closer to the American data, although still much higher: Bulgaria at 52 per cent; Czech Republic at 47 per cent; Slovak Republic at 49 per cent; but Poland at 63 per cent (higher than many Western Europeans but still lower than Germany). To the extent that, in the aggregate, the East European results are closer to the American, one finds a corroboration of an aspect of the "new Europe" thesis: the formerly Communist countries discovering an affinity with the United States that divides them, even in terms of values orientation, from parts of Western Europe (Ibid., T-7). In any case, Germany is least like the United States on this point: where Americans trust individual initiative, Germans look to the power of larger social forces.

One final variant of the same subject matter shuffles the deck again. Asked to choose between two desiderata, 58 per cent of Americans chose to be "free to pursue goals without interference from the state" as opposed to 34 per cent for a "state guarantee that nobody is in need." No other advanced industrial country displays as stark a profile. Comparing only the "state guarantee," which received 34 per cent in the United States, the United Kingdom measures 62 per cent, France 62 per cent, Italy 71 per cent and Germany 57 per cent (Ibid., T-42). In fact, if one were to look only at West Germany (in other words, excluding the post-Communist effect from East Germany), the result would be lower at 52 per cent. Interestingly the Germans are in a liminal position: very much within the European range on this question, but at the American end of the spectrum. Arguably the severity of the decline of the positive American image in Germany is a result of this particular values structure: Germans are, in some ways, most like the United States, at least within the Western European group, and therefore they are most susceptible to identification but also to disappointment. While they are the Europeans closest to the American apprehension regarding an intrusive state, they are also furthest from Americans in their deterministic estimation of the power of social conditions over individual initiative. Skepticism with regard to a strong state (presumably a legacy of the Nazi experience) coexists, counter-intuitively, with less of an individualistic ethos. The combination suggests an orientation toward conservative stability, implying potential discomfort with the dynamic changes sometimes associated with the United States and American society.

Conclusion

The various data suggest the complexity of the German perception of the United States, a result of a long and intricate history. As soon as one concedes that different nations may respond to the United States differently, one has to recognize the role of local cultures and therefore internal factors. It is hardly surprising that fragments of the long German-American history resurface to shape the cultural context within which contemporary American policy and actions are judged.

The complexity of German-American relations explains the fragmented results in the print media data survey: strong opinions of support for and opposition to United

States initiatives. This bipolarity explains a curious aspect of the debate around German attitudes to the United States: assertions of anti-Americanism typically elicit denials and demonstrations of extensive appreciation for the United States. The distinctiveness of the German case is that anti-Americanism and philo-Americanism may well exist side by side. As much as Germany as a whole shares many American values, it can also nurture the anti-western and anti-American subculture where the September 11 conspiracy germinated.

* * *

Editorial Remarks

The collapse of the Soviet Union in 1991 meant the emergence of the United States as the sole superpower. Such a global ascendance of America did not happen overnight. Being particularly apparent after the end of the Cold War, the trend was underway long before the 1990s. Therefore, in Germany, perceptions of the United States and its new changing role have been in the making for some time. These perceptions, of course, were impacted by the significance of the events in 2001. On the other hand, the views of America had deep roots in recent history. Several arguments comprise the contemporary view of the United States in Germany.

First, Germans tend to believe that the single superpower cannot, ultimately, avoid global responsibilities; however, such responsibilities should be pursued without the consent of other countries, especially those, such as Germany, with the economic and political potential to accept at least part of such responsibilities. Having taken heavy losses in the wars of the twentieth century and fallen victim to authoritarianism, Germany became a country in which many citizens believe in the moral responsibility of pursuing restraint and non-aggression in international affairs. Moreover, while attempting to build the post-nation-state foreign policy of the European Union, German politicians have to face an exclusive "national" foreign policy conducted by Washington. The paradox of the situation is that Germany, an economic giant of the European Union, has very little to say in the international field, where most decisions are made, apparently, by the United States.

The second argument refers to the psychology of cross-cultural perception. At least two kinds of arguments are apparent here. For many Germans, and most of them grew up in the modern welfare state, the United States is associated with a "wild" capitalism where everybody is against everybody, people lack social protection, and rely exclusively on individualism—"the law of the jungle." Associated with this view is the image of American consumerism: the Americans care for nothing else but profit. This image then easily contrasts with the humane German capitalism, and the "cultured" German nation that has cultivated its cultural heritage for centuries. The other type of argument stems from the communist ideology, a system of beliefs formed and maintained by many Germans who retain sympathy toward socialism— most of these individuals grew up in the East. For pure ideological reasons, American capitalism is viewed as inhumane and the United States is considered an ultimate adversary of the working people of the world, as it was during the Cold War.

The third argument is associated with the events of September 11. The attacks on the World Trade Center and the Pentagon were commonly understood as retaliation for specific United States policies abroad. From the point of view of many Germans, to prevent further terrorist attacks, the United States should change its image abroad by changing its ways of conducting foreign policy, especially in the Middle East. It should be emphasized that the vast majority of Germans did not attempt to legitimize terrorism by drawing a moral equivalent between United States policies and terrorism.

Suggested Additional Literature

Alterman, Eric (2003). USA Oui! Bush Non! How Europeans See America. *The Nation* 10, February.

Diner, Dan (1996). *America in the Eyes of the Germans: An Essay on Anti-Americanism.* Princeton: Markus Wiener Publishers.

Ermarth, Michael (2003). Counter-Americanism and Critical Currents in West German Reconstruction 1945–1960: The German Lesson Confronts the American Way of Life. In Stephan, 2004.

Johnston, Karin (2003). German Public Opinion and the Crisis in Bosnia. In R. Sobel and E. Shiraev (eds.). *International Public Opinion and the Bosnia Crisis.* Lanham/NY: Lexington.

Kagan, Robert (2003). *Of Paradise and Power: America and Europe in the New World Order.* New York: Knopf.

Stephan, Alexander (ed.) (2004). *Americanization and Anti-Americanism. The German Encounter With American Culture After 1945.* New York: Berghahn Books.

CASE 2
RUSSIA

It was an early September 11th evening in Moscow when the breaking news about the terrorist attacks in the United States began to reach the Russian people in their homes and cars. First there were sketchy radio and Internet reports coupled with CNN live coverage. Later in the evening, however, most major radio and television stations canceled their regularly scheduled broadcasts to cover the news about the events in America. Almost immediately, the terrorist acts activated a wide range of responses. Serious evaluations appeared next to hastily made emotional assessments. Shock and genuine sadness expressed in many comments were accompanied by critical suggestions about what America could have or should have done to prevent the terrorist acts. Facing only limited censorship, the responses came from different corners of Russia's political rink. Some of these reactions were in line with the Kremlin's statements and policies. Others echoed the attitudes of the "old school," which formed during the Cold War and continues to treat the West and the United States with resentment. Yet other reactions reflected a more dynamic, contradictory, and at times confused range of attitudes driven by local political interests, inspired by new ideological doctrines and at the same time, rooted in pragmatic calculations and rational assessments of international events.

Chapter 3

Russia's Views of America in a Historic Perspective

Eric Shiraev

The American leadership, official and private consultants, has been deeply involved in implementing the Russian economic reforms. They arrogantly assumed a large part of the responsibility for the radical transformations of the thousand-years-old way of life of a giant country. This preordained that the failures and excesses of the reforms would be perceived in Russia as linked to the American participation, and this would inevitably reflect itself upon foreign relations with the United States.
Alexei Arbatov (1992), member of the liberal "Yabloko" Party and former Head of the
Defense Committee of the Duma

A Long-term Context

Since the beginning of the eighteenth century, Russia faced a dilemma: which way to go? Two paths of development were, as a fork in the road, associated with two different outcomes or possibilities. One path led toward a predominantly traditionalist and authoritarian provincial country, isolated from the outside world, feared and mistrusted by its neighbors. The other led toward equal membership in the European community as well as openness to innovations and the ever-superior Western social and political system and its lifestyle. Facing this dilemma, all Russian leaders and scores of thinkers, both affiliated with the rulers and opposed to them, confronted the predicament of overcoming the country's economic and social backwardness without losing its political independence and rich cultural heritage. In fact, this was a foundation for the chronically ambivalent attitude toward western countries and America in particular as more advanced and "civilized" than Russia. Such ambivalent views are the most persistent features of the Russian elite's mentality reflected in the everyday opinions of most ordinary Russians. This frame of mind existed throughout many years of pre-Soviet, Soviet, and the most recent Russian history. Today, as well as in the 1980s or a hundred years ago, suspiciousness and resistance to anything western is amazingly combined with the attraction to and acceptance of its customs, values, symbols, and the general way of life (Shlapentokh, 1988; Shiraev and Zubok, 2001).

When Russians discuss government, culture, technologies, or societal progress, they seldom compare themselves to their eastern or southern neighbors. Russians have always been keen to measure themselves against the West. Despite its ambiguous geographic location, people of Russia in recent history persistently considered nations located westward as somewhat closer to them culturally than the kingdoms, caliphates, emirates, and empires to the east and south. This mindset is also rooted in the tradition of singling out one western country at a time in history to be either a paragon for acceptance and imitation or a model for blatant rejection. Historically, the "positive" roles were assigned to countries such as the Netherlands, France, Prussia, and England. Germany was a "villain" during both world wars in the past century. By the second half of the twentieth century, the United States had become such a country, to which most Russians compare themselves and the rest of the world.

Since the 1940s, during the communist years, attitudes about the United States were based on the fortified pillars of a totalitarian ideology, generally limited by the lack of access of the Soviet people to the West. Studying in schools and reading government-controlled newspapers, the Soviet people were given information about some achievements of western democracies in economy and technology. At the same time, the main message conveyed to the people about the United States and the West was that their material success was superficial. The capitalist economic system and liberal democracy, according to the official Soviet ideology, were doomed to fail because they had been based on the false beliefs in a free market (Vasiliev, 1955). The notorious remark, "We will bury you," made by the Soviet premier Nikita Khrushchev was not necessarily a reflection of the deadly intentions of the Kremlin but rather an ideological belief in the inevitable collapse of capitalism. The official point of view in Moscow was that the U.S. and its allies were warmongers. In the Soviet media, the government's statements, and in high school textbooks, U.S. foreign policies were commonly called "imperialist," "colonialist," "Zionist," and "anti-people." In the ideological rhetoric, the distinction was often made, however, between ordinary Americans—especially those who represented the working class—and the elite, including the corrupt politicians, greedy leaders of the military-industrial complex, and the die-hard ideological "hawks" (Kukharkin, 1974).

However, despite the systematic institutional effort to develop anti-Western and anti-American attitudes in the Soviet people, especially in the younger generations, the outcome was ambiguous. Although the majority of the Soviet people by the late 1970s-early 1980s maintained negative or non-supportive attitudes about U.S. foreign policies, few people then believed that the capitalist social system and economy were doomed to fail, and even fewer people rejected the western lifestyle and ideals of material success (Shlapentokh, 1986; Shiraev and Bastrykin, 1988). There are no accurate numbers describing these attitudes because public opinion polls were not permitted to administer surveys without the direct control and censorship of the authorities. Overall, we can offer the rule of the thirds: about one third of the Soviet people generally accepted the anti-American attitudes prescribed by the government; about one third rejected most of the critical information conveyed via the media about the United States; and the remaining third had a mixed opinion (Shlapentokh, 1988).

Perestroika and its Impact on Russia's Views of America

The coming of Mikhail Gorbachev to power in 1985 had indicated a major shift in Soviet domestic and foreign policies. Gorbachev needed a reform to provide all the necessary conditions for the successful restructuring of the failing socialism. Official ideological perceptions of the West have also been changing. Overall, the reforms of the late 1980s affected the Soviet people's attitudes in at least three ways.

First, most people who carried suspiciousness and mistrust toward the United States and the West strengthened their attitudes, regarding the "pro-Western" policies of Gorbachev as treason and the main cause of the failure of his reforms. On the other hand, people who already maintained pro-Western views saw the reforms as a confirmation of their beliefs about the necessity of political reforms in the Soviet Union and cooperation with the West (Shiraev and Zubok, 2001). Second, a significant number of people with mixed views about the West, facing an inevitable collapse of an inefficient regime, had chosen to side with the "pro-Western" views considering them as the only alternative to ideology-driven, pro-communist, and anti-Western beliefs of their opponents who wanted to keep socialism. Third, most of the pro-Western attitudes, the expression of which had been virtually prohibited before 1985, were easily conveyed during the period of Gorbachev's reforms via a growing number of independent media sources, especially newspapers. At the same time, anti-American views in the late 1980s-early 1990s were virtually shut down and their distribution was limited to a few significantly weakened media outlets. Overall, in the struggle among the advocates of the emerging post-communist ideologies, the United States was becoming an important political and cultural symbol: having either a negative or a positive attitude about America was an essential part of an individual's ideological orientation and cultural identity. For most representatives of Russia's new middle class, the free-market and prosperous America became the natural antipode of the inefficient, bureaucratic, and backward Soviet Union (Glad and Shiraev, 1999).

Despite their apparent decline, anti-Western attitudes of the late 1980s were still supported by millions of communists and their sympathizers. Moreover, these attitudes were gaining strength from new and increasingly diverse sources. Some of the advocates of the Cold-War ideology, who sought an evolution of the old regime, promoted the development of a kind of Russian National-Socialism, a version of "Stalinism without Stalin" (Shlapentokh, 1988, 162). A small minority followed the example of Alexander Solzhenitsyn, the famous writer who passionately advocated two national models of development. The first was to be in total opposition to the old Soviet regime. The second was the rejection of Western and particularly American civilization on historical, philosophical, religious, and moral grounds (Solzhenitsyn, 1998). Another, similar and vital movement embraced the nationalist idea of Russia's historic Eurasian mission to become a moral and economic leader of the world independent from the decadent and imperialistic West (Dugin, 1998).

Since December 25, 1991, after the failure of Gorbachev's reforms, the Yeltsin administration continued a pro-American course. It began to act openly and exuberantly on its pro-Western beliefs. During Yeltsin's appearance at the U.S. Congress in June 1992, he gave credit to the United States and praised it for helping Russia slay the dragon of Communism (Ryurikov, 1999). Overall, the pro-Americanism of Yeltsin's supporters was based on specific material reasons. They expected that a massive program of economic assistance, similar to the Marshall Plan, would be provided to a new democratic Russia (Arbatov, 1992).

Attitudes and their Sources in the 1990s

The development of attitudes about the United States among Russians during the decade prior to September 11 was mostly a reflection of the domestic events, as well as a reaction to a range of international developments. On the domestic front, pro- and anti-American attitudes reflected the internal political struggle and ideological and political debates about the future of the country and the role that Russia should play in international affairs.

The economic difficulties that Russians encountered in the 1990s reduced people's trust in western free-market models. Social disenchantment with the course of the reforms grew in 1992 during a severe economic crisis. Serious mistakes were committed in the implementation of market capitalism. The legal reform was slow. Corruption and crime were rampant. The severity of Russia's domestic political turmoil was highlighted in several instances, including the constitutional crisis of 1992–93, Yeltsin's use of military force to disband the Supreme Soviet in September–October 1993, opposition victories in the legislative elections of 1993 and 1995, and the war in Chechnya, which officially began in December 1994 but had actually started months prior. The expected massive influx of American and western assistance never materialized. There was no Marshall plan prepared for Russia. The country's leadership realized that Russia needed to solve its problems using its own, already drained resources. Instead of achieving instantaneous prosperity, the Russian economy took a deep and painful dive again in 1998 thus shattering the beliefs in the self-regulating power of the free market.

One of the psychological consequences of the economic difficulties was the sustained growth of an anti-Western mood. America in particular—with its perceived attitude of indifference toward Russia's troubles, seemingly arrogant advisers, and unattainable wealth—became a convenient source of frustration. In the minds of many Russians, America was a prosperous country that was able to provide to its citizens a standard of living that was impossible to achieve in Russia. America was seen as a rich neighbor who does not care much about the others who fell to their knees.

A substantial portion of the Russian population—almost a quarter of adults, according to the polls—remained largely impervious to pro-Western and pro-market messages. They were critical of western policies, indifferent to western fashion, and disinterested in pursuing wealth of the "Western" type. They believed that the West was responsible for the collapse of the Soviet Union—the dissolution of which was commonly mourned by a majority of people, according to national surveys. Many (up to one third of respondents) believed that the United States was still an enemy desiring to deprive Russia of its hard-won gains. These individuals continued to respond favorably to the themes—promoted unflaggingly by many politicians and the media—that endorsed xenophobic isolationism and the "Russian" way of life and thinking (Grushin, 1994).

For millions of Russians, the fall of the Soviet Union and the sudden emergence of an independent Russia created an immeasurable psychological gap between past and present. Not long ago, they used to be citizens of a gigantic multi-national superpower. It was respected and feared around the world. Suddenly, by the early 1990s, Russia had effectively lost its great-power status. Economically, militarily, and diplomatically, Russia could no longer make a difference on the international playing field. History gives examples of how national humiliation coupled with devastating domestic collapse sparks explosions of xenophobia and fascism. Indeed, the rise of Russian chauvinism and nationalism became apparent after the collapse of the Soviet Union.

Two specific groups became carriers of the great-power ideas. The first was represented by several, mostly disjointed, radical nationalist formations. The new Russian "right" represented a sophisticated blend of ideas about Russian exceptionality, the country's special Eurasian status, and the exclusive way that Russia should be followed as the "chosen" country. The main principles of western capitalism were declared genuinely foreign to the Russian people, who were "destined" to be more spiritual, collectivist, and educated than the average ignorant, egocentric, and narrow-minded European or American (Kurginian, 1992; Dugin, 1998). The second group was the Russian Communists, who in the 1990s were relatively organized and unified. Despite their many ideological differences, nationalists and Communists were among the main carriers of anti-Western and anti-American attitudes shared by approximately 30–40 per cent of Russians (Wyman, 1997; Shiraev, 1999).

The pro-Western course chosen by Yeltsin in the early 1990s evoked criticism from the growing domestic political opposition. Anti-Americanism and anti-Western attitudes were used as a political card to achieve specific goals at home. On more than several occasions, Russian policy toward the West fell hostage to domestic political considerations including national elections (Shiraev and Terrio, 2003). During the 1990s, the left-wing and nationalist opposition, and later even the mainstream press constantly blamed the West for attempts to keep Russia away from economic competition, America's refusal to give Russia the status of a most favored nation, and, as already mentioned, provide any significant financial help.

Overall, support for pro-western and pro-American policies waned during the 1990s. A key turning point was reached in December 1995, when elections to the State Duma resulted in a large majority of seats going to opponents to "soft" foreign policies, including Russia's allegedly pro-American policies. Bowing to pressure from opposition legislators, Yeltsin finally removed the Foreign Minister Kozyrev, known for his pro-western views, a move cheered by the opposition. Kozyrev's fall signaled a new age in Russian foreign policy, which began to be shaped primarily by elite power struggles and the search for a new Russia's post-Cold War identity, which involved a turn away from a "pro-American" foreign-policy period of the early 1990s.

Several international developments of the 1990s and early 2000s have contributed to anti-American feelings among people representing different layers of Russia's public opinion. In particular, NATO's westward expansion in the 1990s was seen as an anti-Russian demonstration of power, and total disrespect for Russia's strategic interests and security concerns. The United States was viewed as a major coordinator of the expansion and accused of deliberate attempts to undermine the strategic balance that occurred in Europe after the collapse of the Berlin Wall. Next, NATO's military intervention in Bosnia in the mid-1990s was perceived by many, including the Russian government, not as an attempt to resolve one of the bloodiest civil wars in contemporary European history, but rather an attempt by Americans and their

European puppets to punish Serbia for its role in the war and establish American control over the Balkans (Sobel and Shiraev, 2003).

Another event had a particularly strong impact on the Russian people's attitudes toward the West and the United States. It was the U.S.-led NATO military campaign against Serbia in 1999. As in the case of the war in Bosnia in the early 1990s, Russians were especially irritated by the actions of Washington and London against a sovereign country. The United States and NATO were called aggressors and a threat to Russia. At that time, anti-Western sentiment crossed party lines. Even cautious moderates began to issue warnings against the dangers of American and NATO politics. Public opinion polls yielded a steady 60 per cent level of anti-Western attitudes. Overall people's irritation spread to other areas of concern. The United States was frequently accused of selling Russia poor-quality food products. In addition, U.S. corporations had been accused of ripping off Russian consumers and manufacturers who dared to compete with their American counterparts. One of the most remarkable cases was a media campaign in support of the boycott of fairly popular American frozen chicken legs (called in Russia "Bush's Legs" in reference to the former U.S. president) as a retaliation for the increase of U.S. tariffs on imported steel, some of which was being produced in Russia (Shiraev and Zubok, 2001). The United States was frequently accused of following the policies of the IMF, the World Bank, and other transnational financial institutions without paying closer attention to the specific circumstances of Russia and other countries "in need" (Kagarlitsky, 2000).

Despite the ambiguity of opinions about the United States, the sudden rise to power in 1999 of a former security officer from St. Petersburg, a young and pragmatic Vladimir Putin, was increasingly seen by Russians as a sign that Russian foreign policy would be based on common sense, rational calculations, and reliable and mutually beneficial relations with the United States. Largely, it turned out to be the case.

How Policies are Made and Attitudes Expressed

In the U.S.S.R., foreign policy-making had been the unquestioned purview of Communist Party elites—Politburo members in particular—who had exercised decisive sway, especially over policy related to the United States. *Perestroika* marked the beginning of serious change in Soviet foreign policy-making. But most of the restructuring came after Russia gained independence in 1991. Institutional reforms required that new policy-makers be designated and their relative powers decided. Also, in accordance with Russia's democratic aspirations, new ground rules had to be set up on how to take into account the views of the political opposition, the media, and interest groups. While the new constitution of December 1993 institutionalized the reform of foreign policy-making institutions, the practical sorting out of new arrangements continued throughout the 1990s and into the new century. As this process has evolved, the number of actors involved in Russian foreign policy has proliferated, and relations among them have been very contentious. This can be seen, in part, as a natural result of Russia's initial steps toward democratization, which, in theory, transferred power over policy from party elites to representative government institutions. However, the expansion of the foreign policy-making arena and sharp struggles among politicians have also been due partially to resistance toward democratizing policy-making—specifically, to the President's efforts to keep decisive control over policy. In the 1990s, president Yeltsin deliberately enlarged the number of institutions involved in foreign policy-making in an effort to dilute the power of any one person or institution which might rival his own. He also played actors off each other for the same reason. Thus, while power over foreign policy decisions was more dispersed by 2001 than it had been earlier, it remained concentrated in the executive branch. The dominance of the president in foreign policy-making was also formalized in the 1993 constitution.

While the legislators did gain some influence in foreign policy-making, an oligarchic style of decision-making, of course, has long been favored by Russian elites. It seems that old patterns are hard to break. The political elite of the 2000s (whether just the executive branch or all political officials combined) appears to remain convinced that they, not voters, are the ones who should decide policy— especially foreign policy, given its concern with central issues of U.S.-Russia relations and security. The public seemed largely content to let their political leaders handle Russia's foreign policy. Yet the circle of political elites who helped decide policy is now broader than in the Soviet era, and political elites are part of an elected government. There are numerous channels for unrestrained public criticism, and critics felt free to put pressure on their government to respond to their views. While the Kremlin hangs on to the power to decide foreign policy in Russia, Boris Yeltsin and Vladimir Putin, who became president in 1999, found it increasingly difficult to do so without taking into account the wishes of critics, especially opposition legislators and the media.

Despite a consolidation of the Russian media since 2000 and the increase of the direct and indirect government control over broadcasting, the media are free of government control. Elements of censorship still exist though. For example, anti-Putin messages are typically not published due to internal "rules" that most editors and producers began to embrace after Putin ascended to the presidency. Criticism is largely directed at the methods by which policies are conducted, but not at the leader. However, printed sources that represent the interests of the political opposition generally express less tolerant attitudes about Russia's domestic and foreign policies than newspapers more loyal to the government.

Surveys taken by the Public Opinion Foundation between 2001 and 2003 showed that Russian people's attitudes about America are significantly influenced not only by immediate events but also by their coverage in the media. The more negative, one-sided the coverage is the worse are the attitudes (Bavin, 2003). Many critical and supportive comments related to the United States launched by the Russian media were obviously echoing the Kremlin's position.

However, many opinion leaders in Russia do not care much about which direction the political wind is blowing. They remain committed to anti-American (and commonly, anti-western) attitudes of the Soviet era. What was different in the 2000s is that instead of the old single radical communist anti-western ideological platform, contemporary anti-American views are rooted in a wide variety of beliefs ranging from militant nationalism, fascism, and racism, to isolationism and post-materialism. The other type of criticism of America was coming from a different ideological and political crowd. These were members of the Russian opinion elite, largely former or current officials, renowned pundits, and respected journalists, many of whom during Gorbachev's perestroika held pro-Western, liberal attitudes, and who were confronted by the developments in the early and mid-1990s after the United States had become the world's only superpower and, as a result, Russia ceased to play a dominant role in international affairs.

Public protests are regularly organized by different organizations, in particular, by pro-communist, pro-nationalist, or other radical groups. The vast majority of such gatherings are peaceful. During the war in Serbia, for example, when the public mood was especially irritated by the apparent U.S. and NATO invasion, the Russians did not puncture the tires of Fords and Chevrolets on the streets and pour out bottles of Pepsi or Coca Cola — something that some Americans had done to the cars of Soviet diplomats and bottles of Stolichnaya vodka in 1983, when the Soviets shot down the Korean airliner due to a negligent mistake. In the late 1990s and 2000s, the Russians continued to wear Nike and Reebok, watch Hollywood movies, buy American cars, use American computers and communicate via Microsoft's Hotmail or AOL's instant messenger, and listen to western and American pop, rock, and hip-hop. Thousands traveled to America and applied for immigration. Today, the consumption of western products and services is increasing. Boycotts and other forms of active resistance are not common. For instance, in 2001, it was widely reported that several leading Russian representatives of the presidential administration and the government were considering a boycott of the reception at the U.S. Embassy in Moscow in the evening of January 20, commemorating the inauguration of the U.S. president-elect. However, this action went generally unnoticed by the press.

Chapter 4

"Sorry, but …": Russia's Responses in the Wake of 9/11

Eric Shiraev

Russia ought to use the presently advantageous situation to attempt to resolve at least some of our problems in Chechnya and Georgia.
                                        Mikhail Leontiev, TV Host, September 15, 2001

We should be interested only in how, during the period of this war, Russia will be able to position itself in the new changed world.
                                        Gleb Pavlovsky, Political Commentator, October 24, 2001

The Week of September 11th: The Government's Immediate Reaction

The reaction of the top Russian officials to the violent acts against the United States was quick and unambiguous. On September 11th, Putin made a brief televised statement broadcasted on all networks. He called the acts "barbaric," emphasized that they were directed against innocent people, and referred to the feelings of "indignation and revolt" directed against the perpetrators of the attacks. Later the media reported on a telegram sent by Putin to George W. Bush, in which the Russian president not only expressed sympathy to the American people but also stated that the attacks must not go unpunished (Interfax, 9/11). Putin issued a decree to lower the flags and observe a moment of silence throughout Russia at noon Moscow time on September 13th. On that day, Putin held a telephone conversation with Bush, the second in a matter of hours to discuss joint actions. The prime ministers of Russia, China, and four Central Asian states issued to the media a joint declaration on September 14th condemning the brutal terrorist attacks in the United States. Earlier, Russia and NATO issued an extraordinary joint statement expressing anger at the devastating attacks on the United States and calling for international efforts to combat global terrorism. Public officials from Defense and Foreign Affairs ministries also issued statements or made public comments that resembled Putin's statements made on September 11th. On a rare occasion, Sergei Lebedev, head of the Foreign Intelligence Service, who usually keeps a very low public profile, stated publicly that his agency was working closely with national security offices of other countries to prevent or respond to new attacks. He also called for renewed attempts to fight international terrorism, suggesting that the events of September 11th were perpetrated by terrorists (Uzelac, 2001).

While President Putin did not make public comments about what Russia and the United States would do jointly and how the events would affect specific domestic and international developments, politicians and public officials of various ranks had more than an ample opportunity to express their reactions to the events, make assessments, and draw predictions for the future. Boris Nemtsov, leader of the Union of Right Forces and the person known for his conciliatory approach to conflicts, said on September 13th that Russia should get tough on terrorists because otherwise they would soon strike against the Kremlin. Grigory Yavlinsky, a politician known for his long-term support of the principles of liberal democracy and market economy, said on September 15th that the terrorist attacks in Washington and New York signaled the beginning of a new era of cooperation between the United States and Russia in the sphere of combating international terrorism.

Many politicians, however, expressed ambiguous opinions. Some were anxious. Irina Khakamada (2001, 09/14), Deputy Speaker of the Duma, said that she could foresee a nuclear war. Alexander Shokhin, Head of the Duma's finance and crediting committee was quoted by the *Kommersant* paper on September 12th as predicting with regret that the United States would not listen to reason and would choose to undertake unilateral actions to punish other countries. Another Deputy Speaker of the Duma, Vladimir Zhirinovsky (2001, 09/14), notoriously famous for his flamboyant behavior said that the terrorist attacks meant that the rest of humanity would no longer put up with the U.S. dominance. The leader of the Russian Communist Party, Gennady Zyuganov (2001, 09/14), has voiced concern that Russia's partnership with America would foist upon the country's relations with the Islamic world and other neighbors in Central Asia. Politicians' concerns over a possible destabilization lead to a Duma resolution of September 19th. The resolution, while stating that the perpetrators of the attacks had to be brought to justice, also underlined that any use of force—presumably by the United States—must be rigorously monitored and should not provoke any destabilization in the region.

The reactions to the September 11th events: A summary

Issue	Descriptions of general reactions
How America should react to the September 11th events	America should coordinate its actions with the world community and Russia; America may retaliate only against those responsible for the attacks and must make sure the civilians are not hurt. In less than 15 per cent of the publications, unilateral U.S. military actions were suggested. An emphasis on multilateralism was strongest in October and waned in December. *Komsomolskaya Pravda* was among the most pacifist-oriented papers; in basically all *K.P.* publications related to the events, sobriety of judgment, self-restraint, and non-violent solutions were suggested. The pro-communist *Sovetsjkaya Rossia*, while leaning toward the non-interventionist approach (18 per cent of articles) and suggestions about how the U.S. should change its foreign policy (30 per cent), displayed a greater variety of opinions.
How Russia should react to the September 11th events	Overall 40 per cent of publications suggested offering support to the United States, although the enthusiasm declined by the end of the fall. *Zavtra* was the most consistent in suggesting isolationism and no support to the U.S. *Sovetskaya Rossiya* expressed both the opposing and supporting views (help and isolationism). Local newspapers expressed mostly pro-internationalist views (70 per cent).

Identifying the perpetrators of the September 11th attacks	More than 54 per cent of all publications pointed to Islamic militants or fundamentalists, including Bin Laden and/or Al Qaeda; another 10 per cent mentioned Arab terrorists as perpetrators. The remaining third of references included a wide variety of guesses including America's government or "homegrown" terrorist groups (15 per cent), but these were largely earlier reactions and suggested primarily by *Sovetskaya Rossiya* and *Zavtra*. In newspapers such as *Moskovski Komsomolets*, *Komsomolskaya Pravda*, and *Trud*, more than 70 per cent of suggestions referred to Islamic or Arab militants.
The words to describe the September 11th act or its possible perpetrators	The vast majority of descriptions of the events in America contained negative or very negative adjectives referring to cruelty, murder, extremism, insanity, and evil. Only about 1 to 2 per cent of references advocated rationalizations for the suicidal actions (newspaper *Zavtra*).
The root causes, motivations, or conditions that led to the September 11th events	U.S. foreign policy or specific actions were named as root causes in 35 per cent of the publications. Religious and political fanaticism, religious fundamentalism, or prejudice against the United States were suggested in 36 per cent of the articles. Poverty and suffering were mentioned in 8 per cent of the cases; self-targeted conspiracy was also mentioned (5 per cent) but mostly in the earlier September issues. *Vek* is the steadiest supporter of "non-US" causes of the terrorist actions (77 per cent of its publications); *Zavtra* and *Sovetskaya Rossiya* pointed to the U.S. as the cause of the attacks more than any other newspaper (66 and 62 per cent of their publications respectively).
The abstract phrases used to describe the conflict brought to light by the September 11th events	The events were regarded as an attack against freedom, democracy, humanity, or the civilized world in 36 per cent of articles, mostly by *Izvestiya*, *Trud*, and *Rossijskaya Gazeta* and by the local newspapers. A clash between religions or civilizations was suggested in about 22 per cent of reports. A class conflict was suggested in 9 per cent of articles. In October–November these abstract evaluations were used significantly less frequently.
The motivation of the U.S. officials or government in the war in Afghanistan	Strengthening its own power, or political and economic influence in the region or in the world was suggested by a plurality of articles (48 per cent). A desire to stop terrorism was mentioned in 15 per cent of publications, whereas revenge was referred to in 21 per cent of articles. *Sovetskaya Rossiya* mentioned the power-driven U.S. motivation in all its publications; *Nezavisimaya Gazeta* and *Zavtra* did the same in most of their articles; whereas *Moskovsky Komsomolets* was particularly insistent about punishment as the prime motivation. Motivations such as the defense of freedom, democracy, humanity, or protection of the Western civilization were largely ignored.
The words or phrases used to describe the U.S., its government, and people	About 11 per cent of descriptions were associated with positive features attributed to the U.S. and Americans. About 72 per cent of descriptions were negative, including those that underline U.S. and people as weak and shaken (18 per cent), greedy (5 per cent), belligerent and oppressive (20 per cent), indifferent and selfish (11 per cent), and unfair, hypocritical (9 per cent). The number of accusatory descriptions increased through October and December. At the same time, the number of sympathetic descriptions decreased. *Sovetskaya Rossiya* displayed the most negative evaluations, followed by *Zavtra*, *Moskovsky Komsomoles*, *Vek*, and *Novaya Gazeta*. *Vek*, on the other hand, gave frequent positive evaluations as well.

Assessments of the U.S. war in Afghanistan and its outcomes	The vast majority of assessments were negative, including statements that the U.S. actions harmed civilians (30 per cent), did not lead to the capture of Bin Laden, or increased anti-American feelings. There was practically no mention of the positive outcomes of the war, such as the liquidation of terrorist camps.
General appraisal of attitudes about the U.S.	The overall picture reflects an even distribution of both favorable (33 per cent) and unfavorable (34 per cent) opinions and an equal share of mixed attitudes (33 per cent). In September, favorable comments were somewhat more frequent (39 per cent) than negative ones (25 per cent), but the tendency reversed in October (22 per cent positive and 48 per cent unfavorable) and in December (only 9 per cent of positive vs. 37 per cent of negative comments).

Instant Reactions: Media and Elites

The authorities of the four national networks—ORT, RTR, NTV and TV6—all chose to provide a commercial-free coverage of the events in the United States on September 11th and other developments taking place later. The networks picked up CNN live reports and accompanied them by simultaneous Russian translation. All regularly scheduled programs were canceled (with the exception of local coverage in some areas provided by smaller, regional television companies). Immediately after the attacks, a few editorial comments were added and some footage was edited in, such as the reaction of President Putin and pictures of Muscovites bringing flowers to the U.S. embassy.

The newspaper headlines in the morning of September 12th were dramatic. "Armageddon Now," read across the issues of *Kommersant*, a respectable daily newspaper. Commenting on the aftermath of the events in the United States, the newspaper mentioned on several occasions the ongoing market collapse and a chaotic situation in currency exchange operations. The expressions, "Armageddon" or "end of the world" were used by other printed sources, including a popular newspaper *Izvestia*, which also proclaimed the beginning of the war among civilizations. The doom-and-gloom metaphors and apocalyptic phrases were featured on the front pages of most newspapers. *Vremya MN* issued a headline that read: "The Apocalypses Happened Yesterday." *Komsomolskaya Pravda* in the September 12th issue referred to a Third World War, which had been started by terrorists.

Newspapers were also filled with reports about Americans coping with the devastating consequences of the terrorist attacks. Articles written by Americans—in which they thanked Russians and their government for the sympathy and compassion—began to appear in the Russian media, such as one titled, "Thank you Russia" by Michael McFaul (2001, 09/17). Only a few newspapers in the first four days after the terrorist attacks provided a relatively rational and comprehensive analysis of the developing situation. *Rossiyskaya Gazeta*, as an example, on September 14th had been already discussing military plans, strategy, logistics, and other operational issues related to a possible retaliatory strike by NATO in Central Asia against terrorist camps.

Analysis provided for this book shows that the vast majority of descriptions related to the Russian media's immediate reactions to the tragic events in the United States, contained negative, condemning, and disapproving comments referring to the cruelty, murder, extremism, insanity, and evil of those who perpetrated the attacks. As an example, the newspaper *Izvestia* put together the following headline: "Armageddon. Big country. Big sorrow. Big suffering." Only a very small proportion of the printed comments (mostly from the ultranationalist newspaper *Zavtra*) offered a justification for the murderous actions against the United States.

While many Russians were laying flowers outside the U.S. embassy in Moscow, some people began to panic. Several money exchange offices refused to accept dollars on Tuesday and Wednesday, just hours after the attacks, as reported in *France Press* and *Reuters* (AFP, 09/11; Reuters, 09/12). Some businesses stopped operating, anticipating the imminent collapse of the dollar. However, the overall initial fall of the U.S. dollar against other currencies as a result of the attack was as small as one per cent and was covered by an upsurge, which was reported by most newspapers, two or three days later.

Instant Reactions: Opinion Polls

The first results of opinion polls were published as early as September 13th. A telephone survey of 500 randomly selected adult Muscovites conducted by ROMIR, an independent public opinion company, revealed that almost 35 per cent of respondents believed the attacks were part of a campaign of terror against the United States. About 30 per cent of the surveyed considered the attacks to be the starting point of a massive global terrorist warfare. About 39 per cent expected the United States to retaliate against the states suspected of being related to the attacks. Four out of ten of the respondents said that the United States would attempt to destroy the strongholds of international terrorism. About 50 per cent of the respondents believed that Islamic extremists were behind the attacks; less than 8 per cent thought that other religious extremist groups conducted the attacks. Similarly, small proportions of the surveyed attributed the blame for the terrorist acts to the secret services of some countries (7 per cent, the names were not mentioned), anti-globalization radicals (5 per cent), and the U.S. secret services (3 per cent). Almost one quarter of the surveyed did not have an opinion on the issue. At the same time, more than 47 per cent of the respondents of this ROMIR poll believed Russia could also be hit by a similar wave of terrorism. Three quarters of the Muscovites expressed confidence that president Bush was able to deal with the situation, as compared to 20 per cent who said he was not. The respondents split their opinions about whether the United States would find the perpetrators of the terrorist attacks. About 48 per cent expressed confidence that the perpetrators would be or were likely to be found. To the contrary, more than 45 per cent said that the people behind the attacks were not likely to be found or would not be found at all. The opinions were divided about the economic impact of the recent events. About 35 per cent believed that there would be no consequences on the global economy, whereas 33 per cent of the respondents worried about the harmful effects of the terrorist acts on the Russian economy. However, less than 8 per cent anticipated a global economic crisis.

Another early poll was conducted on September 11th and 12th by the Moscow Academy for Humanitarian and Social Issues (MGSA). According to this survey, 21 per cent of the respondents agreed that the attacks were a justified punishment for the Americans. A similar question asked in a poll by the All-Russia Public Opinion Study Center (VTsIOM) showed that 35 per cent of Muscovites polled two days after the events spoke of the terrorist act as well-deserved punishment of Americans for the "past" bombings of Hiroshima and Nagasaki, Iraq, and Yugoslavia. However, in the MGSA survey, 37 per cent disagreed with the statement about a "justified" penalty and in the VTsIOM poll, a significantly larger number of respondents (61 per cent) disagreed with the idea that the United States brought the punishment on themselves.

The Russians also expressed concerns about their own safety in the wake of the events in the United States. Some 59 per cent of Muscovites believed that Russian law-enforcement agencies could not protect them from terrorist acts. A hypothetical appearance of Taliban units at the border with Tajikistan worried 72 per cent of Russians and more than a half of the respondents expected the Taliban's infiltration into Tajikistan in the near future (Stepanov, 2001). Opinions split when people were asked whether Russia should support U.S. retaliation if it turns out that Islamic extremists were responsible for the September 11th attacks. Overall, 43 per cent of the surveyed agreed with this action, whereas 47 per cent expressed disagreement (VTsIOM, 09/18).

A majority of the Russian people sympathized with the victims of the attacks. In a poll taken on September 15th–16th by the Public Opinion Foundation, 77 per cent of the 1,500 respondents across Russia said that they experienced strong emotions when they first heard about the attacks in the United States. Only 8 per cent of the respondents said they did not care about the events. At the same time, about 15 per cent reported that they were greatly satisfied with the attacks and 15 per cent said they had experienced some satisfaction. More than one third of the respondents who were satisfied with the attacks identified with Communist leader Gennady Zyuganov (www.fom.ru, 09/20).

A telephone survey conducted on September 23rd by the independent Russian television network TV-6 and the popular weekly program *Itogi* hosted by Yevgeniy Kiselev showed that many people supported direct military help by Russia to the U.S. campaign against terrorism. Almost four thousand out of ten thousand phone calls received by the show's organizers suggested that Russia should have provided military assistance to the war and almost five thousand thought Russia should provide both political and diplomatic support. Although the host of the show suggested a substantial growth in support of a pro-active position of the Russian government in the war against terrorism, his conclusions were based on the results of two straw polls, which are viewed in public opinion studies as generally inaccurate (TV-6, 09/23).

Plans to retaliate against unknown terrorists caused an ambivalent reaction. According to the data of the MGSA research institute, 19 per cent of the polled failed to give any answer, whereas 48 per cent of Muscovites spoke confidently in favor of a powerful attack on the areas where terrorists live. Several hours later, only 3 per cent of the polled (VTsIOM) favored an immediate strike. Some 72 per cent of the polled insisted that first the culprit should be found, and military action taken after that.

Only 4 per cent of the polled failed to give an answer to this question. At the same time, only 40 per cent of Muscovites thought then that the target for military attacks could be determined. Fifty-two per cent of the respondents did not believe that the masterminds of the terrorist attacks could ever be found (Stepanov, 2001).

Naming the Causes of September 11th

More than 54 per cent of all analyzed Russian publications pointed to Islamic militants or fundamentalists, including Bin Laden and/or Al Qaeda and another 10 per cent mentioned Arab terrorists. In search of immediate evidence, reporters quoted mostly foreign information services. Others referred to "domestic" facts, such as a map confiscated from Chechen rebels displaying directions of strikes at the World Trade Center in New York (RIA, 09/24). Most publications underlined the international nature of the sophisticated plot (Ovcharenko and Umerenkov, 2001). Approximately one third of the published references included a wide variety of guesses including America's own government or "homegrown" terrorist groups (Kagarlitsky, 2001, 09/18). To illustrate, Vladimir Zhirinovsky, leader of the Liberal Democratic Party of Russia and whose name was mentioned earlier, drew parallels between the September 11th attacks and the burning of the Reichstag, the House of Parliament, in Berlin in 1933 after which Hitler assumed dictatorship in Germany.

Zhirinovsky predicted in a television interview on October 18th that, in a fashion similar to what Hitler had done, the United States would identify an innocent "scapegoat" and would attack it (www.ortv.ru, 10/18). General Boris Agapov, a well-known expert on Afghanistan, also expressed reservations about Afghan groups as perpetrators of terrorist acts. He said that it was impossible to imagine how "primitive" organizations such as the Taliban or Bin Laden groups could have executed such a complicated and large-scale act of terrorism (Kagarlitsky, 2001, 10/30). Other commentators also raised doubts about Arab terrorists, as did Leonid Shebarshin, the former chief of the Soviet Foreign Intelligence (2001, 10/17). But these skeptical reactions were largely expressed earlier in the studied period mostly by opposition newspapers such as *Sovetskaya Rossiya* and *Zavtra*. In other newspapers, including *Moskovski Komsomolets*, *Komsomolskaya Pravda*, and *Trud*, more than 70 per cent of references accused Islamic or Arab militants.

Threats against Russia

The tragic events in America sparked concerns about Russia's own national security. Two sources of such threats were identified. First, journalists and commentators suggested possible attacks from terrorists against targets in Moscow. *Komsomolskaya Pravda*, on September 13th, for instance, speculated about a kamikaze pilot who could change course and hit the Kremlin or any other strategic target in the city. The newspaper warned helplessly that nobody could prevent a terrorist act if someone had plans to do it. Some experts referred to statements by Chechen separatists in which they had made threats in the past about a suicide terrorist on board an airliner that would target the Kremlin (Fedorov, 2001, 09/14).

Some commentators called for the acceleration of a military buildup to reduce the probability of such suicidal actions (Ptichkin, 2001, 09/14) and not wait for too long and thus invite the enemies to launch their strikes against the country (Pavlovsky, 2001, 10/24). The other source of potential threats to Russia was primarily strategic. Analysts referred to the country's regional instability, the growth of insecurity of Russia's southern borders, and the significant loss of revenues from weapons deals with Arab countries, which would not commit billions of dollars to Russia if the country decided to help the United States in its future wars (Pushkov, 2001, 09/15; Pronina, 2001, 09/24).

Seeking Gains for Russia

Most media reactions, however, were not necessarily about the threats and imminent dangers to Russia as a result of the events on September 11th. After a few days of emotional responses, the media began to focus on rational assessments of the political and economic impact on Russia. One of the earliest suggestions made by the commentators was about the vulnerability of the world's infrastructure and the inability of countries to guarantee their own national security using the old methods. In a live interview on the *Russia TV* network, devoted solely to the terrorist attacks in the U.S., Dmitry Rogozin, chairman of the State Duma's International Affairs Committee said that recent events showed that the United States before September 11th paid attention to the wrong threats. He emphasized the need for the United States to rethink the missile defense program because the enemies could strike this country by nontraditional means. The U.S. missile defense program, as Rogozin concluded, was the wrong way to deal with the security challenges of the modern world especially in the face of terrorist threats (Gornostaev, 2001).

Most published comments, however, dealt with one of Russia's most serious domestic problems: the breakaway republic of Chechnya. In the past, Moscow repeatedly accused bin Laden and the Taliban of helping Chechen guerrillas. Hours after the attacks in the United States Russian politicians were already drawing comparisons between the U.S. tragedy and the troubling situation in this southern region of Russia. On September 11th, Dmitry Rogozin, whose name was mentioned earlier, said that that the events in the U.S. could make a positive impact on western attitudes toward Russia's policy in Chechnya (*Russia TV*, 09/11). Sergei Yastrzhembsky, the presidential spokesman on Chechnya, referred to the Russian campaign in this breakaway region as part of the overall struggle against international terrorism. Nikolay Patrushev, Director of the Russian Federal Security Service also said that the West must rethink its views on Chechnya (*ORT*, 09/15). Many Russian politicians—including those who had earlier urged a more moderate stance in Chechnya—have become distinctly hawkish since the attacks against the United States. Boris Nemtsov (2001, 09/13), the leader of the Union of Right Forces, and one of a few active supporters of a political settlement in Chechnya, changed his position. In an interview with Moscow newspaper *Moskovsky Komsomolets* on September 13, Nemtsov was clearly skeptical about negotiations and insisted on the toughest measures against terrorist of all kinds. Alexander Dugin, leader of the Euro-Asia movement said in *Nezavisimaya Gazeta* on September 13th that Russia should use the momentum, put aside concerns about human rights and rush headlong against the Chechen resistance. Nikolai Kovalev, former director of the Russian Federal Security Service, deputy chairman of the committee of the State Duma for Security, expressed hopes that the western media would stop using double standards and would finally consider Russian fighting in Chechnya as a struggle against international terrorism (Kovalev, 2001, 12/06). Scores of columnists and television commentators began to use harsh remarks about Chechnya and insist on tough measures against the terrorists (Russia TV, 09/13; Leontiev, SMI.RU, 09/15; Solovei, 09/21; Safonov, 10/23; Reuters, 09/23). The reports also reminded that Russia had repeatedly claimed in the past that there was a connection between the international terrorist groups on one hand and Chechen terrorists on the other.

While citing missile defense systems and the situation in Chechnya in association with September 11th, the Russian media started to discuss the direct and indirect benefits that the country should receive for its support of the United States and the war on terror (Osipov and Palshin, 2001, 10/02), or what benefits Russia should ask for (Markov, 2001, 10/23). Vladimir Zhirinovsky said to *Nezavisimaya Gazeta* (09/13, 2001) that the U.S. administration should start negotiations with Russia and write off Russia's foreign debts. He suggested further that the Kremlin—in the face of international terrorism—should reactivate the KGB, triple servicemen's salaries, and raise the salaries of the special forces by five times. The military, he mentioned in another interview, should be built up to 3 million men (Zhirinovsky, 2001, 09/14). At the same time, while Russian defense minister Sergei Ivanov emphasized the importance of profitable arms deals with the Northern Alliance in Afghanistan (gazeta.ru, 10/29), publications started to appear in which the West was criticized for the lack of benefits given to Russia for its cooperative role in the war on terror (Nikonov, 2001, 10/27).

In September 2001, Putin stated that Russia was ready to cooperate with the United States during the anti-terrorist campaign (*RIA Novosti*, 2001, 09/24; *Komsomolskaya Pravda*, 09/24). Various commentators immediately acknowledged that Russia should become an equal partner of the United States and play a major role in any international coalition of the countries. To secure Russia's participation, NATO should stop its expansion eastward, the Americans should drop their plans to develop a strategic defense system, and Russia should not be criticized for its Chechen policies. These three suggestions were repeatedly mentioned in publications (Pavlovsky, 2001, 10/24). There were also voices, including Deputy Foreign Minister Georgy Mamedov (ITAR-Tass, 2001, 09/17) who maintained that the tragic events in the U.S. could stimulate the development of a new world order, in which Russia would actively participate in a stronger U.N., a non-ideological NATO, a more humane World Trade Organization, and an efficient G-8 (Bogaturov, 2001, 09/28). Some authors recommended the creation of a new antiterrorist alliance, modeled after the anti-Hitler coalition of the 1940s, this time on the basis of NATO. If such a coalition was created, Russia was anticipated to take a leading role along with the United States (Markov, 2001; Uzelac, 2001). Commentators also brought to attention that the post-September 11th situation gave Moscow a chance to draw closer to the United States. In some reports, Russia was called to revise its foreign policy and defense doctrines and provide more positive and cooperative foreign policy. If Russia did not approach the West, the reports warned, the country would face huge debts, hostilities by its southern borders, and fierce competition from China (Vasiliev, 2001; Khamrayev, 2001; Alexeyev, 2001).

Support of the Unfolding Campaign in Afghanistan

Although the immediate plans of the Washington Administration were not clear yet, the Russian media began to publish commentaries about a forthcoming military action against Afghanistan almost immediately after September 11th (Pavlovsky, 2001). President Vladimir Putin and Russian Foreign Minister Igor Ivanov made several statements about the importance of balanced and intelligent decisions. They did not rule out, however, that the United States would use force in the fight against terrorism (Interfax, 2001, 09/15). Some of the media's predictions were gloomy about Afghanistan's future, predicting the immanent destruction of an entire country by the U.S. armed forces, if it is confirmed that the Taliban government aided terrorists (Ovcharenko and Umerenkov, 2001). Other predictions estimated the "price" the Kremlin would demand for its involvement in the conflict, as it was done in a radio interview by the head of the Foreign and Defense Policy Council, Sergei Karaganov (Radio Ekho Moskvy, 09/17).

Cautious voices sounded louder by the end of September 2001. Military and civilian experts, while expressing an overall positive opinion about a forthcoming retaliation from the United States, warned about potential problems and casualties (Arbatov, 2001). Moscow Region Governor Boris Gromov, the top military commander in Afghanistan during the Soviet occupation in the mid-1980s, ruled out any deployment of infantry in Afghanistan for fear of heavy casualties (RIA, 09/18). These opinions reflected generally the views of the public. In October, different sources published reports about the split public opinion on the potential air strikes against Afghanistan (Shusharin, 2001, 10/26). Dmitry Rogozin (2001, 09/13) suggested that the result of any military action initiated by the United States would be innocent victims and further terrorist retaliatory acts.

Later in the fall and winter of 2001, the comments acknowledged the success of the international coalition. Some politicians even began to take credit for the successful U.S.-led campaign, as did Alexei Arbatov, Vice Chair of the Duma Committee for Defense (Federal News Service, 2001, 11/26). In a similar fashion, a few articles praised American technological advancement and made sarcastic, self-depreciative remarks about looting that would have been widespread if the Russian army, not the United States, were to lead in a military operation of this magnitude (Bitsoyev, 2001, 12/28).

Critical Reactions to the Unfolding Campaign in Afghanistan

After the Kremlin promised to support the military campaign in Afghanistan and possibly elsewhere (*Russia TV*, 09/15), many articles and interviews published in September–October began to spell out possible limitations to what Russia and other countries could do. Early in the fall, several Russian officials had clearly ruled out the use of Russia's ground forces in any foreign military engagement. Defense Minister

Sergey Ivanov told *Russia TV* that the Kremlin was not planning to participate in any military action against terrorist bases in Afghanistan (ORT, 13 September). Anatoly Kvashnin, head of the general staff of the armed forces, said it was highly unlikely that Russian troops would take part in an anti-terrorist operation (Ulyanov, 2001, 09/19). Assurances of the governments of several former Soviet countries to participate in American-led actions against international terrorism were criticized in the media.

These reactions were another indication that some powerful officials were somewhat reluctant to witness any military action conducted by the United States. Military officials and national-security bureaucrats were unhappy about NATO troops in Central Asia. The "open letter" of a group of the generals and admirals of the Russian armed forces published on November 10th, 2001 criticized Putin's policies as too pro-Western. Left-wing political parties and groups did not welcome even a hint at the new pro-Western orientation of the Kremlin. Russian Communist Party leader Gennady Zyuganov warned about a possible war with the entire Islamic world, which could begin in the wake of the U.S.-planned actions (Interfax, 2001; 09/24). The leaders of the Russian parliamentary factions of the Unity Party, the Communist Party of Russia, the Peoples' Deputy Group and the Liberal Democratic Party all stood firmly against any form of Russian military participation in the evolving anti-terrorist coalition (Ulyanov, 2001). Russian conservatives too felt defeat in Putin's newly declared political course. Their dream to rebuild Russia's independence, while keeping distance from the West, and strengthening the country's military power was apparently rejected by the president (Shlapentokh, 2001). Some business groups saw a potential loss of business with many partners in the Middle East or Central Asia. On top of that, some feared that Moscow's good-neighborly relations with the Arab world would be wrecked (*Komsomolskaya Pravda*, 2001, 09/25). Other voices predicted a depressing scenario for Russia's security as a result of the war in Afghanistan, which could spark off another wave of terror (Primakov, 2001; Kovalev, 09/14).

Duma Speaker Gennady Seleznev expressed a common objection in a television interview. He declared on September 18 that Russia should distinguish between governments and simple people and not deliver blows to entire nations for the sins of the few (www.ortv.ru, 09/18). Some extremist and nationalist politicians displayed their direct hostility against the West. For instance, Vladimir Zhirinovsky of the LDPR said that the only way for Russia to become a great power again was to stop supporting the United States, sign a deal with the Taliban, and create a new powerful alliance with the Arab world (Khamrayev, 2001; *NTV International*, 10/02). Of course, there were individuals who vehemently supported the new foreign policy of cooperation. They voiced their opinion mostly through a few consistently pro-liberal, pro-Western media, such as TV channel 6, the newspaper "*Kommersant*," and the weekly "*Itogi*." But the moderates, representing a solid majority of the Russian political elite, were divided between the supporters of the course announced by president Putin and its critics.

The media's reaction to the events in Afghanistan was cautious too. One of the most common themes was a convenient objection to violence. A well-known political commentator wrote in the *Moscow Times* in October that U.S. air strikes were killing large numbers of ordinary Afghan civilians; the Northern Alliance, an opposition to the Taliban government, was incapable of effective offensive action; the situation was a terrible strategic impasse, and the United States seemed caught in the middle of it (Felgenhauer, 2001, 09/20; Felgenhauer, 2001, 10/25). It was common for the media to doubt the effectiveness of the military actions and to suggest that Russia should stay away from the conflict (Shelia, 2001, 10/11). Overall, according to the media analysis, unilateral military actions against the Taliban regime were supported in fewer than 15 per cent of the articles. An emphasis on multilateralism (such as a military coalition) was strongest in October but waned in December. *Komsomolskaya Pravda* was among the most pacifist-oriented newspapers: basically all of its publications related to the events appealed to sobriety of judgment, self-restraint, and non-violent solutions. Pro-communist *Sovetsjkaya Rossia*, while leaning toward the non-interventionist approach (18 per cent of articles) and suggestions about how the U.S. should change its foreign policy (30 per cent), displayed a greater variety of opinions, both supporting and opposing the war.

In evaluation of the U.S. actions in Afghanistan, outcomes such as strengthening America's power, its political and economic influence in the region or in the world were suggested by a plurality of articles (48 per cent). Desire to stop terrorism was mentioned in 15 per cent of publications, whereas revenge was referred to in 21 per cent of articles. *Sovetskaya Rossiya* mentioned the power-driven U.S. motivation in practically all publications during the period under observation; *Nezavisimaya Gazeta* and *Zavtra* did the same in most of their articles; whereas *Moskovsky Komsomolets* was particularly insistent about punishment as the prime motivation. The media largely ignored the arguments about the necessity to defend freedom, democracy, humanity, and Western civilization. The vast majority of assessments were negative, including statements about the U.S. actions harming civilians (30 per cent), and causing anti-American feelings. There was practically no mention of the positive outcomes of the war.

Criticism of American Foreign Policy

Only about 11 per cent of the newspaper materials were associated with positive features attributed to the U.S. and Americans. About 72 per cent of descriptions were negative, including those that depicted the U.S. and its people as weak and shaken (18 per cent), greedy (5 per cent), belligerent and oppressive (20 per cent), indifferent and selfish (11 per cent), and unfair, hypocritical (9 per cent). The number of accusatory descriptions increased through October and December, and the number of sympathetic descriptions decreased.

There was no shortage of comments about the U.S. bullying behavior, arrogance, and overconfidence. One type of argument held that the attacks against the United States were, in part, caused by America's own sense of superiority (Fochkin, 2001, 09/13) and its attitude toward international law (Markov, 2001, 09/22; Kagarlitsky, 2001, 10/30). Another type of comment underlined the false sense of unity that the Americans have about the world following them (Arbatov, 2001; Tretiakov, 2001). The White House's argument that the attacks on September 11th must be considered an attack on the whole world was rejected (Tretiakov, 2001). The prominent Russian political scientist Gleb Pavlovsky, head of the Fund for Effective Policies, referred to the "traditional" U.S. demonstrative retribution, which the Americans used to resort to time and again to show the world how tough they were (Pavlovsky, 2001). Moreover, some publications suggested that the war on terror was an excuse to start a campaign against any state that dares to express anti-American attitudes (Dugin, 2001, 09/13). America was commonly accused of bullying the rest of the world (Pankov, 2001, 09/18).

Numerous articles in Russian newspapers and magazines contained personal accounts from Russian officers who fought in Afghanistan and who predicted a tough time for the American troops in that country. Plenty of warnings came from former military veterans who referred to the U.S. inability to learn from other countries' mistakes, like ones that the Soviet Union committed in Afghanistan in the 1980s where the military took serious casualties (Aushev, Interfax, 09/17). Colonel General, First Deputy Chief of the General Staff Yuri Baluyevsky said, while expressing a positive attitude about the U.S.-Russia strategic cooperation, that the ability of rogue states, including Afghanistan, to create weapons of mass destruction is exaggerated and, therefore, military strikes against such countries are not justified (2001, 12/09). State Duma Deputy Andrei Kokoshin, who was also former secretary of the Russian Security Council, said during a radio interview that the United States should change its arrogant attitude and turn to cooperation with the international community (*Mayak*, 2001, 09/12). Other reports questioned the ability of the American people to persevere under adversity. For example, Yulia Latynina, a journalist with *ORT* called Americans intellectually lazy and incapable of fighting to the bitter end. She said that the U.S. government always removes its soldiers from the places that were too frightening to them (2001, 09/19).

The most negative opinions came from nationalist and communist newspapers, which accused the United States of barbaric actions, hegemonic policies, and disrespect to the international law (Zyuganov, 2001, 09/13). However, a distinct anti-American sentiment was also present in a range of articles appearing in "liberal" publications, which for a decade were in strong opposition to nationalist and communist publications. In the wake of September 11th, at least three of such newspapers, *Izvestia*, *Obshchaia Gazeta*, and *Novaia Gazeta*, published several poorly-substantiated, openly-prejudiced, anti-American articles, which practically gloated over the tragic events in America and suggested that terrorism was a necessary redemption for America's arrogance (Shlapentokh, 2001).

In general, articles, interviews, and columns that supported the U.S. actions in Afghanistan and approved of the anti-terrorist campaign were most likely to be published in late September. Voices that discussed a balanced opinion about the events in Afghanistan in October–December 2001 were practically silenced by the critics.

Conclusion

The initial reaction of most Russians to the tragic September events in the United States was concerned and sympathetic. The media undoubtedly identified Islamic radicals as the perpetrators of the attacks. Conspiracy theories involving Israel or the CIA and their alleged participation were quickly dismissed. Nevertheless, after the initial emotional shock caused by the TV footage and pictures of the falling buildings was over, the reactions in Russia began to change later in September and in the fall of 2001. Although the official policy appeared unchanged, the media's assessments became increasingly ambivalent and critical. If we look at the numbers, the overall picture reflects a practically "even" distribution of both favorable evaluations of the United States (33 per cent), and unfavorable (34 per cent) opinions, and an equal share of mixed attitudes (33 per cent). In September, favorable comments were somewhat more frequent (39 per cent) than negative ones (25 per cent), but the tendency reversed in October (22 per cent positive and 48 per cent unfavorable) and in December (only 9 vs. 37 per cent).

Each individual's opinion is unique and generalizing about how an entire nation reacts to an international event is difficult. However, if we look for the general tendency, we will find that there was a substantial difference between how the events of September 11th were perceived and explained in the United States and Russia. For most Americans, and numerous polls support this assumption (Shiraev and Sobel, 2004), the U.S. military responses in Afghanistan and other places were inevitable actions to the grave threats to America imposed by terrorists. For most Russians, on the other hand, the military responses launched by Washington were primarily a reflection of Washington's longing for global domination realized in the opportunity to gain ground in South Asia and in former Soviet republics. America was often described as a proud and strong nation. Nevertheless, in so many cases, America was also depicted as a faceless, arrogant, and greedy monster, an image far too familiar to those who lived in the Soviet Union during the Cold War.

As several Russian commentators admitted, most Russians, while responding to the tragic events of 2001, were sorry for Americans as individuals but were not particularly sorry for America as a country. As a matter of analogy, in the 1970s, one of the officially promoted ideological doctrines in the Soviet Union was that the Soviet people did not, in fact, dislike the American people but they despised America's rotten capitalism and democracy. Remarkably, fifteen years later, during Perestroika, most Russians maintained that they were neither against the American people nor were they against America's social system. The imaginary pendulum of attitudes swung again in the last decade. There is always hope against hope that this pendulum of Russian people's attitudes would swing back again in the 2000s and the Russians, who were bitter or prejudiced in 2001, would tomorrow regret and ridicule themselves for the things they said yesterday. Actually, they had already done this so many times in the past.

* * *

Editorial Remarks

Why did the media and opinion polls in Russia reflect such an ambivalent and critical view of the United States and its foreign policy? As we do in each chapter, let's look at institutional, political, and psychological factors that might have contributed to such reactions.

Unlike in the Soviet Union, the Russian people in 2001 had a much broader access to information, including independent media, the Internet, and satellite television.

The Kremlin could no longer dictate what people thought and how they interpreted international events. Moreover, President Putin, since taking power in 1999, had maintained a pragmatic foreign policy aimed at partnership with the United States. Since 2001, the Kremlin and the White House shared similar attitudes on several policy-related issues, including the fight against terrorism, non-proliferation of nuclear weapons, trade, and regional stability. Obviously, the Kremlin would not support every action initiated in Washington and there were points of disagreement. Nevertheless, official relations between the U.S. and Russia in 2001 and 2002 were warmer than at any time since the collapse of the Soviet Union.

Despite the official policies, a majority of opinion leaders in Russia remained genuinely committed to their anti-Western attitudes. The political climate in Russia in 2001 was such that pro-American attitudes were widely regarded as non-patriotic. The anti-American card was eagerly played by nationalist groups and the Communist Party, the members of which maintained a genuine hatred, cultivated since the Cold War, for western democracy and free-market capitalism. International developments contributed to the arguments of the Russian political opposition, including NATO's expansion, U.S. promises to walk away from the Anti-Ballistic Missile Treaty, the perceived unfair trade policies, and, of course, the unfolding military campaign in Afghanistan.

The most significant factor contributing to ambivalent and critical views of the United States seems psychological and rooted in Russian political culture. As in the late 1980s, a substantial proportion of Russians in the beginning of the 2000s associated America, more than any other place on earth, with prosperity and advanced technologies. Overall, Russians respect American economic success and are impressed by its democratic form of government. But they tend to be concerned about U.S. international ambitions. Surveys taken by the Public Opinion Foundation between 2001 and 2003 also showed that the Russians' attitudes about America are significantly influenced by "immediate" events and their coverage in the media. Most Russians remain proud of the country's victory in World War II in 1945. These reflections on their country's history give many Russians a sense of moral superiority over Americans. But more and more, in Russia, nostalgic feelings of superiority and security have been replaced by a sense of personal and national insecurity. Many ordinary people maintain the view that the United States represents a general threat to Russia's national security, a threat that has significantly diminished since the end of the Cold War, but still remains a viable menace. Surveys conducted by leading polling organizations showed that many Russians, up to fifty per cent, believe that since America was so quick to bomb Afghanistan, there is a strong likelihood that they might patrol the streets of the republics of the former Soviet Union. Most people in Russia held an opinion that superpower America is capable not only of making statements but also of undertaking decisive unilateral actions. Russia, meanwhile, remained a passive bystander. In the face of Russia's own relative weakness, this perceived American ferocity is feared and distrusted. Although the tragedy of September 11th brought Russia and the United States closer together for a short time, the war on terror has served to drive the two nations somewhat further apart.

Suggested Additional Literature

Goldgeier, James and McFaul, Michael (2003). *Power and Purpose: U.S. Policy Toward Russia After the Cold War.* Washington DC: Brookings.

Shiraev, Eric and Terrio, D. (2003). Russian Decision-making Regarding Bosnia: Indifferent Public and Feuding Elites. In R. Sobel and E. Shiraev (eds.). *International Public Opinion and the Bosnia Crisis.* Lexington Books/Rowman & Littlefield.

Shiraev, Eric and Zubok, Vlad (2001). *Anti-Americanism in Russia: From Stalin to Putin.* New York: St. Martin's Press/Palgrave.

Shlapentokh, Vladimir (1988). The Changeable Soviet Image of America. In T. Thornton (ed.). *Anti-Americanism. The Annals of the American Academy of Political and Social Science.* Vol. 497, 157–171. Newbury Park: Sage Publications.

Shlapentokh, Vladimir (1998). The changing Russian view of the West: From admiration in the early 1990s to hostility in the late 1990s. In Tom Casier and Katlijn Malfliet (eds.). *Is Russia a European Power? The position of Russia in a new Europe.* Louvain: Leuven University.

CASE 3
COLOMBIA

On the afternoon of Tuesday, September 11th, 2001, United States Secretary of State Colin Powell was scheduled to arrive in Bogotá as head of a diplomatic mission to underscore the United States commitment to fostering peace, human rights, and above all, the eradication of drugs in Colombia (Brownfield, 2001). Obviously, he never arrived, but flew instead from an Organization of American States (OAS) conference in Lima, Peru, directly to Washington D.C. Meanwhile, the reaction in Colombia to the tragic attacks of 9/11 was decidedly mixed, as indicated in the pair of remarks quoted below. On one hand, as U.S. Ambassador Patterson noted, many Colombians expressed sincere regret over the loss of life in the attacks and subsequently identified with the vigorous reaction of the Bush administration. On the other hand, as exemplified by Antonio Caballero's comments, a significant number of Colombians also manifested a distinct lack of sympathy for the plight of the United States. While not approving of the attacks themselves, these Colombians believed that the United States was directly or indirectly responsible for the attacks, and should not respond unilaterally or with military force.

Chapter 5

Colombian Attitudes toward the United States after 9/11

John C. Dugas

Following the horrific terrorist attacks in the United States today, the Embassy has been overwhelmed by public and private expressions of sympathy and support from Colombians of all walks of life. President Pastrana, his cabinet, the military high command, and editors of Colombia's leading media have all communicated their condolences to us. The Embassy has similarly received hundreds of telephone calls and e-mail messages from private Colombian citizens expressing sorrow and solidarity.
Anne W. Patterson, United States Ambassador to Colombia

It was only natural that after half a century of cruelty by U.S. governments against the cities of half the world – Tokyo, Dresden, Hiroshima, the villages of Korea, Hanoi, Beirut, Panama, Tripoli, Kabul, Baghdad, Belgrade – the time for horror would also arrive in New York and Washington. They have spent their lives sowing the seeds of rage throughout the world; they shouldn't be surprised that the harvest of storms has arrived.
Antonio Caballero, renowned Colombian journalist

A Historical Context

In previous chapters, different types of anti-Americanism were described. Let us turn to the view that distinguishes issue-oriented, ideological, instrumental, or revolutionary types in the Third World (Rubinstein and Smith, 1985). Issue-oriented anti-Americanism is mostly episodic and rooted in policy disagreements between a foreign government and the United States over specific issues. Ideological anti-Americanism is more sustained and consists of a belief system in which the United States is viewed as a decadent society, the government of which is conducting hegemonic, imperialist policies. Instrumental anti-Americanism is based on hostility toward the United States instigated and manipulated by a government for ulterior motives, such as to consolidate supporters or identify an "external" enemy. Finally, revolutionary anti-Americanism, similar to ideological anti-Americanism, is used by a political opposition seeking to overthrow a regime allied with the United States. Should this oppositional movement come to power, their ideological anti-Americanism becomes a key, legitimizing tenet of their foreign and domestic policies.

Such a classification of different types of anti-Americanism is valuable because it allows analysts to form a better understanding of the reactions of people and elites to

71

the events of September 11th. Any deviation from the United States Administration's viewpoint should not be deemed "anti-American" because such a categorization might produce a distorted view of attitudes about the United States. It is argued by some experts that differentiating among various types of seemingly anti-American attitudes is important because "there is the danger of dismissing all criticism of the United States as the product of a mindless and homogeneous anti-Americanism and thus of failing to address the issues that give rise to criticism of the United States" (Crockatt, 2003, 46). For example, staunch disagreement with Washington's military response to the terrorist attacks does not necessarily indicate a visceral hostility toward the United States. Rather, such opinions are probably better classified as situational and related to issue-oriented anti-Americanism.

Cross-national and cross-regional variations occur with regard to different forms of anti-Americanism. Latin America has often been regarded as a bastion of ideological and revolutionary anti-Americanism. The explanations for this are various and not mutually exclusive. At the broadest level of generalization it has been suggested that Latin America, like much of the Third World, evinces a certain envy and resentment of the power and success of the United States (Haseler, 1985). Often, this resentment is mixed with a simultaneous admiration, leading to what Rangel describes as "Latin America's undeniably true feelings—a mixture of admiration and envy, of love and hate, toward the overbearingly successful North Americans" (Rangel, 1977, 63). Indeed, Rangel goes so far as to suggest that ideological anti-Americanism is the result of a psychological need to compensate for their feelings of inferiority and humiliation with reference to the United States.

Most analysts, however, point to more concrete reasons for ideological anti-Americanism in Latin America. Of particular note is the long history of United States interventionism in the region. While a specific intervention might be the cause of immediate issue-oriented anti-Americanism, the repeated history of interventions, even into the 1980s and 1990s (e.g., Panama, Grenada, Nicaragua, Haiti), goes a long way toward explaining the development of ideological anti-Americanism among many elites of the region. The negative effects of this history have been compounded by racial and ethnic prejudice, in which Latin Americans often perceived United States officials as treating them as inferior human beings. Lars Schoultz (1998) in his extensive history of the relations between the United States and Latin America has argued that this was not a misperception by Latin American elites: the belief in Latin American inferiority was the essential core of United States policy toward Latin America.

Nevertheless, despite the many reasons for ideological anti-Americanism, it must be kept in mind that people in the region also share with the United States a form of Western Judeo-Christian culture. As Horowitz has noticed, "for most people of Latin America, a sense of common and shared values with North America is taken for granted" (1985, 51). The source of anti-Americanism, as this author implies, is the frequent failure of the United States to keep faith with its own highest ideals and values. This argument may underline the reasons why the history of repeated United States interventionism and prejudice have fostered ideological anti-Americanism in the region. In general, anti-Americanism is a phenomenon associated with elites. In particular, ideological anti-Americanism is an attitude held primarily by intellectual elites—that is, academics, journalists, teachers, university students, and some politicians. As Horowitz argued, it was dangerous and erroneous to view anti-Americanism as an indigenous and mass phenomenon within Latin America. Such a contention appears to be backed by recent empirical evidence showing broadly favorable attitudes toward the United States among the general populace of the vast majority of countries in Latin America (Lagos, 2003). This is worth keeping in mind as we examine the data from Colombia. The bulk of the data reviewed in the next section consists of elite opinions, and thus may well overstate the general ideological anti-Americanism present in contemporary Colombia.

Post 9/11 Attitudes toward the United States in Colombia

To appreciate the range of attitudes in Colombia about the United States after the September 11th attacks, it is useful to consider public opinion in terms of three principal groups—the general public, government officials, and elites. The available evidence indicates that the Colombian general public exhibited a broadly favorable attitude towards the United States. For example, a poll conducted by Latinobarómetro in 2002 found that 76 per cent of Colombian respondents had a "good" or "very good" opinion about the United States (Lagos, 2003, 99). However, such a positive opinion was reduced considerably when Colombians were questioned about the effects of United States foreign policy on Colombia. In a Gallup Poll conducted in September 2001 after the 9/11 attacks, only 41 per cent of respondents asserted that American foreign policy generally had a "positive effect" on Colombia (Gallup International 2001). This same poll revealed that only 11 per cent of Colombians (compared to 54 per cent of United States citizens) believed that once the terrorists were identified, the United States should launch a military attack on the country where they were based (Ibid). In short, there appeared to be relatively little deep-seated ideological anti-Americanism amongst the Colombian general public. Nonetheless, strong disagreement with specific United States foreign policy measures (e.g., a military response to 9/11) did appear to elicit issue-oriented anti-Americanism among many ordinary Colombians.

Meanwhile, the reaction of Colombian government officials to the 9/11 attacks was one of unambiguous support for the United States. As discussed below, the administration of President Andrés Pastrana (1998–2002) had actively courted United States support for several years. Indeed, by the time of the September 11th tragedy, the Pastrana administration had succeeded in convincing both the Clinton and Bush administrations to support a massive program of security and economic aid to Colombia ("Plan Colombia"), which had made Colombia the third largest recipient of United States aid in the world. Furthermore, Colombian government officials saw in the 9/11 attacks a means of consolidating the support of the United States for the Colombian armed forces in their struggle against the Revolutionary Armed Forces of Colombia (*Fuerzas Armadas Revolucionarias de Colombia*, FARC) and the National Liberation Army (*Ejército de Liberación Nacional*, ELN). These revolutionary movements arguably engaged in terrorist tactics and, indeed, were designated by the State Department as "foreign terrorist organizations" (United States Department of State 2001).

Thus, the Colombian Embassy in Washington sought to demonstrate empathy with the United States by noting that "the deep sense of insecurity and anger that have overwhelmed the U.S. are feelings that Colombians have had to endure for the last 40 years" (Embassy of Colombia, 2002). Moreover, it explicitly drew parallels between the Colombian government's struggle against armed opponents and the Taliban: "what is happening in Colombia is not very different from what has happened in Afghanistan … [T]he Taliban have financed their revolution, and a good part of their activities by taxing the heroin industry, much in the same way as the guerrillas and the paramilitaries in Colombia" (Ibid). Building upon these parallels, the Colombian foreign minister, Guillermo Fernández de Soto, in an address to the OAS on September 21, 2001, sought to use the 9/11 tragedy to reaffirm close U.S.-Colombian relations: "I wish to express my recognition, that of my government, and that of the people of Colombia, for the effective solidarity that the government of the United States has shown in the struggle that we are facing against the global problem of drugs and its innumerable terrorist effects. My country today is on the side of the U.S. people and their government, victims of these acts that placed the soul of the nation in mourning and shook the world" (De Soto, 2001).

The attitude of Colombian elites, as revealed in a content analysis of their opinions in the major organs of the Colombia print media after 9/11, was more mixed than that of either the general public or government officials. However, to begin with the least ambiguous result, the overwhelming majority of elite opinions found the September 11th attacks and/or their perpetrators to be outrageous and clearly morally unacceptable. Fully 77 per cent of the opinions viewed the attacks/perpetrators in negative terms ranging from "criminal" to "fanatic" to "despicable" and "cowardly." Another 16 per cent of opinions utilized more neutral terms such as "well-organized," "shrewd" or "intelligent" to describe the attacks and/or their perpetrators. Only 2 per cent expressed the seemingly sympathetic opinions that the attacks were part of a "Holy war" or that the perpetrators were "victims of oppression, exploitation, or persecution." Thus, in describing the September 11th attacks, Colombian elites demonstrated almost no sympathy for its perpetrators. Colombian elites also (although to a lesser degree) accepted the official United States explanation of the perpetrators, with 48 per cent pointing to "Osama bin Laden" or "Al Qaeda," and another 10 per cent signaling "Islamic militants" more generally. Still another 4 per cent more equivocally blamed "Arab militants," while 10 per cent thought that "Palestinians" were guilty and 4 per cent believed that "Iraq" was behind the attacks. Notably, not a single Colombian elite expressed the view that domestic terrorists were behind the attacks, nor did any venture the conspiratorial view that the United States government itself was responsible.

In describing the conflict underlying the September 11th attacks, Colombian elites demonstrated a greater degree of autonomy from the official position of the United States. Overall, 39 per cent of elite opinions took the position of the Bush administration that 9/11 was "an attack against freedom, democracy, or the civilized world," or "a clash between good and evil." Another 35 per cent held that this attack was better understood as the manifestation of a conflict between civilizations or religions. This position, although it did not accord with the Bush administration's interpretation of events, was certainly not anti-American per se. Only 9 per cent held the more anti-American positions that this was "a conflict between rich and poor" or "a war of the United States against the world."

A stronger indicator of the existence of ideological anti-Americanism might be found in the opinions ventured on the root causes or motivations for the September 11th attacks. Of those Colombian elites who ventured such opinions, some 38 per cent opined that the United States was directly or indirectly responsible for the attacks due either to specific foreign policy actions taken in the past or more generally to the arrogance of the United States. Nonetheless, another 48 per cent held the more pro-American view that religious or political fanaticism was at the root of the attacks or that the attacks were motivated by jealousy or hatred of the United States. Finally, 3 per cent of elite opinions pointed to conditions of poverty or human suffering as the root cause.

Colombian elites distanced themselves still further from the official position of the United States government when opining on how the United States should respond to 9/11. In general, the opinions expressed by elites reflected the belief that the United States should not respond to the September 11th attacks with force. Indeed, only 4 per cent of opinions in the print media felt that the United States should react to 9/11 with military force. Fully 17 per cent explicitly urged Washington *not* to declare war against terrorism. Another 50 per cent urged the United States to pause and soberly reflect or to work primarily through the world community to counter terrorism. Finally, 16 per cent placed the onus fully on the United States, urging it to reform its own foreign or intelligence policies. Although these results may indicate a lack of identification with United States' government policy (cf. Shlapentokh and Woods), it would be erroneous to interpret them as indicators of strong ideological anti-Americanism. Rather, they are probably best interpreted as rational disagreements with a specific United States' policy response. Thus, to the extent that the opinions reflected any anti-Americanism, they were most likely a manifestation of issue-based anti-Americanism.

This benign interpretation is bolstered by an examination of the opinions expressed with regard to how the Colombian government should react to the events of September 11th. Overall, the elite opinions encountered in the print media were decidedly sympathetic toward helping the United States. About 77 per cent of the recorded elite opinions expressed the belief that Colombia should in fact help or support the United States *in some fashion* (although not necessarily militarily). Indeed, given the fact that the Colombian military had its hands full trying to contain Colombia's own long-standing internal conflict, it would be surprising in the extreme if elites actually supported sending Colombian troops abroad to fight. Notably, on this same issue, only about 2 per cent of elite opinions indicated an explicit rejection of supporting the United States.

The preceding argument is not to suggest that Colombian elites evinced no anti-American feelings. That would have been surprising, especially given Colombia's position as a Latin American country that has experienced first-hand the effects of United States intervention. Such ideological anti-Americanism is perhaps best captured in the abstract phrases that elites used to describe the United States. These opinions frequently did not distinguish between the United States government and its citizens. When referenced in this fashion, 24 per cent of the opinions expressed generally positive views of the United States. Another 43 per cent of elite opinions were neutral descriptive statements to the effect that the United States was "the world's only superpower" or that it was "a country whose superpower status had been shaken by the events of September 11th." Such descriptive statements, by themselves, reveal neither antipathy nor friendliness toward the United States. However, some 31 per cent of elite opinions regarding the nature of the United States were clearly negative. These opinions held that the United States was "belligerent," "vindictive," "chauvinistic," "arrogant," "materialistic," "culturally imperialist," "unjust," "hypocritical," etc. Such strongly worded evaluations go beyond issue-oriented disagreements with the United States and point to the existence of a more ideological anti-Americanism among a minority of Colombian elites.

Nevertheless, such ideological anti-Americanism appeared to be directed primarily against the United States government rather than the citizenry as a whole. Thus, when elites commented directly about the government, 68 per cent of these opinions were negative, and only 26 per cent were positive. On the other hand, when the citizenry was referred to, more than one half of elite opinions showed favorable sentiments toward the public, while only 22 per cent were negative. If we combine the general statements made about the United States with those specifically referencing the United States' government and those referring to citizens, we have a total of 434 coded opinions regarding the nature of the United States. Overall, 35 per cent of these opinions were negative, about 27 per cent were positive, and almost 34 per cent were essentially neutral. In sum, the opinions expressed by Colombian elites in the print media toward the United States covered a fairly broad spectrum— as a whole, they were neither unequivocally hostile toward the United States nor unquestioningly friendly. Perhaps a third of the elite opinions evinced an underlying ideological anti-Americanism, but such sentiments were counterbalanced by more positive or neutral opinions about the United States.

An analysis of the media publications provides evidence in support of this picture of Colombian elite views. Overall, coders examined 283 articles from the Colombian press. For each article, the coder was asked to state his or her own opinion regarding whether the article presented the United States in a favorable or unfavorable light. Notably, coders found that 40 per cent (113 articles) were either completely or mostly favorable toward the United States. At the opposite end of the spectrum, 22 per cent of the articles were judged to be completely or mostly unfavorable toward the United States. Finally, almost 38 per cent of the articles were determined to be neutral, mixed, or too difficult to judge.

The preceding review of the evidence indicates that Colombians, by and large, were sympathetic to the United States in the period immediately after September 11th. Among the general public, this sympathy did not, however, extend to a more generalized support of specific United States foreign policy actions. Moreover, this skeptical stance regarding the country's foreign policy was evident among Colombian elites, as revealed in their opinions in the written press. Meanwhile, the Colombian government was unambiguous in its efforts to demonstrate complete solidarity with the United States in the aftermath of 9/11. The challenge for the analyst is to explain these seemingly contradictory aspects of Colombian attitudes toward the United States—broadly positive attitudes toward the United States in general combined with an evident unwillingness to approve of its foreign policy actions—a skepticism that, in the case of a minority of Colombian elites, appeared to reflect a substantial degree of ideological anti-Americanism.

Explaining Colombian Attitudes: External Factors

The complexity of Colombian attitudes about the United States is best explained as the "product" of several overlapping factors. Many Colombians, as well as their counterparts in Latin America, tend to maintain distrust of the United States, particularly with regard to its foreign policy. This attitude is especially notable among Colombian intellectual elites, who frequently evince a marked ideological anti-Americanism. Moreover, as in most Latin American countries, this attitude was shaped largely, although not exclusively, by specific historical encounters with the United States. On the other hand, negative attitudes in Colombia are assuaged by a variety of factors including growing emigration to the United States and the apparent need for United States' support to help end Colombia's decades-old internal armed conflict. These seemingly opposed tendencies—both pro- and anti-American—have evolved simultaneously, although during any given period of time one or the other appears to predominate. Furthermore, while some Colombian elites are rigidly anti-American and others are staunchly pro-American, most of them occupy an uncertain middle ground, manifesting seemingly ambiguous, conflicting attitudes toward the United States. Let us examine separately the reasons why Colombians hold anti-American and pro-American attitudes.

To some extent, ideological anti-Americanism in Colombia is the result of an understandable wariness of the overwhelming power that the United States exerts in the Western Hemisphere. This suspicion has been compounded among many intellectual elites by their adherence to variants of Marxism or dependency theory, which view the United States as inherently exploitative. Nonetheless, such negative predispositions have been consolidated by the history of U.S.-Colombian relations, in which the United States on various occasions has utilized its dominance to exert undue pressure on reluctant Colombian leaders. Moreover, concrete United States' actions have not infrequently been accompanied by an ill-disguised disdain exhibited by American leaders and representatives for their Colombian counterparts. The combination of these elements goes far toward explaining why many Colombian elites harbor feelings of ideological anti-Americanism.

The seeds of an anti-American sentiment were initially planted in the first half of the nineteenth century. Although relations between the United States and the newly-independent Colombia had begun on a promising note, by the time of the American Civil War "affairs between the two nations had deteriorated to the level of bitter recrimination, hostility, suspicion, and, at times, open contempt for the other society and its political culture" (Randall, 1992, 42). From the perspective of the United States, the tense relations stemmed from the prevailing conditions in Panama, Colombia's northernmost province, which had become a major transportation route for American citizens heading to California in the wake of the 1848 discovery of gold. The United States was concerned about the inability of Colombian officials to maintain peace on the isthmus, protect American lives and property, and ensure the uninterrupted flow of traffic. These tensions were undoubtedly exacerbated by the prejudicial attitudes demonstrated by United States' representatives in the nineteenth century. For example, in the mid-1830s, United States Chargé Robert McAfee described Colombia as "a bigoted Catholic country controlled by the Priests" (Schoultz, 1998, 165). Twenty years later, United States Minister James Bowlin characterized Colombians as "miserable wretches," arguing that "even in contrast with Nations of her own kind, formed of the same revolution, from the same people, she occupies the lowest round on the ladder" (Ibid).

The Canal Issue

The central issue in U.S.-Colombian relations from the latter half of the nineteenth century through the first decades of the twentieth was the construction of a canal across the Isthmus of Panama. The United States insisted on a dominant role in the construction of any trans-isthmian waterway, and was irritated when the Colombian government awarded a concession in 1879 to a French company. After the French went bankrupt, the United States and Colombian governments negotiated the Hay-Herrán Treaty of 1903, which authorized the United States to construct and operate the canal. Nevertheless, the Colombian Senate, concerned about the amount of the initial payment as well as the abrogation of Colombian sovereignty in the proposed Canal Zone, rejected the treaty unanimously in August 1903. President Theodore Roosevelt was outraged by the decision, calling the Colombians "contemptible little creatures," "jack rabbits," and "foolish and homicidal corruptionists" (Schoultz, 1998, 164). He described Colombia as "the worst forms of despotism and of anarchy, of violence and of fatuous weakness, of dismal ignorance, cruelty, treachery, greed, and utter vanity," and concluded that, "You could no more make an agreement with the Colombian rulers than you could nail currant jelly to a wall" (Ibid, 164–165).

Washington's displeasure with the Colombian rejection of the Hay-Herrán Treaty led to one of the more dismal episodes in United States' foreign policy history—its complicity in the separation of Panama from Colombia in November 1903. This sordid tale has been recounted in detail many times (cf., Randall, 1992, 72–106; Schoultz, 1998, 152–175). Suffice it to note that the United States encouraged secessionist leaders in Panama, intervened to ensure that Colombian military forces could not put down the insurrection, quickly recognized the independence of the rebel government, and within two weeks negotiated a new canal treaty with representatives of the fledgling Panamanian government. Colombians held the United States directly responsible for the Panamanian secession, and their bitterness is reflected in the statement of Colombian General Daniel Ortíz: "It is preferable to see the Colombian race completely extinguished than to submit ourselves to the infamous policy of President Roosevelt" (Randall, 1992, 87). Colombian writer José María Vargas Vila subsequently expressed the generalized Colombian sentiment in those years that the United States was "the unruly and brutal north that despises us" (Safford and Palacios, 2002, 279). In 1921, the United States' government agreed to pay Colombia an indemnity of $25 million for the loss of Panama. Nonetheless, as Randall notes, "the political and cultural legacy of the Panama episode was of both greater duration and depth, shaping Colombian perceptions about the nature of the imperialist threat that it was believed the United States had come to pose to Colombian sovereignty and self-respect" (Randall, 1992, 77).

In the decades following 1921, ideological anti-Americanism was fostered by rapidly expanding United States investment in Colombia and the concomitant apprehension of some elites that this posed a threat to Colombian sovereignty. A key episode in cementing this fear was the 1928 massacre of banana workers employed by the United Fruit Company. In response to a plea from its local United States manager—and in part to avoid any pretext for an American military intervention—Colombian President Miguel Abadía Méndez had sent the army to maintain public order after 25,000 workers had declared a strike. On December 5, 1928, the troops fired on a gathering of between two and four thousand striking workers in the town of Ciénaga. Although the exact number of deaths is unknown, the incident became part of the collective memory of Colombians and was immortalized (although in exaggerated form) in Gabriel García Márquez's celebrated novel *One Hundred Years of Solitude* (Safford and Palacios, 2002, 281). An additional source of anti-American sentiment originating during this period was the United States' investment in the oil industry, wherein companies such as the Tropical Oil Company (a subsidiary of Jersey Standard) and Colombian Petroleum (a joint subsidiary of Gulf and Socony) came to control much of the production and export of oil from Colombia. Moreover, as in the banana industry, American oil companies faced massive labor unrest and relied upon Colombian state security forces to suppress their striking workers (Bushnell, 1993, 177–78).

The Post-Cold War Developments

During World War II and the Cold War, official U.S.-Colombian relations were notably amicable, a phenomenon that will be discussed later. Nevertheless, relatively cordial relations became progressively strained beginning in the 1970s, as the issue of illicit drugs became an increasingly prominent item on the bilateral agenda. The drug problem has fostered greater ideological anti-Americanism as the United States exerted unrelenting pressure on Colombian officials to confront the drugs on the streets of American cities. The drug problem, many Colombians believed, had its origins in the insatiable demand of United States' consumers. The effects of a "hyper-narcotized" United States policy toward Colombia—one that relegated all other issues to a distinctly secondary status—were manifold (Tokatlian, 1997). For the purposes of this analysis, it is worth highlighting four aspects of Washington's counter-narcotics policy that produced animosity toward the United States.

First, Colombians, in general, resented their country being portrayed in an extraordinarily negative light as a result of the U.S.-led war on drugs. Many Colombians felt unfairly stigmatized as a result of the flood of negative media reports about their country, the unflattering portrayals of Colombians in American films and television programs, the stern consular warnings issued by the State Department to limit visitations to Colombia, and the humiliating search procedures that Colombian travelers were subjected to upon their arrival in the United States. As Robin Kirk has noted, the American perception of Colombians is brutally simple because they are largely seen as drug traffickers (Kirk, 2003). Polling data support the contention that Americans view Colombia in a negative fashion. For example, a Gallup Poll conducted in 2001 found that 59 per cent of respondents had an unfavorable view of Colombia, a lower ranking than that accorded to China, Vietnam, and North Korea (Gallup Organization 2002, 43–44). Colombians, particularly elites, are very aware of this perception and naturally resent it.

Second, Washington's counter-narcotics policy has become, as many Colombian elites believed, an unjustifiable intervention in domestic Colombian politics. This aspect culminated in the nadir of contemporary U.S.-Colombian relations during the administration of Ernesto Samper (1994–1998). Samper was accused of having knowingly accepted money from the Cali drug cartel to finance his 1994 presidential election campaign. These accusations led to impeachment proceedings against Samper in both 1995 and 1996. On each occasion, the Colombian Chamber of Representatives voted against impeachment, and Samper served out the remainder of his term (Dugas, 2001). Throughout this crisis, however, the United States played an exceedingly high profile role. Indeed, American intelligence operatives gathered the information that led to the crisis in the first place. Subsequently, the United States used the threat of "decertification" to pressure the Samper administration to appoint or remove specific Colombian officials, as well as to adopt specific policies such as lengthening sentences for convicted traffickers, introducing legislation to counter money laundering, and renewing the extradition of Colombian drug traffickers to stand trial in the United States. Despite such cooperation, the Clinton administration chose to express its displeasure with Samper by "decertifying" the country in its 1996 and 1997 annual reviews of international cooperation in the war on drugs. Ironically, these de-certifications came after the Samper government had effectively dismantled the Cali cartel. In a more personal rebuke, the State Department cancelled Samper's visa to the United States after the Chamber of Representatives failed to impeach him. Such actions "generated an unusually hostile reaction and sense of betrayal among the Colombian populace" and had the unintended consequence of bolstering public support for the flagging Samper presidency (Crandall, 2002, 42). In effect, Samper was able to portray himself as the defender of Colombian dignity and sovereignty against the United States, which refused to respect the decisions of Colombia's elected representatives.

Third, for those Colombian peasants involved directly in the cultivation of coca, United States pressure on Colombia to engage in intensive aerial fumigation to eradicate their crops generated intense hostility toward the United States among population. For example, in 1996 tens of thousands of peasants protested the planned fumigation in the department of Putumayo. Their protests ended only after the Colombian government agreed to allow farmers to manually eradicate their own coca crops and to provide funds for alternative crops (Crandall, 2002, 123–124). Subsequently, extensive U.S.-funded aerial fumigation destroyed legal food crops and raised significant concerns about its environmental and health effects (WOLA 2002, 6–7). For example, the Colombian Public Advocate's Office conducted studies in 2000 and 2001 that underscored the health problems associated with both skin contact and the inhalation of the herbicide used in aerial spraying (Tickner, 2003, 78–79). Moreover, the Public Advocate's Office harshly criticized the U.S.-funded coca fumigation campaign after receiving some 6,553 complaints from farmers that their *legal* crops had been erroneously sprayed. Many of these small farmers, including several from indigenous communities, had previously signed social eradication pacts to manually remove their coca plants, only to find that their new alternative crops were sprayed (Haugaard, 2002, 3, 5). Notably, this spraying occurred in November 2001, precisely when the United States was hoping to receive foreign solidarity in the aftermath of the September 11th attacks. Fourth, Colombian human rights activists have been justifiably concerned that the United States war on drugs has had the unintended consequence of deepening human rights abuses stemming from Colombia's decades-old internal armed conflict. Since 1989, the United States has provided several billion dollars worth of military aid to the Colombian National Police and the Colombian Armed Forces for the purposes of fighting drugs. Notably, this policy of massive military aid has been carried out despite the fact that these state security forces have directly or indirectly engaged in egregious human rights abuses (Dugas, 2004). This aid intensified in the late 1990s under the auspices of "Plan Colombia," a supposedly comprehensive strategy meant to eradicate drugs, support a negotiated settlement with the guerrilla movements, and revive the floundering Colombian economy. Nonetheless, the vast bulk of United States money went toward security assistance. Indeed, between 1999 and 2002, the country gave Colombia $2.04 billion, of which 83 per cent ($1.69 billion) went to Colombia's military and police forces (Vaicius and Isacson, 2003). The current human rights situation in Colombia is appalling, with over 15,000 persons killed in political violence *outside of combat* just in the 5-year period of 1997–2001. Right-wing paramilitary groups are estimated to have carried out 70–80 per cent of these killings, often with the direct complicity or acquiescence of the Colombian state security forces (Fundación Social-UNICEF 2002). Not surprisingly, human rights activists and leftist politicians are furious that the United States continues to fund the Colombian state security forces despite their record of human rights abuses and their continuing ties to the abusive right-wing paramilitary groups.

There are numerous reasons why Colombians may be distrustful of the United States, and why some elites have developed a marked ideological anti-Americanism. Thus, it is not particularly surprising that many Colombian elites did not "identify" with the position of the United States' government in the aftermath of the September 11th attacks. This is not, however, the whole story. Equally notable is the fact that many other Colombians—including elites—exhibited a marked degree of sympathy toward the United States after 9/11. In order to understand this mixed picture it is thus also necessary to explore the reasons why many Colombians held a more positive view of the United States.

Internal Factors: The Perception of Common Interests with the United States

Just as ideological anti-Americanism may originate from seemingly abstract beliefs (e.g., a distrust of inordinate power; an adherence to Marxism or dependency theory), so too pro-American sentiments may be partially rooted in a perception of shared values with the United States. Moreover, such positive attitudes may be bolstered by the widespread admiration found throughout the region for the United States' technological prowess and ingenuity. Pro-American sympathies exhibited by many Colombian elites appear to be related to their social-class position. These people are attracted to the prosperity of the United States and seek to establish a similarly comfortable lifestyle for themselves.

Nonetheless, ideological anti-Americanism further consolidated as the result of specific experiences. The argument here is two-fold: First, pro-American attitudes have been nurtured in part by positive experiences with the United States government or with individual citizens of the country. Second, and at least of equal importance, positive sentiments toward the United States have developed as a reaction to internal conditions within Colombia. Specifically, a growing despair over the prolonged armed conflict in their country has caused many Colombians to look to the United States for support—whether in the form of increased military or economic assistance, or as a desirable destination for those who chose to emigrate from their country.

For extended periods the United States and Colombia enjoyed quite amicable relations, particularly in the twentieth century. President Marco Fidel Suárez (1918–1921), a fervent admirer of the United States, attempted during his administration to establish an overarching principle for Colombian foreign policy, which he labeled the "Doctrine of the Polar Star." In brief, this meant that "Colombia must look northward, toward the pole (the United States), to find a model of social and political democracy and a natural collaborator in political and economic affairs" (Bushnell, 1992, 165). More generally, the Suárez Doctrine entailed "a perception that ties with the United States were inevitable and should be constructively pursued" (Randall, 1992, 109). This more general understanding of the Suárez Doctrine has, in fact, largely guided Colombian leaders from the time of Suárez to the present day. Although different presidential administrations have demonstrated greater or lesser degrees of autonomy from United States foreign policy, nearly all—if only for pragmatic reasons—have made substantial efforts to maintain positive relations with the United States.

From the period of World War II through the duration of the Cold War, formal U.S.-Colombian relations were exceedingly close. Thus, Colombia broke diplomatic relations with Japan the day after Pearl Harbor and with Germany and Italy less than two weeks later (Randall, 1992). With the advent of the Cold War, Colombia also broke relations with the Soviet Union in 1948 (Ibid, 196). In an even greater show of solidarity with the United States, Colombia was the only Latin American country to send troops to fight as part of the United Nations forces in Korea, contributing both a battalion and a frigate to the war effort (Ibid, 199). It should be underscored that such actions were not taken merely to court favor with the United States. As Randall has stressed, Colombian ruling elites shared essentially the same values as their American counterparts. Thus, Colombia needed little additional encouragement to move into the anti-Soviet and later the anti-Castro camp. If the United States had a vested interest in free enterprise, anti-Communism, a free labor movement, and political pluralism, Colombians had an equally strong vested interest in ensuring that this was the direction of Colombian politics. One errs in attributing too much influence to the United States in the achievement of these goals (Randall, 1992).

Colombia reaped the rewards for its seemingly pro-American stance by becoming one of the major Latin American recipients of United States military aid in the 1950s. Subsequently, in the early 1960s, it became a "showcase" for the Alliance for Progress, an endeavor that was embraced positively by most Colombian elites, particularly during the Kennedy administration. Even during the more strained period of the American-led war on drugs, recent Colombian administrations (e.g., Andrés Pastrana, 1998–2002; Alvaro Uribe, 2002 and later) have enjoyed excellent relations with the United States government, which has in turn reciprocated with massive amounts of military and economic aid. Indeed, at the time of the September 11th attacks, Colombia had become the third largest recipient of American foreign aid in the world.

Productive economic and social ties have generally complemented these positive official relations. Thus, most Colombians, and especially elites, are well aware that the United States is the principal market for their exports, as well as the leading producer of the goods and services imported by Colombians. For example, in 2000 the United States was the destination of almost 51 per cent of Colombian exports, and the source of 40 per cent of its imports, with bilateral trade reaching $11.2 billion in that same year (Embassy of Colombia, 2003). The United States is also a principal destination of Colombian elites for both tourism and higher education. The ability to study in the United States has been facilitated by governmental programs such as the United States Fulbright Program, which has enabled nearly 2,000 Colombians to travel to the United States for educational or cultural programs since 1957 (Comisión Fulbright-Colombia, 2003). Finally, it should be noted that aspects of American pop culture are ubiquitous in Colombia, ranging from fast food restaurants to movies, music, and satellite television, particularly in the larger urban areas and in middle and upper-class neighborhoods. Randall has properly cautioned that we must "be careful not to exaggerate either the degree or the impact of such 'culture'" in Colombia (Randall, 1992, 228). Nonetheless, it serves as an indicator of the relative degree of openness to certain aspects of American society among Colombians.

Despite the important role played by economic, social, and governmental relations in creating a positive attitude toward the United States, of equal significance has been the internal factor of armed conflict. In particular, a growing sense of despair over Colombia's four-decade-old internal conflict has led many Colombians, elite and otherwise, to look to the United States for support in bringing this conflict to an end. The Colombian conflict is both appallingly bloody and exceedingly complex. It originated in the 1960s, when a period of restricted political democracy facilitated the emergence of a variety of left-wing guerrilla movements that, while differing in ideological specifics, shared the goal of toppling the established political and socio-economic order. The guerrilla movements waxed and waned over the course of the succeeding decades, and several of them demobilized after lengthy peace negotiations with the government in the early and mid-1990s. Nonetheless, the two largest movements, FARC and ELN, have continued their armed struggle to the present day.

Over the years, several factors have intensified the conflict and made its resolution more difficult. First, right-wing paramilitary groups emerged in the early 1980s to fight the leftist guerrillas or, more commonly, to target their supposed collaborators in the civilian population. The paramilitaries flourished as they benefited from an influx of drug money, the support of sectors of the Colombian state security forces, and a slow process of institutionalization, which resulted in the 1997 creation of a national federation, the United Self-Defense Groups of Colombia (*Autodefensas Unidas de Colombia*, AUC), to coordinate their activities. The paramilitaries are gruesomely bloody in their methods and frequently engage in torture. As noted in the previous section, they are responsible for 70–80 per cent of all political homicides committed outside of combat in Colombia (Fundación Social-UNICEF 2002).

A second factor that complicates the conflict is the fact that the left-wing guerrillas have also engaged in an array of abuses that have kindled deep hostility on the part of most Colombians. Like the paramilitaries, the guerrillas have engaged in political killings outside of combat, accounting for 17–28 per cent of such victims annually over the past five years (Fundación Social-UNICEF 2002). Of equal concern, however, is their participation in the crime of kidnapping. It is a sad fact that roughly half of all kidnappings in the world today occur in Colombia, making it the global leader in this violation of international humanitarian law (UNHCHR 2002, 34; WOLA 2002, 1). In the five-year period 1997–2001, nearly 15,000 Colombians were kidnapped, the vast majority of them by the leftist guerrillas. In 2001 alone, over 3,000 Colombians were kidnapped (Fundación Social-UNICEF 2002). Moreover, like the paramilitaries, the guerrillas widely employ child soldiers, often under the age of fifteen, and frequently recruit them by force (HRW 1998, 192–196).

Finally, the drug trade has intensified the conflict. Both paramilitary and guerrilla forces are involved in the drug trade, reaping tremendous profits that are then invested in uniforms, rations, and armaments for their respective soldiers. Historically, the FARC and the ELN have limited their participation in the drug trade to charging taxes on the coca leaves grown in the territories that they control. Many of the paramilitaries, on the other hand, have engaged directly in the processing and distribution of cocaine. In both cases, however, the earnings from the drug trade have fueled the conflict, making it more difficult to resolve.

Most Colombians have little sympathy for either the left-wing guerrillas or the right-wing paramilitaries. Indeed, they have generally supported government efforts to negotiate an end to the armed conflict. Nonetheless, in recent years a critical mass of Colombians appears to have reached the end of their patience with the armed insurgents, particularly with the FARC, the largest of the guerrilla movements. This sentiment stems most directly from the frustrated effort of the administration of Andrés Pastrana (1998–2002) to negotiate peace. For over three years, the Pastrana administration engaged in a fitful dialogue with the FARC leadership, during which the guerrillas were actually ceded a 16,000 square-mile demilitarized zone intended to facilitate peace talks. Nonetheless, the talks ultimately failed to produce much more than a detailed agenda for negotiations. Over time, the Pastrana administration grew increasingly concerned about abuses committed by the FARC in the demilitarized zone, whereas the FARC repeatedly charged the government with failing to act decisively to curtail the cruelties of the paramilitaries. The peace talks broke down definitively in February 2002 when the government ordered the military to retake the demilitarized zone after the guerrillas had hijacked a commercial airliner and kidnapped its passengers, including a Liberal Party senator. Pastrana's abrupt termination of the peace talks received broad support from the Colombian public. By then, most Colombians had come to believe that the president's good faith efforts had been cynically abused by the FARC, which continued to prepare for and engage in war instead of negotiating seriously for peace.

The hardening of the public's attitude was subsequently confirmed in the presidential elections of May 2002, when Liberal Party maverick Alvaro Uribe won the election with 53 per cent of the votes (Registradura Nacional del Estado Civil 2002). More than anything else, Uribe was known for his unyielding stance with regard to the country's left-wing guerrillas. He had been extremely critical of the peace negotiations engaged in by Pastrana, particularly the ceding of the demilitarized zone, which Uribe dismissed as a "paradise for delinquents" (Aznarez,

2002). Uribe's fundamental position was that "violent groups can only be stopped when the state exercises authority and demonstrates to them that it is able to defeat them" (*El Espectador* 2002). Thus, he stressed the need to reestablish state authority by greatly strengthening the state security forces. Specifically, Uribe proposed nearly doubling the number of professional soldiers in Colombia, from 54,000 to 100,000 (Primero Colombia 2002). He pledged his complete support for Plan Colombia, and called for its expansion in order to help Colombia prevent "terrorism, kidnapping, massacres, and the taking over of municipalities" (Uribe, 2002). More polemically, he suggested that Colombia should invite multinational forces, under the auspices of the United Nations, to reinforce national troops. He called for an anti-terrorist statute to facilitate searches and detentions. And he emphasized the need for citizens to support the state security forces, pledging to create a network of one million citizen informants to provide timely intelligence to the police and armed forces (Uribe, 2002).

Although outside observers found such proposals to be both extreme and militaristic, they clearly resonated with many in a populace grown weary of guerrilla violence. For many middle and upper class Colombians, as well as for many poorer Colombians who had been harmed by guerrilla actions, Uribe represented the rare politician who had the backbone to confront the leftist guerrillas. Notably, one year after his election to the presidency a survey of public opinion in May 2003 revealed that 71 per cent of respondents approved of Uribe's performance in office, while a whopping 79 per cent approved of the measures that he had taken to strengthen public security (*Cambio* 2003, 32).

Uribe's evident popularity, his full backing for Plan Colombia, and his unreserved support for the United States since his arrival in office are all indirect indicators of a significant reserve of goodwill toward the United States. Uribe has clearly conveyed that Colombia needs the assistance of the United States if it is to confront effectively its leftist insurgencies and, if not defeat them, at least pressure them to negotiate an end to the armed conflict. For its part, both the Clinton and Bush administrations endeavored to meet Colombian needs through massive outlays of primarily military aid under the auspices of Plan Colombia. Although the merits of Plan Colombia are certainly open to debate (particularly given the human rights concerns noted above), what must be underscored here is the broad acceptance that this strategy has had with the Colombian public. In short, despair over the inability of successive Colombian governments to resolve the armed conflict has led many Colombians to embrace United States aid. Some do so with enthusiasm and others with reluctance, yet the end result is that many Colombians have come to view United States support as necessary for ending their terrible nightmare.

While the armed conflict has caused many Colombians to look to the United States with hope, it has also increased the attractiveness of the United States as a place of political and economic refuge. Until the mid-1980s, emigration from Colombia to the United States had been relatively moderate. Between 1961 and 1986, for example, some 206,000 Colombians immigrated to the United States (Randall, 1992, 227). As Randall has noted, this was before the intensification of both the war on drugs and the internal conflict, and most of these Colombians were pulled by the attraction of economic and political opportunities in the United States. However, by 2001, the rate of immigration to the United States had doubled, with some 16,000 Colombians arriving in that year alone (Office of Immigration Statistics, 2001). By the late 1990s, the Colombian news media began to speak of an "exodus" of Colombians leaving the country, primarily as a result of the growing violence. Indeed, a Gallup Poll undertaken in 1999 revealed that an astonishing 56 per cent of Colombians desired to leave the country (*Semana*, 1999). The number of asylum cases filed by Colombians in the United States grew rapidly from 334 cases in 1999 to 7,307 cases in 2001 (Office of Immigration Statistics 1999, 2001). Although the "push" factor was now clearly more important in the decision by Colombians to immigrate, it is notable that the United States was the preferred choice of most Colombians, with Spain and Canada vying for second place (*Semana*, 1999).

In sum, there have been a number of important sources of pro-American attitudes in Colombia, ranging from shared values and admiration for American technological feats to a history of generally amicable relations between Colombia and the United States for most of the twentieth century. Notably, internal conditions have also helped to foster a favorable predisposition toward the United States among some Colombians. In particular, the prolonged and intensifying nature of the Colombian armed conflict has led them to look to the United States for support. At the same time, other Colombians have come to view the United States as a desirable destination to which they can escape from the current violence.

Conclusion

Colombians, as people in other countries, reacted in a variety of ways to the events of September 11th. The vast majority of people unequivocally condemned the attacks. However, while some identified with the White House's vigorous military response, others criticized it and went so far as to place the blame for the terrorist attacks squarely on the shoulders of the United States. Some Colombians, particularly among the intellectual elite, demonstrated an unambiguous ideological anti-Americanism, while others—including many elite groups—reflected a clear sympathy for the United States.

The complexity of the Colombian reaction is best explained as the result of overlapping influences. That is, there are sufficient reasons for Colombians to hold very negative as well as extremely positive opinions of the United States. On one hand, many Colombians viewed the United States with suspicion. The long history of U.S.-Colombian relations provided to them sufficient reasons to distrust and dislike the United States. Other Colombian elites, however, believe that the United States and Colombia, despite setbacks, share a range of fundamental values. They, too, can point to numerous instances of friendship and solidarity in U.S.-Colombian relations, and see the country as an important source of support for resolving the current armed conflict in their country. Still, other Colombians are likely to find themselves conflicted in their feelings about the United States, caught amidst the seemingly contradictory arguments about the impact of the United States on Colombia.

Most Colombians hold opinions about the United States that are somewhat tentative in nature: they are less ideological and more issue-oriented and, therefore, apt to change in accordance with the context of the times. This conclusion appears to be supported by a Gallup Poll in Colombia indicating that the proportion of

Colombians holding a favorable opinion of the United States dropped from nearly 60 per cent in July 2002 to only 31 per cent in February 2003, as the United States prepared to go to war unilaterally against Iraq (Londoño, 2003). The Colombian case thus serves as an instructive reminder that American policymakers cannot simply count on popular support from a country, even when ideological anti-Americanism is the minority point of view.

* * *

Editorial Remarks

When viewed in comparison to the other countries examined in this book, Colombia, as well as most other countries, occupies a somewhat "intermediate" position. On one hand, as Ambassador Patterson noted in the beginning of the chapter, many Colombians expressed sincere regrets over the loss of life in the attacks and subsequently identified with the vigorous reaction of the Bush administration. On the other hand, as exemplified by Antonio Caballero's comments, a significant number of Colombians manifested a distinct lack of sympathy for the plight of the United States. While condemning the attacks, these Colombians had a ready explanation for why these tragic events took place. They believed that the United States was directly or indirectly responsible for the terrorism caused by the country's foreign policy. Many of them also maintained that the United States should not respond unilaterally or with military force.

Most people in Colombia have access to information. However, their particular experiences, especially in cases when the United States foreign policy influenced their wellbeing, had a tremendous impact on how the events in the United States were perceived. Overall, the complex reactions of Colombians are likely to be viewed as a continuum between (a) attitudes of resentment and even animosity toward the United States given its history of domination in Latin America, and (b) attitudes of hope and sympathy rooted in beliefs and expectations for a greater solidarity with the United States.

The history of United States foreign policy toward Colombia certainly provides numerous examples that help understand the reasons why anti-American feelings have been occurring among Colombians. Such examples include United States' complicity in the separation of Panama and, more recently, tremendous pressure exerted on the Colombian government to carry out a punitive war on drugs. Such actions have been particularly resented by elites, who were the principal focus of this study. Nonetheless, anti-American sentiments are attenuated by the country's long-standing internal armed conflict and the widely perceived need for American assistance if Colombia's leftist guerrilla movements are ever to be defeated or, more likely, pressured into serious negotiations. An additional attenuating factor is the large-scale immigration of Colombians to the United States in the 1990s and 2000s, helping to create the perception of the United States as a place friendly toward political refugees and welcoming for economic opportunity. On balance, these factors helped to generate a set of complex attitudes—a moderately favorable position about the United States, yet colored by an evident distrust of United States' foreign policy.

It is remarkable how cultural factors are incorporated in the debates about the United States and its relations with Colombia. People carrying anti-American sentiment are likely to maintain that Colombia represents a relatively poor and oppressed country exploited or neglected by the rich and arrogant United States. Supporters of the United States are likely to point out that Colombia, like the United States, is a western country with a dominant Christian religion, a formal political democracy, and a major recipient of aid from the United States.

Suggested Additional Literature

Kirk, Robin (2003). *More Terrible than Death: Massacres, Drugs, and America's War in Colombia*. New York: Public Affairs.

Lagos, Marta (2003). Terrorism and the Image of the United States in Latin America. *International Journal of Public Opinion Research*, 15, 1, 95–101.

Schoultz, Lars (1998). *Beneath the United States: A History of U.S. Policy toward Latin America*. Cambridge, MA: Harvard University Press.

Tickner, Arlene (2003). Colombia and the United States: From Counternarcotics to Counterterrorism. *Current History*, 102, 661, 77–85.

Vaicius, Ingrid, and Isacson, Adam (2003). *The "War on Drugs" Meets the "War on Terror."* Washington, D.C.: Center for International Policy.

CASE 4
CHINA

"What will be the new world order in the post-Cold War era?" This was one of the most widely discussed topics before September 11th 2001. It seemed that the most educated guess suggested that communist China would soon surge up to replace the former U.S.S.R. as the "evil superpower" that would compete with the United States for oil, political influence and military power. An internal Chinese official report on the analysis, assessment, and study of the development and crisis of Sino-U.S. relations also implied that in the next 10 to 20 years, these relations would be in a "mixed state of tension, détente, antagonism, cooperation, challenges, and anti-challenges, with each of them being spectacular at one time or another" (Li, 1997). No matter how biased political interpretations are, one thing is true: the diplomatic relationship between China and the United States remains fluctuating and dependent upon leaders and events. Some external events aggravate the Sino-U.S. relationship while some soothe it.

Chapter 6

China and Hong Kong Reporting on the United States: Ambivalence and Contradictions

Anthony Fung

The NATO military campaign against Yugoslavia in 1999 and the bombing of the Chinese embassy in Belgrade were important "external events" that influence the perception of the United States in China. At the time some experts even suggested the outbreak of a limited Sino-United States war (Li, 1997). Immediately after the bombing, which Washington claimed was accidental, the *People's Daily*, the official newspaper of the People's Republic of China (PRC) published an article lashing out at NATO and charging the United States with attempting to "intervene and destroy China's development" (N.A. 1999: A4). NATO's air strike convinced China that America had turned to hegemonic policies thus forcing China to reevaluate and withdraw from its all-embracing and multi-lateral diplomacy. It also intensified Chinese domestic politics by polarizing the pro-American reformist camp headed by the former Chinese Premier Zhu Rongji and other conservative groups (Jian, 1999). By April 2001, the Sino-American relationship was put to an additional critical test when an American spy plane collided with a Chinese jet, causing the death of the Chinese pilot.

Despite these events, the global scene has been totally transformed by the events of September 11th. In Chinese, the word "crisis" or "*weiji*" can be dissembled into "wei" and "ji." While the former means danger and risk, the best signifier for the 9/11 attack, the latter can be translated into "opportunity"—in this case, an opportunity for China and the United States to redefine a new working relationship. The subsequent reaction of the Chinese media to the event created a united propaganda front (including the print media and Chinese Central Television, CCTV), and represented the shift away from anti-Americanism and toward the accommodation of a new Chinese foreign policy.

The state's political position, however, has created at least two contradictions. First, while the official view has China leaning toward the United States, it cannot be so pronounced as to embarrass Chinese leaders with the charge that it is ingratiating itself to the West. Second, the restoration of the ties should not be made too explicitly with respect to a public that was educated to safeguard against capitalist "spiritual pollution" and "American imperialism." With these dual considerations, as it is argued in this chapter, reporting about the 9/11 events required both ambivalence and ambiguity in the Chinese press. This argument is substantiated by a systematic content analysis of Chinese newspapers, in-depth analysis of the coverage, online public discussions, and interviews with veteran journalists in Hong Kong and the PRC.

Chinese Media Coverage: Consistence and Contradictions

In the wake of 9/11, the Chinese authorities attempted to restore Sino-American ties by suppressing anti-Americanism in the media and maintaining a coherent and consistent international foreign policy image. As a sort of warning to the international community to keep its distance from China's "internal problems" with Taiwan and Tibet, the PRC advocated a policy of non-interference. To remain consistent with this policy, the press generally avoided giving overt policy directions to the United States, particularly in contradiction to existing American policies. The limited advice that was forwarded in the Chinese press tended toward a peaceful solution to the international conflict. In the sample of studied articles and comments on how the United States should react to 9/11, 43 per cent suggested working with the United Nation or the "entire world" to find a solution to the problem of terrorism (in 18 per cent of these articles, the suggested solution was a nonmilitary one).

However, given that the United States had signaled possible retaliation against the terrorists, China could not shut its door on its American support and lose the opportunity to show its support. Thus, in terms of China's reaction to the terrorist attacks, the second most prominent category was to support America's proposed action to launch military attacks against terrorist camps or military targets. In general, the Chinese government newspapers felt that such action was justifiable so long as the Americans did not cause civilian casualties (24 per cent). Nonetheless, putting together the two diverging views or categories (using non-military means, 18.3 per cent, and using military means, 23.7 per cent), it is not difficult for us to recognize a contradiction in coverage in the Chinese press. Such contradictions seem inconsistent in the eyes of the public. They are consistent, nevertheless, with China's international position *vis-à-vis* the United States.

Internally, China was retaining its political ability to use the military option. Even after decades of retreat by the Nationalist Party to Taiwan, the PRC has never renounced its military plans to target Taiwan. Together with Muslim separatism and terrorism, which are active in the northwestern province, Xinjiang, China would not contradict itself in condemning other nations using military force, particularly nations targeting Islamic terrorists. Thus the press coverage reflected the collective strategic support for these internal and external agendas.

Externally, the PRC, as a growing power, did not want to emphasize the superpower's important global position and supremacy. The events of September 11th, as the Chinese press suggested, were a catastrophe; however, treating these events as a critical event for China would contradict the country's interests. For this reason, 9/11 was played down in the media. Compared to other countries, the amount of coverage of 9/11 in the PRC was limited, with only 205 stories appearing in the September period, and 120 in October. Reports were bereft of emotion and largely deprived of strong political tones. This was also evidenced by the "researcher's opinion" section in the content analysis, which showed that 57 per cent of the Chinese articles gave either a mixed or neutral position.

The Hong Kong Media: Testing the Limits

If we can say that the Chinese press was full of ambiguity, Hong Kong's press was even more "problematic." Hong Kong has to play a dual role. It is a Special Administration Region of the PRC, so the pattern of coverage in Hong Kong should mirror that of the Chinese press. However, Hong Kong is also seen as China's window to the world. It should be international in scope as well as neutral and acceptable to the rest of the world. In other words, the Hong Kong press must stay politically close to China but open to the world.

First, the Basic Law of Hong Kong spelled out that, with the principle of "One Country, Two Systems," the people of Hong Kong are entitled to rule themselves. However, the entitlement does not include its diplomatic and military affairs, which are still in the hands of its sovereign. This is to ensure that Hong Kong presents itself as a Special Administrative Region of the PRC and shares the same nationalist ideology. Thus, it was not surprising that the political tones of the press coverage of 9/11 did not deviate greatly from its motherland. Second, before 1997 there was a significant reshuffling of ownership in the major Hong Kong media. Many newspapers, including the most prestigious English press *South China Morning Post* (which is also one of the most profitable presses in the world), *Ming Pao* and *Sing Tao Daily News*, the two newspapers targeting the professional and educated readers, the popular Chinese press *Sing Pao*, are now in the reins of Chinese businessmen, either local or living abroad, who have strong business ties with China (Fung and Lee, 1994). Despite the lack of evidence showing these newspapers kowtowing to Beijing authorities, there is also no reason why these papers need to be very critical of China. However, observers such as Pery Link, author of *June 4 True Story*, often expressed views that the Hong Kong media exercised a stronger self-censorship after its unification with China (Lee, 2003; Fung and Lee, 2002).

In the case of 9/11, the newspapers mentioned earlier, the three PRC papers in Hong Kong (*Wen Wei Po*, *Ta Kung Pao*, *Hong Kong Commercial Daily*) and other capitalist-owned radio and television stations followed the non-anti-Americanism rule of its motherland. In terms of the amount of coverage, however, as an international city, its press could not de-emphasize the event, as the press in Beijing did. Indeed, the attacks on September 11th stayed in the headlines of all major Hong Kong newspapers. Many of the reports were linked to the local economic implications of September 11th, a relevant angle for this financial city. The news also focused on the trauma, sorrow and shock of the Hong Kong people. An emotional tone was more common in the Hong Kong press than in the PRC. The United States was regarded not only as a trading partner, but also the home for many immigrants who moved there to evade the political transition to China in 1997. Thus, besides the articles about the attacks' negative impact on the local property market, banking industry and employment market, there were articles covering the people's sympathy to the victims in the United States.

As for its national role, Hong Kong papers acted more carefully. One report claimed that the 9/11 events would have positive consequences for China. There was coverage explicating that the potential risk in the United States would probably drive investments from the West to China. Politically, the United States would drain domestic resources on deterring terrorism and therefore need international support, allowing the PRC to widen its international influence. However, despite all these advantageous consequences, the Hong Kong press, even the most critical *Apple Daily*, attempted to refrain from over-reacting to this good news for their motherland lest it trigger a reaction over the PRC's sincerity in commiserating with the "tragedy." The overtone of "restoring a normal diplomatic relationship" was evident in newspapers' commentary and editorial pages. For instance, the *Hong Kong Economic Times* and *Sing Pao* said that 9/11 provided an opportunity for George Bush to befriend the PRC, a position consistent with China's foreign policy agenda. As a matter of fact, for the sake of Hong Kong's own interests, there was no reason for the press to widely present alternative views that could hurt its economic relationship with the United States and its diplomatic relationship with China.

Managing Anti-Americanism in China

Given all the calculated interests, hardly any anti-Americanism was expressed in the Chinese press. But a more crucial question is whether there exists any real anti-Americanism in the PRC. It seems that the government of the PRC—and perhaps the American government as well—pretends to be blind to the fact that there is a strong anti-American mood in Chinese society. The Chinese nationalist ideologies imposed by the authorities, ironically, helped cover up the anti-American mood in China. That is, the Chinese press was deliberately instructed to uphold the supportive position for America, and eliminate opposing views. It ignored or trivialized public opinion in its pursuit of diplomatic relations.

In China, anti-Americanism can be explored at two levels: (1) anti-Americanism in the government or party, (2) and in the public. On the government level, the expression of attitudes is relatively easy to control. In 1999, when the United States demonized China's long-held Serbian diplomatic partner and NATO bombed the Chinese embassy in Belgrade (Bezlova, 1999), the entire government was obliged to react with high-profile vehemence. But that calculated, rational mood can be suddenly changed by an order from the leadership. The September 11th events were just such an example where Chinese governmental officials changed tack on its relationship with the United States.

Thus, contrary to the media in other countries that dug deep for the root causes of the September 11th events, the Chinese media tended to curtain the causes. During the whole period covered by the study, the content analysis showed that there were only 19 articles touching on the causes of 9/11. This was because any explanation could be easily attributed to the inadequacy of the United States' foreign policies. To a certain extent, such a discussion, if it had surfaced, would tend to bring up controversies such as America's role as "big brother" or as an "international policeman" in foreign policies, its backing of Israeli expansion, and imperialism, all of which might worsen the Sino-American relationship.

During the entire period of 9/11 coverage, China managed to unswervingly control its officials' emotional responses to the events. For critical issues such as crucial international events and cases concerning relationships between China and another nation, newspapers are obliged to use reports from the central New China News Agency (NCNA), the official and centralized information release center (interview on September 4, 2003). Although individual media outlets gather their own information, they do not report it until they receive the official release from the NCNA.

The top-down instruction to suppress anti-American sentiment was strengthened by the administrative structure of the Chinese media, which are all owned by the party. The organizational and bureaucratic controls in China are strong. Almost every month, delegates are sent from the Chinese Propaganda Bureau to hold regular meetings with the media heads in different provinces. The meetings aim at ensuring that all media are unanimous on critical issues (interview on September 4, 2003). In-between these meetings, daily "memos" or "guidelines" are sent from the Propaganda Bureau; these "guidelines" served as the base limits of the press in covering critical events. Internally, in most Chinese newspapers, there is a party-monitored department, usually called "news criticism or research units," that assures the higher authorities that the newspaper will not go beyond the limits imposed by the party (interview on October 6, 2003). Thus, when the state wanted to keep a low profile on the coverage of the events of September 11th, it is not surprising that all national, provincial and city newspapers followed suit. Only occasionally, some Chinese publications of 9/11 were different and published more detailed and emotional accounts of the events in the United States. Such variations, however, did not mean that China relaxed its control over some of the papers. Rather, some newspapers, owing to their specific prominence and influence, were strategically allowed to cover the event more widely, thus being supplied with more information from the NCNA. But such a difference was only in terms of quantity while its political overtone remained the same.

As for the Hong Kong press, after 1997, most of the Hong Kong editors were told to be aware of the national foreign policy and Sino-American relationship. As a typical anecdote, an editor from Hong Kong received information about a Chinese delegation in the United States that had showed publicly being overjoyed when they heard about the events of September 11th. Rather than reporting this episode, the editor chose to ignore the story. Her explanation was that such a "boorish act" only made China look ugly, thereby disparaging the image of the Chinese authorities, which had for a long time worked on integrating the country into the world community (interview on June 13, 2003). The editor's experience revealed that the Hong Kong press had deliberately censored itself in order to stay in line with the PRC.

News routines and journalistic experience in Hong Kong inspired the press on how to behave. Editors believe strongly that the government in Beijing watches closely a few prominent websites, which means that content reported on these sites is acceptable and can be reported legitimately. These websites are the "yardsticks" that instruct the editors of Hong Kong newspapers on what to report. For certain news about China, including tragedies, political leadership, or diplomatic relations, Hong Kong papers prefer to follow events that have already been reported by other Chinese media. Such "delayed reporting" can erode the papers' competitiveness. However, as a Hong Kong editor in

China said, "we prefer political correctness to a competitive edge. We can make up for the latter with richness in other sections of the paper" (interview on June 13, 2003).

The Uncontrolled Anti-Americanism Online

The second level of anti-Americanism, the public sentiment, is more difficult to control. Chinese people in general uphold a nationalistic mood and possess antagonistic feelings about the United States. They see the country as an imperialist and a superpower that attempts to dominate the world. To manage a huge Chinese society, especially when its development is connected to foreign investment and trade, the leaders must attempt to suppress these thoughts and sentiments (Ding, 2002). Previous studies (Kuhn, 2000; Fung, 2002) have shown that opposition voices are confined to websites, such as bulletin board systems (bbs), and email.

The contents of two Chinese online sites, the Netease in the PRC and Sina in Hong Kong, both of which provided a forum for the discussion of the 9/11 events, were analyzed for this chapter. All the online discussions (366) of the Netease that appeared on the first three days after the 9/11 events were content analyzed in terms of their anti-American moods. As for Sina, because of the relatively small number of postings, a longer post-9/11 period was studied (377). While the former is one of the most prestigious non-government sites that allows for the discussion of political issues, the latter is one of the most popular commercial sites providing social, cultural, economic and political information in Hong Kong. The results of the content-analysis support the arguments that in China, and perhaps also in Hong Kong, there was a gap between the official discourses that tried to curb anti-Americanism and the civic discourses that upheld opposite views.

In the Netease, only a few postings (13 per cent, 47 postings) showed sympathy toward the United States and 30 per cent (109 postings) were hostile to it, with the remaining postings falling into the category of neutral reporting, personal narratives and analysis. The online opinion clearly tilted toward anti-Americanism and clearly contrasted with the position of the Chinese press. While the Chinese press offered support and even sympathy for the terrorist attacks in the United States, the postings on the Internet were full of messages voicing joy at what they described as a well-deserved lesson for America's arrogance. These antagonistic sentiments were connected to the memory of America's bombing of the Chinese embassy and the death of the Chinese pilot after an altercation with an American spy plane. The 9/11 events were conceived as the ultimate revenge for those who suffered under United States' hegemony. An online posting on September 12th, 2001 said: "Today, the American government finally suffered from its hegemonic ideology. What happened today showed that strong power does not result in peace. Although we are sorrowful for what results from terrorism, what other alternatives did [the terrorists] have? Is there some other method to suppress the arrogance of the big brother U.S.? [I] hope the U.S. will think about what it did in the past. What happened today refreshed my memory that in the plane clash incident, the Americans only compensated 34,567 U.S. dollars as a token. How arrogant they are! This is their attitude toward a strong nation. Let's imagine how bad they are toward the weaker ones. That is why they have today's reparation. I think this is a logical [outcome] and this should happen!"

(Netease, September 12, 2001, 11: 41: 21). In the online discussions, "patriotic" participants often censured those who expressed sympathy toward the United States.

It may be argued that the true intensity of anti-Americanism on the site had been somewhat suppressed. If there had been no "interference," there would have been an even stronger preponderance of anti-American postings on the site. On the day after 9/11, Netease's webmasters suddenly picked up the official view and reiterated President Jiang Zimen's view that the Chinese should back and sympathize with the United States. Later, when the anti-American sentiments reached its zenith, the webmasters jumped in and on behalf of all net users expressed condolence to the American people and disparaged the terrorist attack (Netease, September 12, 2001, 10: 30: 25).

The findings from Netease suggested that the online discourses were not without limits. The Chinese authorities should have envisioned earlier that anti-Americanism would surface in online discussions, but they had not set up a regulatory administrative system as stern as that of the Chinese press to control the web. This is not, in all likelihood, a sign of the failure of the central control mechanism. The authorities do not wish to interrupt the crystallization and formation of online opinion and groups unless the discourses are powerful enough to surface in real politics and influence the foreign policy or the ruling of the party (Weber, 2003).

As for the online medium in Hong Kong, because it is remote from the central control, one might expect that anti-American sentiments would be more obvious. The results of the content analysis support this argument: almost half of the postings (48 per cent, 374 postings) were negative toward the Americans, a higher proportion than that of the national Chinese online site. The online participants tended to justify their anti-Americanism by telling stories and histories of the United States bullying the weak and small nations. Fewer than 10 per cent of the total messages (37 postings) commiserated with the United States over the terrorist attacks, and among these, most advocated a humanistic tone towards the Americans, and not directly to the United States government.

Operating under the shelter of capitalism, Hong Kong's Internet sites, in general, enjoy a higher degree of autonomy than other sites in China. The free nature of the online discussions helps to signify that Hong Kong is a free, non-socialist city under China. Indirectly, Hong Kong can be seen as an extra resource for Chinese economy. However, Hong Kong's nationalistic sentiment does not significantly influence China's domestic politics. Public opinion in Hong Kong does not have the same effect as opinion expressed elsewhere in China. Hostility and resentment toward the United States among the mainland public might block China's entry into the international circle. At the same time, nationalistic feelings and opinions, if manipulated properly, are good for internal unity and harmony, and have an impact upon the nation's future. Thus, the Chinese authorities must carefully control anti-American sentiments without diluting the nationalist ideology.

Patriotism Conflicting Foreign Policy

Nationalism is abstract, intangible, and powerful. It can be used to mobilize the public, and allows the state to call upon its people in wars or in other crises. In general, a state is more secure when the public upholds a kind of nationalism or patriotism that is conducive to blinding the bureaucracy of the state and the people together. However, in China, as manifested in the response to 9/11, the public's version of nationalism did not correspond with the state's policy. The existing nationalist mood among the people is embedded in the anti-imperialist ideology that the people have internalized since the Cultural Revolution. Although the state has changed its foreign policy, the public cannot keep up with such a rapid transformation. Thus, when seeing China's international competitor, the United States, become more vulnerable after the 9/11 events, the public's nationalism was expressed and accompanied with satisfaction, celebration and joy regardless of the foreign policy conducted by Washington.

In fact, the conflict between the public's patriotism and the official national ideology was uncovered by the American media not long after the attacks on September 11th. John Pomfret's article in the *Washington Post* on September 14th, 2001 was among the most widely quoted sources. The article, which blamed the Chinese government for taking no measures to discourage those who rejoiced at seeing the 9/11 attacks, embarrassed the Chinese authorities. After the event, the state took steps to cool the anti-American mood, but they understood that, in doing so, they suppressed the expression of nationalist feelings in the country. An explanation is that the PRC has put the Sino-American relationship on the top of its priority list, leaving aside the domestic opposition and disputes, at least in the short-term period. There is no guaranteeing how long such an imbalance can be sustained in Chinese society.

The immediate, concrete action that the PRC took to deal with the "defiant public" was to increase its surveillance over the Internet with different branches of government monitoring local websites, BBS sites and news discussion groups with a view to curbing dissident opinion. There were reported cases that online users who exposed officials' misadministration were traced, arrested and confined, and their computers were confiscated. Notwithstanding these actions, the PRC was not so stringent as to close down all the dissident sites, concentrating instead on those that went well beyond the baseline set by the government. On one hand, some sites were deliberately left alone as a testing ground for policies and decisions. News reports often hint that officials do keep a close eye on this virtual thermometer of public opinion. On different public occasions, the Party Chief and President Hu Jintao and Premier Wen Jiabao have responded directly to questions posed by Internet users. In 2003, the mayor of Shenzhen, the southern economic administrative region next to Hong Kong, met with an outspoken online user, and this became widely reported news in China (Ho, 2003). These and many similar stories showed that the government had started to develop measures to balance the support of public opinion and that of its own policy. On the other hand, the authorities had developed the tradition of releasing important national policy information from these sites. While many websites are open for free public participation, the PRC has widely expanded its affiliated websites (for example, people.com.cn), which have collectively become another official propaganda tool (Lau, Fung and Ji, 2003).

Nevertheless, there is an assumption that the effort of the government to control and manage these "civic sites" has not been very effective: it did not lessen the public hostility toward America. Various incidents such as United States stance against the United Nations around the conflict in Iraq, reports about the lack of evidence of Saddam Hussein's possession of weapons of mass destruction, and the American military threat against North Korea all continued to undermine the official effort to suppress the expressions of anti-Americanism in the country. According to a survey conducted in June 2003 by a semi-private company for social research and public opinion, the Search and Investment Consultancy Company (SSIC), the Chinese still perceive the United States' hegemony as very intimidating. In the survey, 93 per cent of the Chinese thought that the Americans had a double standard in evaluating countries with strong ties to China, such as North Korea. Also in the report, more than half (57 per cent) the respondents said they would support China in defending North Korea (as was the case in 1950 during the American-Korean war) should a military conflict occur between North Korea and the United States (SSIC, 2003).

Anecdotal evidence also suggests that the society in general was dissatisfied with the Americans. It seems the greater the distance between a region or city and the central government the more difficult it was to suppress anti-Americanism in the given area. For example, in June 2003, in Xian, the ancient Chinese capital, which is now remote from the highly controlled political and economic centers such as Beijing and Shanghai, there were continual reported cases in which American-based businesses such as McDonalds and Kentucky Fried Chicken were threatened and attacked with bombs. Official reports confirmed, however, that these bombs were self-made and primitive.

Public Opinion, Internal Politics and the Press

This evidence suggests that the top-down control of restating a new nationalist discourse may be futile. Administrative orders may have been able to temporarily hide and manage the public's sentiments in the case of 9/11. In the future, however, it will become more difficult for China to direct, control, and present a unanimous view to the world that "China is a friend of the United States." The public, even some officials, would not squarely subscribe to the version of nationalism provided by the nation's top leaders. The gap between the public's nationalist mood and the new version of nationalism proscribed by the leadership is growing, along with the gap between the official agenda and the civic public agenda.

Such divergence, however, is common in foreign policy. The United States faces a similar problem. Ideologically, domestic fear of Communist China still prevails in the United States. American businessmen and women who trade in the PRC circulate stories of the deception and corruption of the Chinese. However, in the past, as Chang's (1993, 237–247) studies showed, in the area of Sino-U.S. relations, the American press and journalists discounted their conventional practices of being independently critical of the Chinese authorities. Instead, first, they become the "magnifiers" of official actions and decisions, paradoxically serving to reshape public opinion to fit and cater to subsequent official actions. Second, the press, together with the officials who tend to withhold information or distort it, depicts an illusive picture of the Sino-U.S. relations that bears little resemblance to reality. Under such a bottom-up cooperation between the press and the administration (if not co-optation), public opinion can be effectively managed, and the anti-Chinese mood in the public discourse can be stifled.

The masses in China are not easily controlled. The top-down control of the Chinese press and the one party system has for a long time instilled a culture of incredulity in the public toward the state media system. Educated readers in China have already developed the practice of "reading between the lines" in order to grasp a more accurate picture of reality. While the party newspapers and the Chinese press can continue to advocate a non-anti-American mood to the rest of the world, the public and the officials in different government or semi-government units simply know the reality, and are conscious that they are the silent majority.

More importantly, local and regional government leaders have become more openly dissatisfied with China's friendliness toward America. Despite their apparent obedience to the party and official orders and duties, their potential challenge to the top leadership of the PRC cannot be underestimated. In recent years, the top leaders have faced immense pressure from party members. Just before the 9/11 events, the ex-president of the PRC, Jiang Zemin, was said to have faced ruthless criticism from conservative party members for a speech he made on July 1st, in which he opened party membership to Chinese capitalists (Pomfret, 2001). Likewise, he was also cautioned for being too sympathetic to the United States because of the 9/11 events. Internal criticism can be dangerous for the government and the leadership. Such unknown factors in the internal politics should always be added into the equation when considering how China responds and reacts to the Sino-American ties in the future. There is always the possibility that the authorities will bolster their domestic political support at the expense of this relationship.

The WTO, Press Reform and Anti-Americanism

Many scholars have high hopes regarding China's current and future media reforms. In 2007, China will open its market to comply with the international requirement for becoming a WTO member. Upon loosening its ownership requirement, and its subsequent industry re-structure, the West might expect that the government would release its grip on the press. Media liberalization might mean a greater range of opinions appearing in the media, but it also implies that the media will have to follow the demands and logic of the market. Because the current media reforms are implemented piecemeal within the boundaries of authoritarian rule, we might not see the entire administrative control of the press break apart right away (Chan and Qiu, 2002). However, it is inevitable that the Chinese media will have to attend more to the audience's needs, and occasionally satisfy the strong anti-American sentiment of the market. In other words, if we applaud China's press reform, we should bear in mind that there is a price to pay. In return for a free press the United States will see more anti-Americanism in the Chinese media.

In the wake of 9/11, while the mainland media de-emphasized its importance, Hong Kong was the only Chinese City that shared the same western tone of sympathy, condolence and pain. In the eyes of optimistic Westerners, the Hong Kong press may look like a role model of reform for China's media. However, quick conclusions are premature. Since Hong Kong's re-sinicization after 1997, Hong

Kong media have tended to swing to the conservative side, and often follow the political limits of the press in the motherland. In the long term, Hong Kong media might become "just another mainland media." At that point, whether the media preach anti-Americanism or whether they continue to defend the Western ideal of freedom and democracy all depends on the direction of China's foreign policy.

Conclusion

With all the uncertainties of the media in Hong Kong and China, the political overtones of the coverage of the United States are bound to become increasingly difficult to predict. Anti-Americanism in China will not just go away. On the other hand, it is not a fixed, enduring and infallible ideology. Both the American and Chinese governments can be more proactive and work together to bring about changes, but to do so requires fundamental grassroots work rather than continuing to fool their respective peoples with various media manipulations.

Chapter 7

Chinese Public Opinion in Response to the 9/11 Events

Xi Liu and Jing Wu

As a newly introduced technology, the Internet seems to offer alternative channels of expression as well as broader access to the "public" forum. Amateurs, though still limited by their economic and technical capacity, can now bypass the editing of professional journalism in articulating their positions on news items by logging on to online forums and news commentary sections. "Publishing" has become easier and more spontaneous thanks to the technology that allows for immediate "printing" and anonymity. The institutional and cultural standards that shape "serious media work" have been greatly relaxed in the world of the Internet, which may explain the more imaginative and colorful language used in online news forums. The current study showed that the Chinese press' assessment of the 9/11 attacks was generally uniform and modest. There was no obvious difference between the party organs and more commercialized papers in this regard. More telling divergences occur when online forums and the printing press are compared. Thus, for this particular occasion, technologies of mass communication and the differing sociological uses of these technologies are key to understanding the varying performances of the printing press and the Internet. The printing press in China, with its historical and institutional linkage to elite discourses, has to be understood in relation to the social category of "intellectual" as well as its political, cultural and ethical ramifications.

Conceptualizing "the Intellectual": The Western Tradition and the Chinese Social Context

As a social role and identity, sociologists and psychologists have studied the "intellectual" extensively. In a contemporary western context, the term "intellectual" commonly refers to people with certain holistic knowledge about society, culture, and life in general. Intellectuals use this knowledge to approach existing realities from a critical distance, either theoretical paradigms or religious and aesthetic utopias, and who produce and articulate ideas as a way of life. Scholars in the humanities and social sciences, writers, artists, and sometimes journalists may be thought of as intellectuals. They differ from those who apply their educations to more instrumental problems with the existing system, such as lawyers, technicians, doctors, and strategists. Intellectuals, from this perspective, are people who have a strong interest in the core values of society, hope to provide moral standards and sustain a universal symbolic system for the culture, and constantly reflect critically upon the philosophical essence of the universe and existing social principles (Shils, 1958). At the same time, they usually stay away from the power "players" of society, either economic or political, and launch their criticism from afar, for fear of corrupting the independence of thought by money and politics. To some extent, this definition of intellectual can also apply to the Chinese situation, but with major modifications concerning the intellectual's relationship to real politics and social management, specific to both Chinese historical legacies and contemporary development.

Though the concept of "intellectual" occurred in China during the early twentieth century, when China was experiencing drastic social transformations from traditional to modern society, a category similar to it had always existed in Chinese history, playing a central role in cultural formations, social institutions and political structures. The counterpart of "intellectual" in traditional China was "scholar," or a member of the "literati," almost a synonym to "people with knowledge." In a form of social organization informed by Confucianism, which put ethics and classical teaching at the center of governance and incorporated scholars into state management by an examination system, learning was by definition the reading and interpretation of texts on philosophy, ethics, history, literature and society. Technical know-how was accumulated through experience, unlike "knowledge" per se, which was obtained from books.

Since the late nineteenth century, modern educational institutions gradually emerged, including the natural sciences and technology. The rudimentary development of modern industry also broadened the venues of professional life for intellectuals. However, for the educated few, who were most sensitive to the impending national crisis, seeking western education was more a means to strike out an alternative for China's social development than an instrument to participate in the modern division of labor. The definition of "people with knowledge" continued to bear an association with the ancient Confucian scholars who aspired to the combined duty of being the conscience as well as managers of society and who could put beautiful visions into practice (Jerome, 1981).

Being an intellectual in China still meant, potentially or in reality, the intermingling of moral, cultural and political leadership in the same identity. Reinforcing the traditional duty of managing the state as a moral project, various important social movements in modern China, such as the May Fourth Movement, the socialist revolution, the Cultural Revolution, and even the most recent economic and political reforms, were all started first as intellectual blueprints for the Chinese nation and secondly as social projects to be carried out in the image of the ideal vision.

As the European-informed project of "nation building" replaced the "ethical edifice" in defining the mission of intellectuals, their relationship to the state, culture and the people also became more diversified, ranging from appreciation to criticism, from attachment to alienation, and from servile to independent. What was *not* changed, however, was the sense of social obligation and purpose (Goldman *et al.*, 1987). The socialist politics after 1949, though critical of and destructive to traditional culture in many aspects, also encouraged the integration of intellectual thinking and actual practice in changing society. Thus, instead of separating realms of cultural production such as academic, artistic and journalistic discourses, from the state, which Weber predicted as the result of modern professionalization, Chinese intellectuals continued to connect the production of ideas and ideologies with the activities of the state in a more or less straightforward way, providing legitimacy for state policies or criticisms that could change certain political visions.

Mass Media in China

In the socialist tradition, the mass media operated as important ideological apparatuses of the vanguard party, formulizing and popularizing theories and directions for the purpose of implementing various social projects (Siebert, 1956). Though there were always contradictions and conflicts between pure ideas of principled intellectuals and political pressure to compromise under practical circumstances, it was hard to clearly distinguish the intellectual stance from the official position in institutional terms.

Recent ongoing reforms in the Chinese press have accelerated the market orientation of some operations, such as advertising and distribution. At the same time, there has been a continued demand for retaining the party leadership's control over mainstream journalism (Zhao, 1998). Once market considerations are introduced, however, it becomes difficult for a newspaper to resist the commercial influence in the selection of materials and even writing styles for the journalistic and editing staff. When market forces and party wishes collude, media institutions are happy that they can make money and maintain political correctness at the same time. When they are in conflict, it is up to negotiation, compromise, and sometimes struggles to decide the actual form of publicized voices, according to specific occasions (Pan, 2000).

Pure ideas and relatively independent theoretical discussions are allocated to the academic field in the form of literary magazines and journals. It is an almost common understanding in Chinese society that press voices are intellectual discourses strongly filtered by political and economic forces. For its perceived importance and power, the press is having less leeway than the publishing industry in articulating aberrant ideas. For key issues concerning strategic national policy, such as foreign relations, mainstream press discourses are especially cautious as to the kinds of voices they air, because they are generally conceived as articulating the official position of the government or elite intellectual communities (Polumbaum, 2001).

Chinese Newspapers' Reactions to the 9/11 Events

Unlike the coverage of 9/11 in most countries described in this book, the reaction in the Chinese press to this extremely dramatic and unexpected event was calm and uniform. China Central Television (CCTV) was under criticism for not following the event closely and for the delays in coverage. The accusation was that CCTV did not interrupt regular programming to show live coverage of the event, as many other national stations did, and only broadcasted the news in scheduled hourly news briefs. In the half-hour evening news segment, the attacks were not even reported as breaking news and were only duly mentioned at the beginning of the second half of the news program.

The criticism was mostly against CCTV's lack of professionalism, and it could be argued that since interrupting regular programming for live broadcasting of unexpected breaking news was seldom practiced by CCTV before, even for important domestic issues, there was no particular reason to break the rules this time. However, the unusual silence and cautiousness characterizing most mainstream media, despite the calamity of the event itself as well as the heated reactions of all other countries, still warrants attention to China's peculiar situation *vis-à-vis* international politics and her own domestic concerns, in addition to the norms of Chinese media.

Institutional Inertia and Print Media Performance

As discussed earlier, Chinese mass media, especially the press, are considered part and parcel of the cultural front of the national project of modernization, under the auspices of the state-intellectual cooperative. For decades, it has not been operated under any form of market system or in competition with other political organs. Thus, except for the years during the Cultural Revolution, the general institutional habit of the mainstream news is to strive for balanced rationality instead of sensationalism, for dry accuracy instead of risky immediacy, and for diplomacy of words at the cost of spontaneous emotions. Though the market reform has brought in forms of commercialism to journalism, 9/11 was still too sensitive and important an issue to be left for the thoughtless spontaneity of the market.

Data from the content-analysis of the Chinese press showed that the print media described the 9/11 attacks using theoretically informed concepts to articulate abstract principles, instead of forwarding personalized judgments on individuals or governments. When discussing how America should react to the 9/11 events, for example, most papers cited the idea of adjusting its foreign policies, cooperating with the United Nations and the international community, and suggested cautiousness in using military force on foreign lands. Both immediately after the event and months later, there are general criticisms of unilateralism as well as the killing of innocent civilians by terrorism. However, these papers only rarely named the specific government, group or individuals that fit in with the critical descriptions.

Extreme words such as "conspiracy," "viciousness," "evil force," and "ruthlessness" in describing either side of the conflict were rarely used in the print media. Direct or emotional attacks on religions were also avoided, which clearly sets the Chinese press apart from the internet forums, where there were more instances of linking specific religion or national culture, such as individualism and aggressiveness, to the actions of governments, groups and individuals. Leaving aside the individual characteristics of the actors involved, much of the coverage was restricted to either the reporting of facts, or the exploration of abstract principles of humanity, peace, mutual respect, multilateralism and equality.

Foreign Policy and Print Media Performance

Though institutional inertia and the intellectual quality of the printing press in China can explain partly the calmness in tone and sophistication in word choice in the coverage of 9/11, China's changing foreign policy stance should also be counted as an influence on the reactions in the mainstream press. Unlike the Internet discourses, the print media's coverage should not be taken as reflecting any social strata's autonomous, organic and immediate sentiment toward the United States, its role in international affairs, and its relationship to China. Instead, these reports can be understood as resulting from the internal negotiations between two basic and diverging understandings of China's national development—whether anti-Americanism or a pro-American ideology should inform China's overall blueprint for its reform and modernization project. The conflicting views are embraced by different sectors and special interests in the government, the intellectual elite, the newly rising economic powers, as well as their media outlets, thanks to the drastic diversification and stratification of China's social interests and visions in recent years.

On one hand, China's revolutionary history and economic status as a developing country necessitate the dominance of a "third-world" perspective in interpreting and evaluating international affairs. From this perspective, many industrialized countries of the West cannot be absolved from their colonial histories that strongly contributed to their own economic and military strength, as well as the underdevelopment of their former colonies. The end of WWII and the beginning of the Cold War brought in a new imperialist era, during which formally independent third world nations continued to be exploited economically and politically by the two superpowers. The end of the Cold War and the globalization of the world economy have brought dramatic changes in the courses of some nations, yet problems such as the unequal distribution of wealth and resources, deepening poverty of some third world nations, rising ethnic and religious conflicts, as well as environmental deteriorations have persisted and even expanded (Harding, 1991).

However, China for the last two decades of the twentieth century has been devoted to an economic and social reform that more or less followed the model of modern industrialized nations of the West. Increasingly strong financial and industrial sectors favor integration into the existing global economic order, rather than an effort to transform it, a position China used to hold. As China has entered the World Trade Organization and become the world's largest receiver of foreign investment, the country's economic, legal, and social institutions are subject to more influences from the American-centered world system than the government and intellectuals are willing to admit. The trend of westernization in economic and political reforms has led to a more pragmatic foreign policy that tones down—but not entirely de-legitimizes—the harsh criticism of America's hegemonic power and shows willingness to cooperate with world powers in maintaining the current world order (Ko, 2001). The new socio-economic situation also renders the old harsh vocabulary in foreign policy somewhat awkward. A new set of discourses on moderate nationalism as a way to integrate a public sentiment fragmented by the novel developments as well as demonstrate China's influence in world affairs is emerging quickly (Zheng, 1999).

From either socialist or nationalistic perspectives, China's official position is usually critical of American hegemony. This can still be seen in the media comments of America's invasion of Afghanistan in 2001, though the wording is much more modest and ambiguous than say, the 1960s and 1970s criticism of America's war in Vietnam. While there are in general quite a few ideologically charged and demonizing descriptions in the entire print media, the ones that touched upon America's military reactions to 9/11 showed the inertia of such a habit of thinking. America was criticized in most papers for its Chauvinist treatment of other countries, using force to impose its own will on other peoples, and self-centered pursuit of its own interest at the expense of others. The historical and institutional commentaries were focused more on military and political issues than on economic and cultural ones. Though in the wider society a war for controlling oil routes was a popular interpretation of America's intention in striking Afghanistan, it was not mentioned clearly and frequently in the press. Reiterations of principles such as peaceful resolution of international conflicts and acting legally with the support of the UN were more common than guesses and judgments on the possible ulterior motives of the military attack.

The response in the press to America's anti-terrorism measures, including the war on Afghanistan, reflected more directly the official position of the Chinese government—a subtle neutrality, or support with certain reservations. There were not many negative commentaries on the measures taken. Moreover, the government promised help and cooperation on financial, legal, diplomatic and intelligent fronts in containing terrorist activities. Yet when it came to the subject of military actions, the wording became ambiguous and mildly critical. The war in Afghanistan was seldom directly opposed, but there were many descriptions of the plight of the Afghan people as helpless victims of the war, who suffered but received no benefits from the conflict.

Where the press expresses an abstract principle of action without specifying whether anyone has, in fact, violated that principle, it can be read as the government's worry or subtle criticism of certain American policies. For example, there are frequent suggestions that bombing terrorist camps should be guided by ample evidence and civilian casualties should be avoided, and that the authority of the UN and the equal rights of other members of the international community should be respected.

Public Opinion Expressed through Online News Forums

In comparison to the print media's coverage of the 9/11 events, online representations of the public opinions were quite informal. Remarks or exchanges in the online forum ranged from a couple-of-word phrases to a few paragraphs, containing slang, distinct regional dialects, or unique combinations of certain symbols, which are understandable to the average Internet surfer in China. China's print media would never behave in such an unserious way when they handle hard international news. Comments posted in the online forum were obviously emotional, speculative, straightforward and judgmental, which, by the print media's standard, could not be more "un-objective" and "un-journalistic."

Compared to mainstream professional journalists, the online forum participants appeared more interested in the character of the American government and the war in Afghanistan. For instance, while the mainstream media basically remained silent about the root causes of 9/11, American foreign policies were widely discussed and scrutinized by the registered visitors to the online forum maintained by the *People's Daily*. Many of them seemed convinced that the United States had been "bullying" other countries in its foreign affairs actions, and its "arrogant, self-centered and hegemonic" attitudes and behaviors finally stimulated revenge from "the bullied." In a similar mode, commenting on America's motivation in launching the war in Afghanistan, China's print media mainly attributed the military action to "revenging against the perpetrators of the 9/11 events." Discussions in the online forum were more imaginative, often associating the war with the strategic concerns of the United States, such as the need to increase its influence over Central Asia, the Islamic World or the Middle East.

Participants of the online forums were quite judgmental and negative in characterizing the United States and the American people. Textual analysis of the online commentaries in the wake of 9/11 showed that the terms "chauvinistic," "tyrannical," "oppressive," "hegemonic," "egoistic," and "uncompassionate" were among the most frequently used descriptors of America. In contrast, direct comments about the United States were rare in the mainland print media, and strong negative descriptors were never used.

As the aftermath of the 9/11 attacks unfolded, discussions in online forums, while not losing their sharp edge, reached a deeper level. While they still articulated their opinions in an emotional manner, quite a few online forum participants historicized the tragedy by comprehensively considering America's past foreign policy strategies and actions across the world. Unlike China's print media, online commentaries did not treat the 9/11 attacks and America's war in Afghanistan as isolated occurrences, but rather as outcomes determined by America's relentless pursuit of its strategic interests.

New Technology and China's Political Legacy

Most Chinese journalists belong to an elite group of intellectuals. Both journalists and the society at large expect the former to contribute to the socio-cultural well being of the nations. For this reason, Chinese journalists are particularly cautious with what they write and say (Xu, 2000; Zhao, 2000). They believe that only through thinking and acting in a rational and sophisticated manner can they as journalists perform their socio-cultural responsibilities of orienting public opinion in the right direction.

Chinese journalists are encouraged to take a cautious approach to their work, especially on the coverage of major problems, and always take the side of the government under "complex" circumstances (Polumbaum, 2001; Zhao, 1998). Echoing and supporting the government's position regarding important or sensitive political and economic issues are widely regarded as the basic responsibilities of all Chinese journalists. The September 11th attacks and the sequence of actions followed in the United States definitely fall into the category of sensitive or complex issues, which explains why the coverage on 9/11 in the print media took a calm, neutral, and even diplomatic tone, glossing over the complexities and historical ramifications surrounding America's situation. China's landscape of news coverage suddenly changed when the Internet emerged together with all the technological possibilities it promised (Harwit and Clark, 2001; Qiu, 1999/2000; Deuze, 2003). Online forums are easy to use. Participants can use whatever style and language they wish and voice their criticism on a wide variety of issues. One important aspect of the change was that the privilege of Chinese journalists to disseminate discourses on public issues was reduced. Chinese web users became fully capable of presenting their own views via online channels, and professional journalists lost their reputations as the only "interpreters" of socio-political events (Vries and Zwaga, 1997).

The Internet's greater significance for journalism in China, however, seems to be its potential of revolutionizing the institutional environment of public opinion (Yang, 2003). In other words, as media organizations incorporate the Internet into their regular operations and practices, news coverage by non-professional journalists will likely increase. Consequently, the grasp by the government and the elite journalists on the popular discourse may weaken.

At the current stage, offering hyperlinks that allow registered site users to publish online their thoughts in response to a relevant web item is commonly practiced among Chinese businesses maintaining frequently visited news sites. These businesses make attempts to attract and keep visitors by satisfying their desire to express their views.

The readiness of online forum participants to demonstrate their negative views of the United States speaks to the mentality of nationalism among the Chinese people at the grassroots level. The nation's collective memory of being exploited by capitalist invaders, along with real concerns about foreign aggression play a major role in the public mindset (Zheng, 1999), suggesting an anti-foreign component in contemporary Chinese nationalism (Fewsmith, 2000). At the same time, negative attitudes toward America should not be generalized to all parts of the Chinese population. In fact, public attitudes are multilayered and negativity is a matter of extent rather than that of kind.

The Difference a Social Class Makes

Another concern in investigating the online representation of Chinese public opinions surrounding the events of September 11th is the identities of the participants who expressed their views. Inequalities in the people's access to information and computer literacy compromise the representativeness of the "virtual" community (Papacharissi, 2002). Given the transitional nature of China's economy together with the country's current distribution of opportunities for higher education, it is quite possible for us to qualitatively tease out the collective characteristics of those participants active in online news forums.

First, those individuals tended to belong to the well-educated social class. This is not because the use of computers requires educational investment. More important is the level of interest in the topic. As the research literature suggests, people who make extensive use of online political information tend to be the same people who are already deeply interested in politics (Bimber, 1999; Davis, 1999; Norris, 1999).

Participants in online news forums develop their communities based on their mutual interest in international politics and military relations, world peace, and the foreign policies of the United States. Their concern and even enthusiasm for certain global themes reflected a social class with a unique dominant ethos in the transitional era in China (Brook and Frolic, 1997; Moore, 2001). As previously mentioned, print media tended to resort to the generic principles of peace, fair negotiation, normal diplomacy and coordinative mechanisms in commenting on the issues related to the 9/11 events. While discussing the same principles, online forum participants appeared more emotional and idealistic, suggesting their true faith in those global themes. In this sense, with a considerable portion of their discussions, those individuals seemed to transcend the nation-based concerns: they disliked America and criticized its policies and behaviors only from the perspective of the world system.

This group of online forum participants differentiates itself from ordinary Chinese people in terms of its value orientation. While the nationalist mentality still shapes their oral and written communication, they take a wider approach to political and social issues through appreciating their global causes and consequences. This group is also distinct from China's journalism elites in that their thoughts and discursive activities are much more independent from the Chinese government. Consciously or unconsciously, this group tends to take a position different from or even opposite to where the government stands. On the other hand, it is obvious that online forum participants still utilized the Internet in a random and spontaneous way and their discussions, mostly, did not demonstrate "the public use of reason" as researchers of the Internet and the public sphere expect. Additionally, they seemed far from achieving the "internalized group memberships" or "social identities" (Postmes and Brunsting, 2002) to consciously pursue "social involvement" in a political and cultural process. We speculate that the transitional nature of the Chinese society partially explains the current situation. Participants of online activities will likely consolidate into cause or interest-based groups as China witnesses more change in its political and economic system.

Conclusion

This case examined how the Chinese print media, in its coverage of 9/11, constructed the news in a way that echoed the foreign policy of China, which, for the time being, is determined to restore the Sino-American relationship. The tragic events of September 11th have been traumatic for both America and the world. Given the graveness and complexity surrounding the situation, it seems reasonable that the established print media played a dominant role in generating and directing the Chinese public's discursive activities. The online news forums, while showing its capability of offering an alternative platform for public expressions, probably has a long way to go to produce substantial impact on the way public opinions are represented in China. Hopefully, when issues of a wider appeal or concern for the Chinese public come along on the horizon, Chinese people will develop more patterned use of the Internet to exchange information on a significant scale.

* * *

Editorial Remarks

The arguments presented in this case provide interesting data and suggestions about how public opinion is formed in China and the role media play in the development of a public's sentiment about a foreign country, the United States in particular, or the international situation in general. It should be taken into serious consideration, however, that unlike in the earlier cases discussed in this book, for example, Germany or Russia, there was no freedom of the press in China in the beginning of the 2000s. Radio, television, and the printed media are under political censorship. The government holds tight control over the expression and dissemination of political opinions in the country, including persistent attempts to control the content of Internet sites. Unlike in democratic countries in which journalists are free to express their political opinions, the ruling Communist Party in China determines what is broadcast and when. The ruling party suggests a set of principles about how government institutions should react to international developments. For instance, there are regular general and specific instructions given to the editors of newspapers and broadcast networks about how to cover specific international events. As a result, attitudes prevailing among the Chinese people are influenced by the media responding to specific instructions given by the ruling party. Printed sources, for example, become the most profound conductors of ideological views transmitted from the government to the people.

Of course, the people are not passive; they are eager recipients of everything that comes from newspapers, radio, and television. There are many other ideological, political, and cultural factors that determine what people think of a foreign country, its people, government, and policies. What people learn, remember, and later express is also mediated by a relatively stable system of values developed through socialization. For many years, since ancient times, people in China maintained a predominantly negative, suspicious attitude about the western civilization. Chinese elites believed in their own cultural and spiritual superiority over other civilizations and, not surprisingly, this attitude was shared by the masses. The attitudes about European countries and the United States worsened during the communist rule for a host of reasons including ideological (rooted in the Marxist classic belligerent stance against capitalism) and political (because of the western anti-communism and support of the renegade regime in Taiwan).

Nevertheless, the media, and especially the Internet, could speak on behalf of the people, thus becoming not only a conductor but also a source of attitudes about foreign policy and international relations. With the development of communication technologies, as described in this case, the government has a limited and constantly diminishing opportunity to influence people's attitudes. On the other hand, China's rapidly developing economy constantly needs new technologies, jobs, energy sources, and expanding markets to sell its products. Without an active trade and other forms of engagement with the industrialized countries and the United States, the achievement of many ambitious goals seems to be difficult. This is understood by the government in Beijing.

Suggested Additional Literature

Kuhn, R.L. (2000). *Made in China: Voices from the New Revolution*. NY: TV Books.

Moore, R.R. (2001). China's fledging civil society: A force for democratization. *World Policy Journal*. 18 (1): 56–66.

Yang, G. (2003). The co-evolution of the Internet and civil society in China. *Asian Survey*. 43 (3): 405–422.

Zheng, Y. (1999). *Discovering nationalism in China*. New York City: Cambridge University Press.

CASE 5
EGYPT

There is perhaps no other country in the Arab world, except Saudi Arabia, where stability is more vital to the overall situation in the Middle East than Egypt. The country's geographic position, resources, military strength, population growth—the largest in the Arab world—and international reputation are major factors that have contributed to its key role in the international arena. For a long time, Egyptian military strength and location elevated Egypt's importance to the Arab world and the United States, as Arab regimes knew that going to war against Israel (a long time source of Middle Eastern consternation) would be impossible without Egypt's support and participation. Egypt has been a cornerstone of U.S. diplomacy in the Middle East and continues to be the second largest recipient of U.S. financial and military assistance. Its military is the strongest and largest in the region amongst Arab countries. Being the most inhabited Arab nation with a population of nearly 70 million, it also has the largest Christian minority in the Middle East. This country traditionally plays the role of a cultural center of the Arab nations because of its science, education, arts and crafts, films, literature, and journalism, to name a few. Egypt is the seat of the thousand-year-old Al Azhar University, one of Islam's oldest learning centers.

The way Egypt sees the United States explains how the country is viewed in many other countries in the Middle East. As the theme of this book indicates, the following discussion will begin by exploring the history of the Egyptian-American relations with regard to both the regional and international settings. As the U.S. began to pursue its goals in the Middle East, we witnessed a rise in negative attitudes toward the country. After 9/11, for reasons discussed below, many Egyptians saw double standards permeating the American involvement in the region, and thus, the anti-American feeling found a fertile breeding ground.

Chapter 8

Egyptian Views of America in a Historic Perspective

Manal Alafrangi

The Beginning of the American Presence in the Region

It is important to briefly trace the American entry to the Middle East. At the root of America's initial involvement in the heartland of the Middle East were three factors: "the failure of Britain's postwar policy, the particular interest in Palestine, and the intensification of the struggle between East and West" (Safran, 1978, 340). While a strong case can be made with the first two motives, the last one seems to lack an argument. The United States has traditionally defined its national interest in the Middle East in terms of the containment of Soviet expansion, under the Cold War banner. As many would agree, the containment doctrine has been pursued as a means of "preventing a shift in the global balance of power, ensuring the security and Western freedom of access to the region's oil supplies, assuring access to the region's markets for American goods, and securing the environment for American investment opportunities" (Rubenberg, 1986, 2). To realize the objectives of containment of Soviet expansion and domination, the U.S. had to develop a strong relationship with the Arab world; Egypt became a priority. As time progressed however, there were misgivings on both sides about this relationship.

According to Hamza, "America's honest, committed, and unfaulted implementation of the Monroe Doctrine (which included policies of non-engagement in world affairs) had been a major contributor to the positive image the Arabs had toward the U.S." (Ahmad, 2003, 11). Because of that, the United States willingly chose not to interfere with issues pertaining to the region it called the "Far East" (later known as the Middle East). After World War I, the United States established a positive reputation for not being "greedy" in terms of controlling Middle Eastern countries and advancing ideas of freedom and independence. To the contrary, it devoted a lot of money and resources to humanitarian endeavors such as building educational facilities, hospitals and orphanages. The U.S. also donated food and assistance to those affected by war or poverty without aiming for obvious political gain. This fact is highlighted in the Syrian and Palestinian demands upon the end of the First World War for the U.S. to replace Britain and France in dealing with their issues (Ahmad, 2003, 12). There was a defensible justification behind the trust granted to the Americans. Arabs saw their dreams of independence in the principles outlined by president Wilson during WWI (especially his doctrine of self-determination). And despite the fact that the Arabs were disappointed with the results that came out of the Paris treaty in 1919, they still held very positive views of the United States and regarded it as a neutral country.

Egypt had paid the price of its crucial geopolitical position by the numerous invasions it experienced throughout history, the last one being Britain's rule. Moreover, this development simultaneously occurred with another important one, the division of the Middle East by European powers in the aftermath of WWI. These developments gave Egypt an impetus to oust the British and the incentive to reshape policy toward its neighboring Arab countries, which consequently determined the alliance system within the Middle East. The latter is an important facet of history; the U.S. often interfered in Middle Eastern countries' choice of alliance, and in some instances, helped create blocs of countries (e.g. the Baghdad Pact) that were detected quite early and suspiciously by the layman Arab.

After World War I, the United States continued to practice its policy of non-engagement, defending the "open-door" policy it had toward the Middle East. Through this period, it found itself quite welcome to invest freely in the oil resources of the Middle East, which were being discovered throughout the region between the world wars. Washington also continued to encourage missionaries in the Middle East and found a way to balance them with missions of its businessmen. During and after the Second World War, there was a shift in American foreign policy from isolationism to major involvement in world affairs, including in the Middle East.

It should be noted that during this time the press of the Arab world was neutral toward the United States. Furthermore, readily available translated American books displayed favorable views of the Middle East and thus played a major role in depicting a positive image of the country. It won over Arab popular opinion, which looked at the literature as an allowable attempt to promote educational and commercial American interests, and most importantly, not containing any political interests. This image inspired Arab populations to see America's way of life as the path to prosperity.

It was not long, however, before America's positive image deteriorated in the Middle East. This occurred for two reasons: first, American support for the Zionist movement (which later became Israel) and second the discovery of America's "true" intentions in the region, which led the West in its conflict with the communist Soviet Union using imperial and hegemonic policies, particularly in the Middle East (Ahmed, 2003, 39). Many argue that the U.S. era began in the Middle East after World War II, since the war highlighted the importance of the U.S. as a world superpower. As Britain became more dependent on the economic and moral support of its American ally and progressively less capable of exercising a stabilizing influence in the region, political turmoil in the poverty-ridden Middle East grew. While Britain and France emerged victorious they were both deeply scarred. America, however, was fresh and ready to enter the politics and society of the Middle East. One should note that the European weakness was not an immediate consequence of the war; the French continued to fight in Vietnam and the British continued to fight in Malaya against Communist domination (Rubinstein, 1985, 73). They also stayed in South Yemen until 1967, in the Gulf until the early 1970s. Yet it was easily concluded that European imperial order was rapidly collapsing. The two ailing great powers still had colonial possessions in the area, but signs of difficulties in managing those possessions became apparent to the Arabs, who witnessed a shift of "domination" from Western Europe to the United States.

America's strategic interests in the region were, among others, to ensure supplies of oil and to guarantee the strength and domination of Israel over its neighbors because of the strong Jewish lobby influencing congress. Concurrently there was a rise of nationalism, which evolved within the Arab countries. The merger of Egyptian and Arab nationalism were combined for several reasons; first because Egypt saw that it would be useful in its struggle against Britain and the creation of the Israeli State and Egypt's involvement in the Palestine war of 1948 (Meyer, 1980, 20). Egypt had a desire to influence major developments in the region, such as the formation of the Arab league and so it made major efforts to become more aware and more active. It should be noted that at the time, Egypt joined with the rest of the Arab world in the widespread resentment after fighting in the 1948 war (in which Israel emerged victorious as a state).

The political and strategic interests of the United States in the area—immediately after World War II—were mainly an outgrowth of the Cold War, and its objective seemed to be to prevent the Soviet Union from taking advantage of diminishing British influence. Most importantly though, the United States took the leading role in dealing with Jewish related issues, such as pushing forward the partition plan through the United Nations General Assembly and putting pressure on Britain to allow more Jewish refugees to enter Palestine (pre-1948). Egypt, on the other hand, wanted to focus on keeping away the abeyant manifestations of imperialism—something unrelated to the Cold War. The region overall sought not only independence from external domination, but also a form of Arab unity and overall economic, social, and political development. Still, countering the British, especially with regard to the security system in the Middle East, became a major priority after the 1952 revolution, and the rise of American power gave Egypt a tool in that task. The net result of that goal can be observed in the 1956 war, when the U.S. opposed the European and Israeli military assault on Egypt, and demanded their withdrawal. Many in the Middle East expected far more from America as opposed to Britain and France. For example, Mosaddeq in Iran originally had high hopes that the U.S. might aid in his dispute with Britain; he visited the U.S. in early 1952 and the Americans had at first seemed more receptive than the British (Katouzian, 1990, Chapter 11). This reiterates the point that anti-Americanism in Egypt and the rest of the Middle East was the result of specific policies as opposed to being inherent in the Arab/Muslim psyche.

After the creation of Israel—in which an entire people were displaced, leading to untenable strains and stresses on the region—the stage was set for an increasingly complex and volatile situation in the region. According to Mohammed Heikal, a former editor of *Al-Ahram* and advisor to Nasser, the West's pattern of armed containment of communism had taken shape with the creation of NATO in the West and SEATO in South East Asia (Heikal, 1978, 5). It was only in the Middle East that a gap in this pattern emerged and the West took advantage of the situation and attempted to fill it through the Baghdad Pact, a British dominated alliance. Heikal points out that for the Arab countries, joining such an alliance represented a new form of Western domination. If they were going to form an alliance with anybody, it was more logical that they formed it with other Arabs (Heikal, 1978, 5). The Arab League came into existence in 1944 and was conceived in part as a defense organization. According to Heikal, this concept was both "comprehensible and attractive" for most

Arabs (since in 1948 they found themselves facing an enemy far closer and more immediate than the Soviet Union: Israel). The creation of Israel in the very heart of the African-Asian land bridge dealt a severe blow to the Arab hopes of unity by cutting off the Arabs of Asia from those of Africa. Certainly, too, the fact that Israel's creation entailed the dismantling of a Palestinian homeland and the suppression of the Palestinian's rights did nothing to endear this new entity to the Arabs. Their hostility was further confirmed by Israel's relations with countries like Britain and the United States, "the one identified with traditional colonialism and the other accused of neo-colonialism" (Heikal, 1978, 5).

The Early Cold War Years

During the first half of the Cold War, anti-American attitudes in Egypt reflected the poor, at times hostile, relations between Egypt and western countries, including the United States. President Nasser's course on political and economic sovereignty turned his government and the country toward the Soviet Union, which began providing substantial economic and military help to Egypt, which did not interfere with his quest for a successful secular national movement. He set off an anti-colonial, anti-monarchist and often anti-conservative revolution throughout the Arab world (that was structured by the oppressive regimes dominant in the region). As a result, Britain, France and Israel launched a war against him in 1956. Eisenhower saved him by opposing the Western powers and Israel. Nasser's aim was to oppose "both Israeli aggression and conservative Islamic regimes, trying to make Egypt a model of secular nationalism for other Muslim states and wrestling with cross-currents of religious traditionalism and modernity" (Ebeid, 2002, 2).

To the American politicians, Nasser was a radical Arab leader. Their aim to unseat him in 1956 was absolutely necessary to maintain influence over the region. The U.S. government was not happy with the Egyptian leader's choice of policies, especially within the Cold War context. President Eisenhower and his secretary of state, John Foster, for example, were "particularly outraged" (Rubenberg, 1986, 11). His purchase of weapons from the Soviet Union (often referred to as the Czech Arms Deal) deeply angered the American leaders. Yet a closer look at Nasser's decision to purchase the weapons will show that his action was only a "direct response to Israel's massive raid on Gaza and after his request for American arms was turned down according to Rubenberg. Nasser's motto of 'I don't act, I react' was emphasized shortly later, when he nationalized the Suez Canal (company), namely because the U.S. had pulled the funding offer for the Aswan Dam Project. It should not be forgotten that at the time, Egypt was a middle power in the international arena, and due to its geopolitical position, had the aim to be the intermediary between the world powers and the Middle Eastern states, whose history of statehood was relatively new when compared with Egypt's. The rivalry between the U.S. and Soviet Russia made this possible. Egypt, until the 1960s when it could afford to remain neutral, could rely on Soviet military aid and American political power, when trying to exercise its foreign policies. On the other hand, the U.S. was moving more toward Israel, and soon enough, it became apparent that America would never act like it had in 1956, defending the Arabs against Israel.

By 1967, the U.S. had shown partiality: it backed Israel as well as oil-rich Gulf states. According to Mona Ebeid, a professor of political science at the American University in Cairo, Nasser's humiliation in the Six-Day War ultimately became the humiliation of secular nationalism in the Arab world. Radical Muslims began to teach the masses that the reason for their defeat was that they had strayed too far from God's path. This defeat was a major blow to the Egyptian population, who immediately conveyed negative feelings toward the United States. To illustrate an example of the rise of anti-U.S. sentiment, in 1967 the governor of Alexandria could no longer guarantee the safety of Americans transiting that city if they happened to be spotted by the mob in the street (Thornton, 1998, 52). On the other hand, Moscow's anti-Israel and anti-American policy and attitudes matched, in many respects, the Egyptian's views on Israel as well as the overall Middle East situation. During the events of 1967 and 1973, the Soviets—contrary to the United States—expressed a staunch support of Egypt and the Palestinians.

Israel's ability to defeat Egypt seemed an important asset to America. During this time, president Kennedy had begun to develop the thesis of a "special relationship" between the United States and Israel, which from then on, was strengthened in every possible way according to Rubenberg, who points out the significance of Israeli influence on U.S. foreign policies toward the region (1986, 12). Of greatest significance, and closely related to Washington's frustrations with Nasser, some individuals in the U.S. administration began to conceive of an Israeli "Sparta" that could dominate the Middle East in the interests of American power. This stance was no longer kept secret. In fact, the U.S. made it explicit that it was angered by Nasser's policy of nonalignment and his regional advocacy of pan-Arabism and internal Arab socialism. Moreover, it believed that the demise of the Egyptian leader (which would later take place with the help of Israel) would open up new opportunities for the U.S. in the region. Therefore it is not surprising to learn that president Johnson gave Israel the backing to initiate hostilities. In addition, in the aftermath of the conflict the U.S. pointedly did not call for Israeli withdrawal to the pre-war lines as it had in 1956 (Rubenberg, 1986). This fact represents a striking example of a common characteristic of U.S.-Middle East diplomacy. As Rubenberg points out, there is a dichotomy between the principles and practices of the United States. "In public and in principle, the U.S. maintained its opposition to Israel's initiation of hostilities, but in practice, they probably encouraged and might have facilitated it" (1986, 12). This detail was seemingly visible to the Egyptian audience, who ultimately produced an opinion of mistrust of the U.S. regarding their Israeli alliance. It was difficult for Egyptians to accept that the U.S. would side with Israel all the time, even if Israel were at fault. As we can see, under Nasser's leadership, Egypt had no plans of improving its relationship with the U.S.—this is, however, a contestable statement since toward the end of the Nasser era, many have speculated that he had softened up toward the West, and specifically toward the United States.

A Turn in U.S.-Egypt Relations

A major reverse of policies and attitudes toward the United States took place during President Anvar Sadat's tenure in the late 1970s and the early 1980s. He led the Arab world into reconciliation with Israel. It was expected that this would lead the Egyptian population and the rest of the Arab world to change public attitudes toward Israel first and consequently the United States second. Indeed, this expectation was built into the 1979 Egypt-Israel Peace Treaty, which called upon the parties to "abstain from hostile propaganda." It is worth noting that almost a quarter century after his assassination, Sadat has become a forgotten and unpopular man in his own country because most Egyptians regard him as having served the U.S. first, not Egypt. It is often said that this iconoclastic Egyptian leader ignored the domestic risks in such collaboration and forged a total alignment with Washington: for his disregard of his country's sensibilities Sadat was assassinated (Rubenberg, 1986, 6). The peace deal with Israel, the establishment of diplomatic ties with Tel Aviv, and an improvement in bilateral U.S.-Egyptian relations have split the country's public opinion. This ambiguity continued into the 1990s. On one hand, the United States was treated as a strategic economic and political "partner." On the other hand, the political opposition—nationalistic forces and religious conservative groups—used any opportunity to launch verbal attacks on the president and the government for being "puppets" of a powerful America. Many people continued to underemphasize the amount of U.S. economic help to Egypt and see the United States as nothing but the biggest supporter of Israel. Both these countries were viewed as trying to dominate the Middle East at the expense of the Arabs, destroy the pan-Arab entity, and pillage natural resources.

Fluctuations in Egyptian Perception of the United States

Prior to 1947 there were sharp distinctions drawn between the French, British and the Americans by Egyptians. Popular opinion in the Middle East held that the United States did not have any imperialistic aspirations and even earned a reputation for supporting self-determination in contrast to France and Britain. Globally, the world was going through a tumultuous time, and traditional imperialism was no longer fashionable. Arguably, it was replaced by the client state system, or a new form of imperialism that did not require control over land. Additionally, the U.S. has openly opposed any possible alliances amongst the Arab countries or nationalist movements, which may have resulted in a stronger Middle East.

One additional point must be made about Arab public opinion: There lies a danger in generalizing the Arab perceptions of the United States, which largely depend on local considerations and events. Egyptians have a profound sense of bitterness and disdain for American politics, represented by the various administrations, but they would never classify an average American walking in the streets as an aggressor. There is much speculation regarding Arab opinion toward the United States and the American people, namely that they make no distinction between the leadership position on foreign policy affairs coming out of Washington, and the American people themselves, who play no role in shaping that policy, specifically regarding the region of the Middle East. Hence, according to this argument, Egyptians would take pleasure in seeing the American people suffer from an outside attack, as the popular Arabic proverb states: "the slave who is happy with his master's catastrophe." This assumption is far removed from the truth for a number of reasons. First, Egyptians are capable of separating the two entities; they are aware of the American governmental system, which gives exclusive power to the president and his cabinet, as well as congress, which conducts foreign policy and not to the people. Second, it is well known that there are a huge number of U.S. tourists who travel to Egypt. Keeping that in mind, when the attack on tourists in Luxor in 1997 occurred (most of the victims were Europeans), the result was public revulsion as well as a schism in the Islamic movements, most of which then rejected violence. Thus, Egyptians empathize with as well as comprehend the reasons behind any terrorist attack, since they witness the injustice that goes on in the occupied territories and the imposed sanctions on Iraq, which are advocated by the United States. However, they wouldn't want to replicate these horrors in other parts of the world, and least of all in the United States. Finally, while they understand that Americans are not Muslims, Egyptians still accept Islam's message that Muslims must respect other monotheistic religions, including Christianity and Judaism. Taking these considerations into account, the next section will explore the historical ties between Egypt and the United States that led to the strong anti-American sentiments leading up to and after the events of September 11.

Chapter 9

The Contradictory Feelings about the United States

Manal Alafrangi

Sources of Anti-Americanism in Egypt

Before discussing the current Arab grievances regarding the U.S., it is important to examine the historical factors that contributed to these attitudes. For some peoples, such as the Palestinians, history is all they have to cling to as a justification of their cause and to establish a peaceful and righteous future. For the Egyptians, the historical events they have shared with the West were decisive in many ways, as it has shaped the present standards. The Egyptians' participation in numerous wars with Israel, which was often supported by the U.S. and fought using American weapons, has never escaped the Egyptian memory. These wars are over now, but for the average Egyptian it has been very difficult to let go of the past.

The United States in its ascent to power has given rise to great antagonism, particularly in the Middle East. Thornton points out that one of the basic reasons for the massive resentment in the Middle East is due simply to the fact that whoever is great is usually envied and whatever he wants some will oppose simply because he wants it. This general approach to anti-Americanism can apply to any region, so one must look at the Middle East in general and Egypt in particular to see how American foreign policy has played out in the region throughout the recent years. American policies have generally led to a profound sense of grievance across the entire Middle East. Take the Palestine issue for example. The U.S. is seen as opposing Arab expectations of self-determination despite a steadfast support of the Jewish right to self-determination. According to Arab perceptions, Israel would not have been born had it not been for the policies of President Truman, a perception widely accepted by Israelis as well. As quoted by Rubinstein, the Chief Rabbi of Israel came to see president Truman in 1949 and told him, "God put you in your mother's womb so that you could be the instrument to bring about the rebirth of Israel after two thousand years" (Rubinstein, 1985, 73). The tremendous efforts taken by the American government to establish Israel were bound to have a negative impact on the Arab psyche, namely because the Americans supported the oppressors according to the Egyptian mindset. Another reason why America has been looked upon negatively is it has been fairly consistent in opposing the more far-reaching forms of Arab Nationalism as exemplified by leaders such as Nasser. This policy has always been interpreted as America's way of supporting Israel and ensuring its existence in the Middle East.

America has been involved in many local disputes such as the Western Sahara issue, the Iran-Iraq wars and the Yemen struggle in the 1960s (Thornton, 1998, 53). Regarding Middle Eastern leaders, the United States has "over identified" with conservative rulers (such as Nuri Said in Iraq, Hussein in Jordan, Hassan in Morocco, Sadat in Egypt and certainly the Shah in Iran). In doing so, the U.S. seemed to always personalize its foreign relations everywhere, and thus make it appear as if these leaders were under American control. This tendency to classify leaders did not go well with the Middle Eastern population, who often felt as if their governments were managed by the United States.

The Islamist Argument

The emergence of political Islam in Egypt was not due to a lack of democracy, but rather a reaction to what was present or more precisely not present. This view is evident in two phenomena: the constant imperial presence and the nationalist or semi-socialist presence, as advocated by the likes of President Nasser. As previously discussed, Egypt's relationship with the West covered a long period—from the Napoleonic invasion and continued with the westernized reforms of Muhammad Ali, which lasted until 1952. The economic and political control was largely in the hands of foreign powers. These encounters with the West created dislocations within Egypt. Key figures like Muhammed Abdu and Al-Afghani provided a common answer: Muslims needed to revive their original heritage, which had been subverted by dynastic empires. There was a visible theme in their advocacy: to return to the roots of Islam, so that Muslims could rival Western progress as in the Golden Age of Islam and thus ending Egypt's inferiority. This premise was referred to as Islamisation, something which the Muslim Brotherhood politicized and used in modern politics.

Between the 1967 defeat and Nasser's death in 1970, the Egyptian society, to some extent, engaged in an examination of conscience. The youth of a generation shaped by Nasserism, which had significantly expanded the number of universities, managed to give themselves a voice (Kepel, 1984, 131). These students demanded not only a firm stand against Israel, but also internal reforms to make the country more democratic. According to Kepel, they "acted as a kind of collective observer, even an internal censor, of government policy" (1984, 131). With Nasser's death in autumn 1970 and his replacement by Sadat, the Egyptian student movement gained greater impetus. Sadat lacked his predecessor's authority and in order to retain power, he had to carry out a palace revolution in May 1971 in which he *neutralized* the leading political figures who were most closely associated with the Soviet Union. This operation, termed the "rectification revolution," gave Sadat "a stronger grip on his political apparatus, while it also gave rise to suspicion on the left that he was about to desert the camp of progress" (Kepel, 1984, 132). The great cause of this camp was the demand for a war of revenge against Israel to erase the humiliation of June 1967. It also demonstrated that the Egyptian government was now getting closer to the other side of the Cold War, the United States.

It seemed most Muslims were bitter and unable to comprehend how the United States (which gives Israel billions annually) could not stop Israeli activities against the Arabs. The emotions awakened in Muslims by the Israeli-Palestinian conflict have poured fuel on a regional climate already smoldering with political dissatisfaction. This conflict has touched the hearts of all the Arabs who see the injustice inflicted upon the Palestinians by the U.S. supported Zionist state of Israel.

A majority of Arabs held the view that the best course of fair action from the Americans would be to wash their hands of any involvement in the Middle East, particularly their steadfast support of Israel. But for a variety of reasons, from the strength of the Jewish lobby in the U.S. Congress to the notion of "divide and conquer" that is arguably adopted by the country, the U.S. would inevitably be involved in the Middle East for as long as it claims to be a superpower. With the collapse of the Soviet Union, the balance of power in the Middle East tipped toward Israel unequivocally. This argument is widely accepted, and it is worth noting that with the end of the Cold War era, Israel's passionate attachment with the U.S. has strengthened.

This surge in Islamic movements can be examined in several ways. First, in the wake of Nasser's demise, it provides another powerful idiom with which to denounce foreign interference and Israeli policies. Second, grassroots activist groups such as the Muslim Brotherhood provided social services and a sense of cohesion that were attractive to the urban poor, who were increasingly left to their own devices, owing to the state's increasingly neo-liberal orientation. To this extent, the Islamic movement had some degree of appeal to the working classes, although it was essentially rooted in the educated but disenfranchised lower-middle strata. For the same reason, it also has a strong cultural dimension (Bayat, 1998, 2002).

Revulsion at the 1997 Luxor attack led most of the movements, including al-Gamâ'a al-Islâmiyya and Islamic Jihad, to call for a truce. Most of these groups see their struggle as one for the hearts and minds of Muslims, and against the "near enemy" in the form of the Egyptian government rather than the "far enemy" of the U.S., as al-Zayyat argues.

Murphy contends that amid a globalizing world, many Muslims feel threatened by a "cultural invasion" committed by the West (Murphy, 2002, 18). In response, they are reasserting Islam as their existential cultural guidepost. They are returning to their Islamic *roots* because they see Islam as a protective armor against a humiliating loss of identity. "American pop culture, particularly with its obsessive flaunting of sex is the first target of what she calls Cultural Islam" (2002, 18). At a more sophisticated level, it is evident in the assertions of cultural independence by Muslim intellectuals as they seek to replace Western concepts with ones grounded in Islamic traditions. "Islamists" have long reproached fellow Egyptians for adopting Western lifestyles and ideas. As quoted in Murphy's book, the Muslim Brotherhood leader, Hasan Al Banna, of the 1930s, called Western lifestyles "undignified, unpatriotic, and insulting to their Islamic heritage" (2002, 268). He advocated thinking independently and in accordance with Islam instead of focusing on imitations, which would tie Egyptians to the theories and attitudes of the West in everything. He wished for the Egyptians to be distinguished by their own traditional values. Many would agree with him that Islam is their vaccination against becoming the West's clones. Others may look to Islam to support the emotional hatred they have adopted toward the West although mainstream Islam entails nothing to support this hatred. In fact, Islam advocates a definite policy of peace and forgiveness.

Western governments often overlook or minimize the social and cultural aspect of Islam's contemporary revival in Egypt. Concerned about the stability of Arab governments, Westerners, particularly Americans, tended to be preoccupied with political Islam's armed rebels and well-organized activists; but culture and politics are conjoined, and what happens in one arena affects the other, sometimes with major consequences. Muslims have begun challenging cultural values and started seeking psychological independence from the West. They reject the assumption that as people around the world modernize, they inevitably will think and act like Westerners. Even as Egyptians made ever-increasing contacts with the West, they managed to keep their strong interpretation of Islamic law (Murphy, 2002, 271). This is arguably because expanding contacts with the West made societies like Egypt insecure and fearful about the survival of their Islamic cultural identity, which gave religious conservatism more control. Murphy points to the fact that whenever a society feels threatened by outside forces, whether militarily or culturally, "self-reflection and internal reform are dampened" (2002, 271). Egypt was no exception to the rule.

U.S. Cultural Presence

While many Egyptians are concerned about America's "cultural invasion," some have actually enthusiastically welcomed it. Like people in most of the world, Egyptians have been "both attracted and repelled by U.S. power, wealth, freedom, technologies—and the Hollywood imagery. The Egyptian government, as a result of the Egypt-Israel peace treaty, has received approximately $2.1 billion in annual U.S. aid." According to Murphy, American businesses have been interested in building factories to produce goods and subsequently to export these goods to other countries. In 1998, for example, U.S. investment in Egypt totaled $543 million, excluding oil and oil products. In total, the Egyptian market accounts for 12 per cent of all U.S. investment in the region. This influx of foreign direct investment could help to shift the Egypt-U.S. economic relationship from aid to trade. Currently, Egypt is the second largest American export market in the Middle East, after Saudi Arabia. Development programs have become more focused on upgrading labor skills and increasing trade and investment (*Al Ahram*, June 1, 2000). According to the Egyptian newspaper *Al Ahram* (August 6, 1998), Egypt's ready-to-wear and weaving exports to the U.S. amounted to $320 million last year, equivalent to 7 per cent of the United States' total ready-to-wear and weaving imports, which exceed $45 billion annually.

But along side this acceptance runs an undercurrent of unease and resentment regarding America's cultural presence, whether in trivial matters like having American fast food chains or the more serious ideas like adopting Western dress codes and behavior. The recurring reminders of American culture in Cairo's streets are signals to some Egyptians of their own culture's weakened influence on the global scene and its domination by a foreign one (Murphy, 2002, 274). Fears of American cultural influences are heightened by the widespread view among Egyptians, from secularists to the most radical of "Islamists" that America has gone too far in its sexual freedoms. Egypt is a very conservative society and its people generally "disapprove of America's acceptance of homosexuality, the sexuality of its entertainment and media industries, and the extent to which it practises gender equality" (Murphy, 2002, 275). Therefore, notions of American life have convinced many Egyptians including moderates that American culture should be kept far beyond reach of the Egyptian people. The assumption that American society is "morally loose" makes it difficult for Egyptians to adopt any of its cultural values for fear that its traits would be transferred onto theirs.

Murphy argues that some conservative "Islamists" feel too much infiltration of Western or American practices can result in high rates of divorce and abortion, broken families, illegitimacy, AIDS, prostitution, and pornography, all of which take place in Western societies and are forbidden and contrary to what should take place in Islamic societies. Some "Islamists" see America as morally irreparable because it has left religion behind. They overlook the fact that the U.S. has one of the most religiously active populations in the developed Western world. Moreover, on the issue of secularism, "Islamists" and moderate Egyptians alike, say secularism practiced in the West should not thrive in a Muslim country like Egypt. This opinion is problematic for Westerners who believe that their secular cultural values have been the reasons behind their success in accordance with the Western Protestant work ethic. The Egyptians, while believing the idea that aid empowers the aid-giver to exert pressure, do not like to contemplate life without this aid. Moreover, the U.S. government has had trouble keeping the promise they made to Jordan when they agreed that they would "forgive" the country's debts if they made peace with Israel. Egyptians today are worried that they might be vulnerable to the same situation.

Anticipating the worst, an opposition Egyptian newspaper put down American aid, asserting that it was tied to the purchase of inferior American goods. Several senior figures, including the Foreign Minister Amr Mousa, have now spoken of the need for Egypt to disassociate itself from foreign aid, or at least not to regard it as eternal. This assertion is fantasy-like to most Egyptians who recognize that while depending on the U.S. for aid and food is dangerous because it keeps them tied up, it is their only source of improving the already very low standards of living. Egypt is unable to provide enough resources for everyone, which results in overtaxing, and a general atmosphere of stress. There is a huge dependence on the Nile as a source of water, which has proven insufficient in supplying a huge number of people. The Egyptian government has continuously struggled to bring about economic reform. As a consequence, an increasing number of Egyptians are joining their fellow Egyptians abroad in order to find work.

Political Development Affecting Egypt

After making peace with Israel in 1979, the prevailing Egyptian attitude at the time was that Egypt had done more than enough to advance the Arab and Palestinian cause. Egypt could sustain itself without the help of the oil-rich Arab states. Coupled with these sentiments was a resurgence of a narrow Egyptian nationalism that stressed Egypt's Nile/Mediterranean roots, as opposed to its Arab identity. The Sadat regime favored intellectuals who wrote on these subjects. One should note that Sadat's policies may have made him the "darling" of the Western media, but domestically they contributed to the simmering discontent that was to eventually lead to his assassination in 1981 (Daweesha, 1997, 42). So again, within the Cold War framework, Egyptian leadership did its best to maximize the economic benefits from the United States, as at the time, this concern was a main priority of their agenda.

By the time Mubarak ascended to the presidency, Egypt was living in a much-changed world. His first major achievement was to bring a balance to Egypt's foreign policy. He did this by restoring relations with the Soviet Union and began the process of reintegrating Egypt with the Arab world. Mubarak made sure that his convenient relationship with Israel and the United States would remain unaffected as he strove to get closer to the Arab-speaking world. In his eyes, the Gulf War of 1991 provided Mubarak with the opportunity to introduce radical reforms and incentives for the international community to reduce Egypt's debt burden. The government was able to sell the reforms at home as being a necessary part of Egypt's international commitments (Rivlin, 2003, 8). The United States wrote off nearly $7 billion of military debt that had cost Egypt about $700 million a year to service. The Gulf Arab states also wrote off about $6 billion, none of which was being serviced. In a sense, Egypt was successful in achieving the goals it set out for itself when it handled the Gulf Crisis. Measuring the incentives for joining in the coalition against Iraq, Egypt was able to take advantage of the Gulf War situation; while appeasing the U.S., they also seemingly formed a unified front against the Iraqi invasion of Kuwait.

On a global level, however, the picture was looking different. The first Gulf War supported the marginalization of Egypt's role in the international arena. As a result of this war, the United States extended military protection to the Gulf, thereby replacing Egypt's image as the potential military protector of the region, and other Arab countries began to "carve out their own political and economic relations with Israel" (Daweesha, 1997, 44). The Americans were now freed from concern over Soviet interference, and Egypt could no longer take advantage of the Cold War atmosphere to maintain its international weight.

Despite their Peace Treaty with Israel, Egypt for the most part has treated Israel like "an angry spouse" (Murphy, 2002, 404). Apart from correct diplomatic ties, the Egyptian government has done little to form closer ties with Israel such as tourist, cultural, and education programs. Egyptian President Mubarak visited Israel only once and that was to attend Rabin's funeral in 1995. This cold relationship is of course a result of the massive solidarity Egyptians feel toward the Palestinians. As Murphy points out, Egyptians gave out anti-Jewish propaganda in public but privately admired Israel for its military and economic sharpness. They resent the United States for its unconditional support of Israel, but feel utterly dependent on Washington to resolve the conflict. They are not totally in love with Palestinians or their leader, Yasser Arafat, but they remain "passionately attached to the Palestinian cause" (Murphy, 2002, 401).

The phenomenon of "anti-Americanism" has become increasingly visible in the Arab world since the beginning of the Al-Aqsa Intifada on September 28, 2000. The anger expressed in demonstrations and in the media throughout the Arab world has been noted in the United States—especially in policy-making circles. Moreover, the attack on the destroyer USS Cole off Aden, in which 17 American sailors were killed, has served to remind Americans that their country can be a target as both the country's presence and biased policies in the Middle East are resented by Arabs.

The standing of the U.S. in the Arab world dropped further following the failure of Camp David peace talks in the summer of 2000. Not only did U.S President Bill

Clinton blame Palestinians and President Yasser Arafat for the dismal outcome of the meetings, but he also praised Israeli Prime Minister Ehud Barak for offering what he described as unprecedented compromises. This partisan position adopted by President Clinton did nothing more than fuel Arab mistrust of the U.S. as well as dissatisfaction with the continual poor foreign policies toward the Middle East viewed by the Arabs.

Many young Egyptians live between two compelling and competing worlds. One easily accepts western culture. The other scorns it. The tension between these two worlds is another reason for Islam's new strength in the Middle East. Pious Islam offers Muslims personal spiritual comfort. Political Islam arises from their demands for new types of governance and a voice in how they are ruled. Cultural Islam reflects their search for true identity.

Opportunity for Opposition and Reaction to 9/11

Violent anti-Americanism in Egypt has been a constant threat in the 1990s. The U.S. Embassy in Cairo has received numerous threats against U.S. government targets in Egypt, and American citizens were constantly reminded to be vigilant while traveling in Egypt. Rallies and protests were infrequent and typically kept under control by police. Public demonstrations are illegal in Egypt without a security permit, which is rarely issued. According to the emergency law, which governs public gatherings, a legal case can be raised against any group of four people unlawfully gathered. If allowed, public protests are usually organized by opposition parties and groups such as the Islamist Labor Party, or student organizations such as those within Cairo University. About two hundred Egyptian journalists staged a sit-in demonstration outside their union office after one of the U.S. bombings of Iraq.

Censorship is practiced in the media. In particular, a publication can be prohibited if it criticizes the Egyptian president or his family. It is against the law to criticize the Egyptian military, or Islamic religion. There is a difference between what is expressed in English, for the consumption in other countries, and what is expressed in Arabic, for domestic consumption. Unsightly and ridiculous anti-American and anti-Israeli denunciations are routinely published in the press or aired on radio and television, and always with either the acquiescence or the prompting of the government. Conspiracy theories are not foreign to the Egyptian press. For example, the data gathered for this book shows that many elites in Egypt believed that 9/11 was carried out by Israel, U.S. Special Forces, or even the U.S. government itself. Name-calling of U.S. officials is a usual occurrence. The lack of political openness and free speech combined with real backroom maneuvers and plots, together with America's relationships with leaders who have few friends, such as the Shah in Iran, create a tendency for conspiracy. In one publication, U.S. Secretary of State Colin Powell was called "stupid" and "a liar" and was said to have "the brain of a bird" (*Al Akhbar*, February 2, 2001). The same newspaper issued an editorial in August 2001 suggesting that the U.S. is not a friend and its task is to impose hegemony on the world, primarily on the Middle East and the Arab world (*Al Akhbar*, August 26, 2001). President Bush was once depicted as a hostage of the Jewish lobby (*Akhbar Al Youm*, September 8, 2001). There are occasional articles about the United States selling bad or inferior products to Egypt (*The Economist*, January 6, 1995).

Elements of anti-Americanism appear in Egyptian performing arts as well. At least three movies released in the 1990s ("The Land of Dreams," "Abracadabra America," and "Visit of Mr. President") criticize U.S. policies and chide Egyptians for wanting to emigrate to the United States (*Al Magd*, 1994). The movie "Visit of Mr. President" also reflects a bitter view of American economic aid. It comes from a novel by leftist writer Youssef el-Qaid about then-President Nixon's visit to Egypt in 1974. In the film, an entire village gets extremely excited when the rumor spreads that Nixon will visit and bring with him U.S. assistance. Peasants abandon their traditional clothes and wear jeans and T-shirts (a sign of Americanization), and soon people are fighting over who will get the American aid. In the end, Nixon never comes; and El-Qaid maintains that his novel is meant to warn Egyptians against the destructive American dream and urge them to reject American aid. Unfortunately, this dream will remain in novels for sometime to come, since it is inconceivable to many of becoming fully independent from foreign aid due to its poor economy and enormous population.

The Egyptian government insists that the Egyptian press is free, and the Egyptian government has no influence over it. However, according to the U.S. State Department's "Country Reports on Human Rights Practices," the Egyptian government maintains considerable control over the press, especially over big daily and monthly publications, as well as radio and television networks. The government owns stock in the three largest daily newspapers and appoints their editors in chief (*Akher Sa'a*, *Akhbar Al Youm*, and *Al Akhbar*). Some newspapers are semi-owned by the government, like *Al Ahram* and *Al ahram Alarabi*, both very influential newspapers. The most visible opposition newspaper is *Al-Sha'b* (or the People), which is run by the Al Sha'b Party Organ, and while they have some opportunities to voice their disagreements with the government, they are aware that crossing the line too much may have serious repercussions. The government also holds a monopoly on newsprint in Egypt and on the printing and distribution of newspapers. Any media attack against the United States would not take place without the right cues or direct instructions from the government. In addition, military courts are legal. Torture of perceived political dissidents is routine. The state also controls a majority of Egyptian mosques and often Khutbas (people giving speeches before Friday prayers) are limited in content and tone.

Newspapers Convey Attitudes

Analysis provided for this book covers newspapers such as *Al Ahram*, *Al Sha'b*, *Al Alam Alyoum*, *Alahram Al Arabi*, *Akhbar Al Youm*, *Al Akhbar*, *Afaq Arabia*, and *Aker Sa'a*. For the purposes of this chapter, and due to length limitations, only these publications will be considered. It should be noted that other forms of media, such as TV and radio, are just as important to look at, and generally speaking, they reflect the results of this data. The content analysis considered several issues surrounding the events of September 11.

Beginning with how America should react to the September 11 events, a big proportion of the press materials (32 per cent) agreed that America should pause and soberly reflect before taking action. Many authors suggested that America should avoid being driven to action by anger, fear, or fervent patriotism. Second, the United States was to change or rethink its foreign policies or actions in general, and in particular toward Palestine and Israel. Thirty-three per cent agreed that America should work with the entire world community to stop terrorism. Most of the newspapers agreed with these options (with *Akhbar Al Youm* mainly emphasizing the change of foreign policy toward Israel and Palestine with 38 per cent). Many Egyptians propagated a policy of "no-help" or support of the U.S. as a result of the September 11 tragedy.

In terms of the newspapers, there was an apparent split; while *Al Ahram, Akhbar Al Youm* and *Al Akhbar* showed a majority in agreeing to help or support the U.S. government in general, *Al Sha'b, Al Alam Al Youm* and *Al Ahram Al Arabi* displayed favorability toward not helping or supporting the United States. *Akhar Sa'a* was most likely to suggest the idea of working with the U.S. to stop terrorism using military force or bombing, but only on terrorist camps or military targets (100 per cent). The option to work with the U.S. to stop terrorism using military force on the governments, states, or groups that harbor or support those who are responsible for the September 11 events was completely ignored by the Egyptians.

In terms of identifying possible perpetrators of the September 11 events, only 16 per cent of the respondents believed Osama bin Laden and Al Qaeda were responsible. As time progressed, this percentage rose to 44 in December. Instantaneously though, the highest percentage (29) chose American radical, militant or terrorist groups as the possible perpetrators of the events. As far as the newspapers are concerned, again there was a split, in which the two camps of either Osama bin Laden and Al Qaeda or American radical or terrorists groups, respectively were selected. The first camp included *Al Ahram*, and *Akhbar Al Youm*, while the second included *Akhar Sa'a* and *Al Akhbar.* The only opposition newspaper *Al Sha'b* was split: 20 per cent blamed it on Osama bin Laden, 20 per cent on Japanese radical militant or terrorist groups, 20 per cent on Israel and 20 per cent on drug lords or Mafia.

These statistics show a similar trend to what happened in Iran up to and during the revolution, where conspiracy theories were rife, and for vaguely similar reasons. As Ervand Abrahamian has argued (1993, Chapter 6), most Iranians knew that American involvement in their country's politics was rife; but they had no way of knowing where it began or ended, leading to limitless speculation on who was "pulling the strings." Edward Said has made a similar point that even intellectuals in the Arab world are often convinced that anything that happens must do so through the will of the U.S., a state of mind that seemingly is the product of moral and political helplessness.

A content analysis also surveyed the words or phrases used in the Egyptian press materials to describe the act itself or the perpetrators of the September 11 events. All chose not to call them freedom fighters or martyrs but instead the majority opted for the choice of calling them horrible, terrible, cruel, malicious, savage, hateful, tragic, gruesome and despicable. The next highest percentage (13) emphasized that they were well organized, planned or coordinated (meticulous, thorough, and professional). This data is significant because it refutes the popular opinion that Egyptians were out in the streets celebrating the atrocities committed in New York and Washington.

Regarding the root causes, motivations, or conditions that led to the September 11 events, most articles (49 per cent) agreed that American foreign policies, actions or arrogance in general were the main reason for this atrocity. This of course includes America's foreign policy toward Palestine or Israel (with 9 per cent emphasizing it). With the exception of *Akhbar Al Youm*, in which 40 per cent of its respondents chose conspiracy (carried out by either America or Israel) the majority of the other newspapers agreed with the choice that American foreign policy was the main root cause. When it came to using a phrase to describe the conflict brought to light by the events, the largest portion of authors (36 per cent) agreed that it was a conflict between rich and poor, between developed and developing countries, or between the industrialized and the non-industrialized world. Second, 14 per cent asserted that the so-called conflict should not be considered a clash between civilizations or religions, nor between the Islamic world and the Western world. The idea that the U.S. had launched a war against Islam became more attractive moving from September to December 2001. Many announced that Islam had replaced communism, America's previous enemy.

Another issue of the analysis looked at how the authors perceived the motivation for the U.S.-led war in Afghanistan. The majority agreed that it was first to satisfy the local and international expectations for a reaction from the government, and second, to protect or enrich American oil interests. The latter sentiment increased between September and December, while the first reason became less favorable. *Akhar Sa'a* was the only newspaper to emphasize stopping terrorism throughout the world as America's motivation behind the war in Afghanistan. *Al Ahram* agreed with the oil motivation, while *Al Akhbar* and *Afagarabia* settled on the motivation to prove to its own people or the world that it was still a strong country, or that it could react firmly or resolutely to the events. In terms of assessing the war, not only did many authors agree that it was wrong, immoral and indifferent, or callous toward the destruction of Afghanistan, the majority believed that the American actions fueled anti-American feelings in one or more regions or countries. *Al Akhbar* was quick to point out that the U.S. had failed in capturing or destroying Osama bin Laden, Mullah Omar, or Al Qaeda. Seventy per cent of the press materials from *Al Sha'b* declared that the U.S. actions increased anti-Americanism.

The last question posed in the press analysis considered the words used to describe America, its government or its people. For this particular enquiry, it was difficult to point to the choice of the majority. On average, there was an alteration between "shaken," "only superpower remaining," "stupid, foolish or ignorant," and "peaceful and friendly." The great majority of the words and phrases were negative. As an interesting ambiguity in the press coverage, many authors thought that the U.S. had been shaken, and its power put into question, yet it was also widely acknowledged that the United States was the only superpower remaining and the strongest country in the world.

Conclusion

One may ask: what can be learned from these findings? It has been widely speculated that the Egyptians were happy or satisfied when the U.S. came under attack on 9/11.

This, however, was not the case. The content analysis of the press did not support this assumption. Moreover, it is obvious that the Israel/Palestine conflict, and the perceived U.S. bias toward Israel played a major role in the Egyptian mindset. As Fuller contended: "Just as the prism of the Cold War warped America's perception of each conflict around the globe so too the Palestinian-Israeli problem warps perception of all events in the Middle East" (1990/91, 31). When discussing the root causes of 9/11, the Egyptian press invariably pointed to U.S. foreign policies, specifically its Middle East policy. When discussing how the U.S. should respond to 9/11, many also suggested that the U.S. should change its policies toward Israel/Palestine.

It can be argued that *Al Ahram, Akhar Sa'a*, and *Al Akbar* are more favorable toward the U.S. than other publications, especially the very negative *Al Sha'b*. At the same time, these differences should not be exaggerated. Also, what should not be exaggerated is the level of anti-Americanism in Egypt. There is evidence of some homogeneity in the Egyptian sample across the different newspapers. It should be noted that it was very difficult to find reliable empirical evidence of Egyptian attitudes toward the United States. This was due to numerous reasons, including the lack of free speech and of a safe, neutral environment in which pollsters can work as well as the difference in levels of commitment to Islam, which seem to effect the level of anti-Americanism in Egypt.

The current situation in Egypt is fluid, but if U.S. policies toward the Israeli Palestinian conflict and more recently Iraq continue, there is every reason to believe that mistrust and conspiracy theories will continue to rise alongside the anti-American sentiment. The anti-American feeling, which has risen since the mid 1950s, has been a direct result of America's often misguided or possibly too guided foreign policy. The position and support the U.S. has given to Israel often at the expense of the Palestinian people has been the major contributing factor to the sentiment displayed in Egypt as well as the rest of the Middle East.

The anti-American feeling is directly related to America's behavior internationally. The only foreseeable way of dispelling this feeling throughout Egypt is to actively change the foreign policy relating to the Middle East. Sympathizing with America in any way has become suspect, even in cases where most people believe America deserves sympathy. One can look at the conspiracy theories in a similar light: people feel that to sympathize with America would be selling out, as they cannot approve of its hostile policies toward the Middle East, and therefore think of a solution (embedded in conspiracy) that lets them maintain their prejudice without infringing on their moral beliefs. Hence what this chapter has argued is that mistrust of the United States has become an ingrained habit because of the history of the last few decades. Fuller made a very valid point when he stated: "Middle Eastern politics have been essentially dominated by a 'Wild West' approach to regional crisis. When things take turns against the U.S.'s apparent best interests, 'strangers' emerge from the wings—usually America or Israel—to set things right with a lightning war, or invasion, or air strike, or commando raid, or flotilla or warship" (1990/91, 32). Coupled with this, America's recent support of such oppressive regimes as Sadam Hussein, Hafiz Al Assad, King Fahd and other Middle Eastern states has created a more visible focus for anti-American sentiment and has demonstrated the double standards that have contributed to the rise of anti-Americanism in Egypt. This support has ensured America's strong position regarding trade and oil policies, while also ensuring that the Middle East stays divided.

* * *

Editorial Remarks

Egypt's recent history, as it is common for the vast majority of today's sovereign countries, was a history of foreign domination. After several centuries under the Ottoman rule after the end of World War I, Egypt began to pursue its own statehood. Foreign domination, nevertheless, continued when Great Britain established military, political, and economic presence in the entire Middle Eastern region. After the end of World War II, during which Egypt was on the side of the anti-German coalition, at least three major problems emerged as challenges to a developing independent Egyptian state: the first was the continuing British rule, the second was its own corrupt and inefficient government, and the third problem was the creation of Israel in 1947 and the escalation of the Palestinian problem. Different political groups within Egypt offered different solutions to these fundamental issues. Three major solutions, supported by three different political groups have emerged.

The moderates believed in gradual steps and steady improvements to resolve the country's outstanding problems. Through negotiations, economic assistance from the West, steady political reforms, including elements of democratization and liberalization, Egypt was believed to have a good chance to create a permanent peace in the region and develop an efficient economy and stable government supported by a majority of people. The moderates, in general, the most educated layer of Egyptian society, maintained a positive view of the West and the United States, as possible models to emulate. The socialists (Baas party supporters) disagreed and demanded radical reforms. They desired a quick and unconditional removal of the British, the establishment of a secular government, and the implementation of socialist principles in all sectors of the economy. Such plans and demands received tremendous popular support associated with the growth of Egyptian nationalism and anti-Western sentiment. The third group followed the ideas of Islamists who believed that the true rebirth of Egypt was only in the establishment of an Islamic government ruled in accordance to the Islamic law—the ideas described in this chapter. Islamists were genuinely suspicious of other political groups and their country and held negative and frequently hostile attitudes about anything western, including capitalism, democratic principles of government, civil liberties, and elements of the western lifestyle.

Although the problems Egypt has to face in the 2000s appear different than those in the 1940s, many essential challenges remain the same. Similarly, people's attitudes about international developments and foreign countries (the United States in particular) are rooted, generally, in the way these challenges are addressed. The first challenge is the government's inability to solve a tremendous number of social problems due to incompetence, corruption, and mistakes in conducting economic and social policies. By supporting an unpopular government, any foreign country should expect criticism, public resentment, and all other forms of negative attitudes from all groups that pursue social change and removal of the inefficient government.

A majority of Egyptians, regardless of their political affiliation, associate the United States with the unpopular government in Cairo. The second stumbling bloc remains Israel and its policies. Although the United States attempts to maintain a balanced approach to the countries in the Middle East and Egypt continues to be among largest recipients of American help, Washington's policies toward Israel are considered hypocritical and unfair to Egypt and other Arabs. As we see in the case of India, mediators always find themselves in an awkward position when two countries are in a state of confrontation. And the third issue is, again, the issue of foreign domination. Like people of many other countries, Egyptians understand that the nation has a tremendous economic and social potential. And yet, for decades, the country has been incapable of making decisive changes in the struggle against poverty, corruption, injustice, and the lack of economic and social opportunities for the young. Frustration, as a dominant feeling, has become a common feature of the country's social climate. As it happened in many other countries, in such a volatile psychological situation, people often find easy targets against which they can vent their frustration. With all its intentions, policies, actions, and mistakes, the United States is an easy target.

Suggested Additional Literature

Al-Zayyat, Montasser (2004). *The Road to al-Qaeda: the story of Bin Laden's Right-Hand Man.* London and Stering, Virginia: Pluto Press, 2004. Translated by Ahmed Fekry and edited by Sarah Nimis.
Haeri, Niloofar (2003). *Sacred Language, Ordinary People: Dilemmas of Culture and Politics in Egypt.* London/NY: Palgrave Macmillan.
Murphy, Caryle (2002). *Passion for Islam: Shaping the modern Middle East, the Egyptian experience.* New York: Scribner.

CASE 6
INDIA

The terrorist attacks on the World Trade Center in New York and the Pentagon on September 11, 2001, engendered a global wave of shock, horror and sympathy for the United States. All over the world, ordinary people grieved and expressed solidarity with the United States in what seemed to be its darkest hour. However, the "we-are-all-Americans" sentiment that seemed to have gripped the world immediately after 9/11 not only dissipated quite rapidly, but since then, international goodwill towards America has been increasingly replaced by anger and antagonism, fueled to a significant degree by the way that America has been prosecuting its global war on terror and its actions in Iraq. According to the Pew Global Attitudes Survey, which used a poll conducted by the United States Department of State in 2000 as the benchmark, the favorable rating for America has dropped in 19 of the 27 nations surveyed. These reactions, moreover, are not simply typical of Islamic countries where such a decline might have been expected, but are manifest even among America's traditional allies such as Germany, Italy and Britain, all of whom have witnessed a significant increase in anti-Americanism (Thibault, 2002). Similarly, in a recent poll commissioned by the Washington-based Council on Foreign Relations, Europeans proved highly critical of the United States, with 85 per cent of Germans, 80 per cent of French, 73 per cent of Britons and 68 per cent of Italians saying that they believed that the United States was acting in its own interests in the war on terrorism (Hale, 2002). As a phenomenon anti-Americanism is not entirely new. As some point out, "it is a trend that has ebbed and flowed" based on American involvement in global affairs (Robertson, 2003). However, its intensity and pervasiveness on a global scale are quite unprecedented and have left many Americans stunned and disbelieving. Commenting on this development, journalist Richard Bernstein of the *New York Times* writes:

In the two years since September 11, 2001 the view of the United States as a victim of terrorism that deserved the world's sympathy has given way to a vision of America as an imperial power that has defied world opinion through unjustified and unilateral use of military force. In interviews by *Times* correspondents from Africa to Europe to Southeast Asia, one point emerged clearly: The war in Iraq has had a major impact on public opinion, which has moved generally from post 9/11 sympathy to post-Iraq antipathy, or at least to disappointment over what is seen as the sole superpower's inclination to act preemptively, without either persuasive reasons or United Nations' approval (Bernstein, 2003).

Anti-Americanism has thus become a highly visible and politically charged issue in the contemporary world since 9/11 (so much so that the State Department has sought to significantly step up its public diplomacy efforts). Yet, the phenomenon is by no means monolithic either in terms of the manner in which it is manifested or uniform in terms of the factors that drive its emergence in countries across the world. Consequently, to obtain an in-depth understanding of America's image abroad, one that extends beyond scattered anecdotal evidence, it is necessary to explore how the country is viewed within specific national contexts, and that is what this chapter seeks to do in relation to India.

Chapter 10

India's Reaction to 9/11:
The Historical Context

Kalyani Chadha, Anandam Kavoori and Katherine McAdams

Friendship and cooperation between our two countries are natural.
Indian Prime Minister Jawaharlal Nehru during his first official visit to the United
States in 1949

Indo-United States Relations During the Cold War: The Big Chill

Prior to India's independence in 1947, American interaction with the country was limited. Compared to countries such as China and Japan, relatively few American traders and missionaries had worked in India and only a small number of Indian immigrants had settled in the United States. Also, as Limaye (1993) points out, the traffic in ideas between the two nations was neither deep nor widespread and as a result their views of one another were often ambiguous and oversimplified. Moreover, even after direct political contacts were established between the two sovereign nations following India's independence in 1947, the latter tended to be focused on matters of national development while the international interests of the United States were centered on European reconstruction and apprehensions regarding Soviet political penetration into Western Europe.

India only gained importance in the American strategic worldview as the rise of communism in China generated American fears about Sino-Soviet expansionism in Asia. At this juncture, the United States believed that India with its democratic polity and faith in religion could be held up as an "alternative" to communism in Asia and thus serve as a counterbalance to China (Stebbins, 1953). As the *New York Times* put it, "Washington wants India to be a bulwark against communism … India is potentially a great counterweight to China" (Editorial, 1949).

Furthermore, officials in the State Department believed that the "latent power and moral influence of such leaders as Mahatma Gandhi and Jawaharlal Nehru, if exerted in line with American views would be capable of producing an effect favorable to United States policy in South Asia" (Saha, 1990). On the Indian side too there was an interest in fostering economic and cultural contacts with the United States. Consequently, when Indian Prime Minister Jawaharlal Nehru made his first official visit to America in 1949, he received a warm welcome. And in his address to Congress in 1949, Nehru said: "I have come here on a voyage of discovery of the mind and heart of America and to place before you our own mind and heart. Thus we may promote the understanding and cooperation, which I feel sure both our countries earnestly desire ... Friendship and cooperation between our two countries are natural ..." (1949).

Yet despite this promising beginning, Indo-United States relations were not cordial and the hopes for amicable and constructive ties between the two countries were soon tempered by the fact that the two countries had vastly different priorities and perspectives in the international system that had begun to develop in the post-1945 era. With the weakening of the European states and the rise of the Soviet Union, the United States, which had emerged as the strongest economic and military power, reappraised its historic isolationism and adopted a far more activist foreign policy. The chief linchpin of this policy was to prevent the expansion of communism, which was seen as a mortal threat not only to the "American way of life but life itself" (Chary, 1995, 14).

As a result, the leading priority of the United States in most of the developing world was to garner support for its policy of containment. This objective effectively took precedence over all other considerations, such as promoting democracy or remedying economic injustice or fighting colonialism. Thus while the United States saw itself as "an anti-colonial power, and sympathized with anti-colonial rhetoric, which was the rhetoric of its own war on independence" (Bull, 1984, 217), to much of the developing world it seemed that the United States behaved in a way that de-emphasized the very economic and political issues that were of the greatest significance to developing nations.

In South Asia, an area with which America had few historical connections and in which it had little real interest, its primary goal was to find allies against communism and its relationships with countries came to be based on their willingness or ability to aid the achievement of the United States' geo-strategic objectives—a fact that had profound, long-term implications for its relationship with India. For its part, as the largest nation in South Asia, India viewed its "independent entrance onto the world stage in August 1947 as a profoundly significant and unique event" (Limaye, 1993, 15). And although at this juncture its power was more potential than real, it too sought an activist role in the shaping of the new international order. However, unlike the United States, with its main interest in finding partners in the battle against communism, India's foreign policy was essentially based on a rejection of the idea of power blocs and the exposition of the doctrine of non-alignment. Through this policy, which implied a distance from great-power conflicts, India hoped to keep the Cold War out of South Asia and to establish India's leading position in the area.

India was, moreover, not particularly concerned by the rise of communist regimes in Asia, which it considered "legitimate expressions of self-determination and not, as Washington proclaimed, the creations of Soviet expansionism in Asia" (Chary, 1995, viii). In fact, Indian leaders such as Nehru questioned the use of Western military alliances to stem communism in Asian countries and felt that economic development rather than American military might was a far better antidote to the spread of communism. In addition to their widely divergent responses to communism, the two countries also clashed over India's adoption of a socialist model of economic development.

India's insistence on a neutral stance and refusal to adopt a strong anti-communist position as well as the country's rejection of the American-style economic policies baffled and frustrated American policymakers who not only resented what they termed Nehru's "holier than thou" lecturing on the virtues of restraint in international relations but increasingly saw nonalignment as immoral and even emblematic of anti-Americanism (Smith, 1972; Kux, 1994). The stage was thus set early for an adversarial relationship between the two countries and although there was some bilateral economic assistance provided to India by the United States in the 1950s, there was little trade, investment or technological collaboration. Instead, discord remained persistent with Indians feeling that United States' aid was "begrudgingly given and only with political motives while the U.S. and especially many members of Congress resented India's apparent ingratitude for American largesse" (Limaye, 1993, 6; Rubinoff, 2001).

During this period, disagreements between the two countries were manifested over a series of issues ranging from the way in which the United States responded to Indian requests for grain assistance during a famine in 1951 and the role of China in the Korean War to the situation in Kashmir and the creation of the Palestinian homeland. The most significant conflict of the 1950s, however, came during the Eisenhower administration when the United States government's belief that the rise of communism in China was synonymous with Soviet expansionism in Asia led it to not only provide military aid to Pakistan, but to enter into a military alliance with it by including Pakistan in the Southeast Asia Treaty Organization (Tahir-Kheli, 1997).

Although President Eisenhower assured Nehru that the arms would not be used against India, saying that, "if our aid to Pakistan is misused ... I will undertake to thwart such aggression (Eisenhower, 1954), the Indian government viewed this action as an act of open hostility towards India. From the Indian perspective, Pakistan's involvement in a U.S.-sponsored military alliance not only challenged the idea of non-alignment but also destroyed what Nehru called the "no war area in Asia." "From the Indian standpoint, the U.S.-Pakistani alliance resembled the initial stages of many imperialist ventures in India. It reminded many Indians of the British phase of Indian history when a weak local power attempted to increase its strength *vis-à-vis* its neighboring state by accepting a foreign military alliance and embracing alien influence. The government of India also worried that increased Pakistani strength would also adversely affect India's position in Kashmir" (Chary, 1995, 93). The transformation of Pakistan into a satellite state and the efforts to equalize the military powers of the two rival nations by the United States convinced the Indians that the American government did not accept India as an independent center of power in Asia and was attempting to contain it.

By its later years, the Eisenhower administration altered its approach towards India and sought to collaborate economically and politically with it, both as part of its new policy to counter Soviet efforts to woo developing nations and as a result of India's growing stature among Asian and other non-aligned Third World countries. As part of this shift, Eisenhower undertook a state visit to India in 1959 during which he expressed respect for India's neutrality in international relations and promised increased economic aid to the country. But while Eisenhower certainly exhibited a more flexible attitude towards India and he and Nehru even developed a good working relationship that was aided by their mutual distrust of China, the fundamental differences between the United States and India continued to persist, particularly with regard to the United States' relationships with Pakistan.

The United States under President John F. Kennedy seemed to build further on its policy of flexibility toward India. Unlike previous American presidents, Kennedy did not view Indian non-alignment as the product of opposition to the United States. Instead he argued that no one "should be put off by the Indian commitment to neutralism," and actually saw in India a counterweight to China. As he said in 1959, "The struggle between China and India for the economic and political leadership of the East would determine the future of Asia ... We want India to win the race against China. If China succeeds and India fails, the economic balance of power would shift against us" (Kennedy, 1960, 143).

Consequently, when India was attacked by China in 1962, the United States supported India and provided emergency military aid as a means to consolidate Indo-American friendship. The American readiness to help India militarily (particularly in light of the Soviet unwillingness to do so) was widely welcomed in India and America was seen in extremely positive terms. Yet, despite a marked improvement in relations during the Sino-Indian conflict of 1962, United States' policy toward India ultimately remained grounded in the framework of the Cold War and the two nations soon found themselves at odds over a variety of issues ranging from India's takeover of Goa and the status of Kashmir to the American refusal to help India construct a steel plant due to Congressional opposition to India's foreign and economic policies and, of course, America's military support of Pakistan. Thus, despite Kennedy's interest in India and his desire to see it emerge as a balance to China in Asia, eventually Cold War considerations on both sides limited the development of the U.S.-India relationship.

Under Kennedy's successor, President Lyndon Johnson, America's growing involvement in Vietnam resulted in a lesser interest in South Asia's affairs. Tensions between the United States and India mounted, nevertheless, over the India-Pakistan War of 1965. India felt that in view of the previous American assurances that arms supplied to Pakistan would never be used against India, the United States was obliged to act to prevent this from happening. India was also deeply angered at the United States' decision to cut off aid to both India and Pakistan, feeling that this was deeply unfair since Pakistan had initiated the conflict using American arms. India and Pakistan clashed once more when President Johnson instituted the so called "short tether policy" whereby he sought to make food assistance to a drought-ravaged India conditional upon Indian support of the United States' policy in Vietnam and the introduction of a more market-oriented development strategy.

By the end of the Johnson's administration, Indo-United States relations were quite discordant and only worsened under President Richard Nixon. His administration's Asian policy was based on the dual principles of the establishment of detente with communist China and the maintenance of the regional balance of power in South Asia. These two policy developments were deeply troubling to India because it not only made India less important to the United States but also signaled the United States' desire to normalize relations with a country with which India had fought a bitter war. The worst phase in the Indo-United States relations came during the presidency of Nixon in 1971, when a revolt in East Pakistan sent almost ten million refugees streaming into India. As the refugee crisis intensified, it was almost inevitable that India be drawn into hostilities with Pakistan whose planes suddenly attacked Indian airfields on December 3. India's involvement in the conflict was decried by the United States, which not only sanctioned a $40-million weapons package to Islamabad, but also dispatched the nuclear-powered carrier U.S.S. Enterprise to the Bay of Bengal. While the ostensible purpose of this step was to ensure the safe evacuation of Americans from East Pakistan (later Bangladesh), the real motive, as Kissinger wrote, was to give emphasis to "our warnings against an attack on West Pakistan" (1979, 905).

This example of gunboat diplomacy generated powerful anti-American feelings in India. Indians were appalled by President Nixon's failure to understand the Indian position, his partisanship for Pakistan and by the Enterprise affair. There were widespread demonstrations against Nixon and for the first time many Indians came to see the United States as a real threat to their country (Van Hollen, 1980). This strained relationship was further exacerbated by India's explosion of a nuclear device in 1974 and thus the early to mid 1970s were characterized by a marked coolness and distance between India and the United States.

President Jimmy Carter attempted to shift United States' foreign policy away from its traditional Cold War orientation and seemed to recognize India's importance in South Asia. He pursued constructive engagements between India and the United States. There were frequent calls for initiatives to be taken towards India by the new administration, which re-instituted an economic aid program and also emphasized the kind of personal diplomacy that had been totally missing in previous years. President Carter made a state visit to India in 1978 where he was warmly welcomed and spoke of India as being "a repository of shared values and a natural ally for an America that hoped to base its policy on moral values and see those policies extend to the rest of the world" (Chary, 1995, 151). In fact, the administration seemed to seek identification with India as a way of strengthening and even legitimizing Carter's approach to American foreign policy and the stage seemed to be set for a vast improvement in Indo-United States relations. This, however, did not happen. The combination of the passage of the Nuclear Non- Proliferation Act in the United States Congress (which India refused to sign), the Iranian hostage crisis and, finally, the Soviet invasion of Afghanistan that renewed Cold War concerns and led the United States to once more turn to Pakistan as a frontline state against the Soviets, resulted in renewed tensions between the United States and India. From the United States perspective, India's position on the Soviet invasion was ambivalent and appeared to reveal a pro-Soviet bias, while India was deeply threatened by the arming of Pakistan by the United States. Once again, Indo-United States relations entered a downward spiral that persisted through the initial period of the Reagan administration.

Through much of the Cold War period, Indo-United States relations were characterized by a "roller coaster" quality. "The high water-mark in this relationship was reached when the United States pledged arms aid to India after the Sino-Indian border conflict in 1962; and the nadir was reached in 1971 when a U.S.S. Enterprise-led task force entered the Bay of Bengal during the Indo-Pak conflict" (Chari, 1999, 3). Thus, while one might have expected that two nations who on the surface had much in common, including democratic political systems, a free press and a shared language among elites would have been natural allies in the post-1945 international order, this proved not to be the case. While there was never any open conflict between the two countries, their relationship certainly oscillated a great deal and there were frequent and often lengthy periods of hostility between them. Dividing the two countries were differences in policies and perspectives, particularly with regard to the Cold War and issues of national security.

From the American point of view, the Indian insistence on non-alignment was at best naïve and at worst immoral. The United States was also quite resentful of what it saw as India's willful opposition to American foreign policy and its tendency to point out numerous moral shortcomings in the policy as well its apparent ungratefulness for American aid (Kux, 1994; Kronstadt, 2003). However, the most significant issue for the United States in its relations with India during the Cold War was undoubtedly the latter's close alliance with the Soviet Union. While the Indo-Soviet relationship was driven by India's need to find a reliable ally against the perceived threat posed by a U.S.-armed Pakistan and China, it evolved due to India's adoption of a socialist economic strategy as well as the Soviet Union's willingness to supply India with both weapons and defense technology. The United States was deeply suspicious of the economic and military ties between the two countries. While India emphasized that its relationship with the Soviets although anchored in trust and mutual respect, did not imply a "tilt" or "bias" towards the Soviet Union, the United States deemed India's stance hypocritical given its commitment to non-alignment and felt that the Indo-Soviet relationship was detrimental to the stability of the region.

India had little appreciation of the dynamics of Cold War politics and felt that the resources devoted to the military buildup could be better used to fight poverty and engender a more equitable economic order, which would serve the interests of developing countries better than any military pacts or alliances. Moreover, India which espoused the idea of non-alignment, based on the realization that its internal development needs prevented heavy military expenditure and its hope that distance from both blocs would enable it to develop an independent political and moral voice in the emerging world order, was also resentful of what it saw as America's tendency to perceive everything through the prism of Cold War politics and to befriend nations based on their willingness or ability to aid the United States' strategic objectives, i.e. the containment of communism.

India, which viewed itself as a significant player on the world stage, felt deeply slighted by the United States' attempt to create a so-called balance of power in South Asia by supporting Pakistan militarily. Indian leaders believed that by treating India as a "country old in thought and experience" (Nehru, 1949), as a mere regional power on par with Pakistan, the United States failed to give the country its due as a potential great power. Moreover, it was deeply threatened by the nexus between the United States and Pakistan which had been anchored in defensive pacts such as SEATO and CENTO and felt that the United States was profoundly insensitive to India's national security concerns as evidenced by its relationships with India's rivals Pakistan and China as well its opposition to India's nuclear program.

Differences between India and the United States were also rooted, to a lesser extent, in their divergent approaches to economic development. While the United States espoused a capitalist system of private enterprise and promoted it as the solution to the economic woes of developing nations, India preferred the socialist model of development in which both private and public sectors co-existed and the state played a critical role in the management of the economy. Aware of the economic impact of colonization on India, nationalist Indian leaders were deeply suspicious of capitalism and many actively disliked capitalist societies and the disparities that characterized them (Saha, 1990). Instead, they held that growth in countries such as India could be best achieved only through socialist methods. Nehru, who as India's first prime minister helped establish the country's economic system, argued that India's mixed economy "represented a new approach to development that would avoid the errors of both communism and capitalism" (Chary, 1995, 4). As a consequence, India not only resisted American attempts to influence its pattern of economic development but also the latter's efforts to use its economic strength to leverage policy outcomes that it desired.

India and the United States were thus divided on a variety of fundamental political and economic issues and their relationship was characterized by indignation and mutual recrimination as each sought the high moral ground in their discussions. While the United States' images of India were those "of acute moralism, ungratefulness and misplaced pride" (Gahlaut, 1999), India saw the United States as an overbearing upstart that had no sense of history and prescribed policies without any regard for the needs or sensitivities of others. In fact, to many in India the United States appeared as an unabashedly materialistic and opportunistic nation that sought to use its economic might to extract concessions in return for assistance and considered everything, including the national pride of other countries, as essentially negotiable.

India and the United States after the Cold War: A Gradual Thaw

These longstanding, mutually negative perceptions were held during the first years of the Reagan administration in which the principal focus of United States' foreign policy was the containment and overthrow of communist regimes. In South Asia, this translated to the condemnation of India for its refusal to publicly criticize the Soviet invasion of Afghanistan in 1979 and the strengthening of its military relationship with India's archrival Pakistan, as part of its vigorous attempt to shore up international defenses against the Soviet Union.

However, the Reagan administration gradually retreated from its dogmatic position *vis-à-vis* the subcontinent: it not only developed a more realistic appreciation of the Indo-Soviet relationship, but also seemed to be more willing to recognize Indian primacy in South Asia. As a White House staff member said at a briefing prior to the Indian Prime Minister's visit in 1982, "we recognize which country is the most powerful in South Asia. No one has to explain that to you" (quoted in Limaye, 1993, 36). As the decade progressed, America increasingly implemented a two track policy in South Asia, whereby while aiding Pakistan militarily, it also accommodated India on a variety of economic and military issues, particularly after the Soviet withdrawal from Afghanistan and the adoption of increasingly liberalized economic policies by India. Consequently there was a substantial increase in Indo-United States cooperation in the areas of science, technology, education and culture.

This relationship continued to develop under the administration of George W.H. Bush, and with the election in 1992 of Bill Clinton who had expressed a personal interest in India and believed that relations could get better. It was "widely anticipated that the Clinton administration, which had pledged to support democratic regimes abroad, would build on the foundation established by its predecessor and further improve bilateral ties" (Rubinoff, 2001, 43). And initially this did seem to be the case, as the Clinton administration identified India as one of ten major growing markets and stated that it saw India emerging as a significant center which had a critical role to play in the balance of power in Asia.

Yet diverging approaches on the issues of nuclear proliferation and human rights persisted between India and the United States (Kronstadt, 2003). The Clinton administration criticized what it saw as human rights violations by India's government in suppressing separatist groups in Punjab and Kashmir and also sought to contain nuclear proliferation in the region based on the perception that "if a nuclear weapon was to be detonated in anger in the next five years or so ... the most likely place would be South Asia" (Gallucci, 1994).

Angered by the United States' stance, India refused to sign the Comprehensive Nuclear Test Ban Treaty (CTBT). While the Indian government's official position was that it had rejected the treaty since it was discriminatory in that it did not lay down a time-bound framework for the elimination of *all* nuclear weapons, its decision was critically driven by what it saw as the intertwined threat from Pakistan and China. By Clinton's second term as president, however, the India-United States relationship seemed to be less contentious. There were growing references to "cooperative engagement" and "strategic cooperation," as both nations renewed efforts to establish a better relationship. In May 1998, this mutual intent was, however, challenged when India conducted five underground nuclear tests at Pokharan. The United States responded by invoking the Nuclear Non-Proliferation Prevention Act of 1994 and imposed a series of wide-ranging economic and military sanctions against India—an action that prompted widespread anger and resentment in the country (Kronstadt, 2003).

Following several rounds of talks between India's Defense Minister Jaswant Singh and United States Deputy Secretary of State Strobe Talbott, some normalcy was restored to the bilateral relationship. By late 1998, Prime Minister Vajpayee talked of India and the United States being "natural allies" and in 1999 Indian feelings were further mollified by the fact that the United States exerted pressure on Pakistan to withdraw from Kargil and did not seek to appoint a special envoy to examine the Kashmir issue as Pakistan had desired (Kapur, 2000). In fact, in 2000, when President Clinton visited India, he was warmly welcomed and there was once again talk of the vast common interests between India and the United States (India News, 2000).

Chapter 11

India's Reaction to 9/11: From Estrangement to Hopes for Partnership

Kalyani Chadha, Anandam Kavoori and Katherine McAdams

When Indians hear about American failures they cheer; when we hear about American foul-ups, we giggle; and when we see the Americans lecturing the world about conflict between good and evil, we first sneer and then we seethe.

Vir Sanghvi, Editor of The Hindustan Times *(2003)*

After the election of President George W. Bush, the process of greater engagement between India and the United States gathered real momentum. During the presidential campaign in 2000, Bush not only disavowed the Comprehensive Test Ban Treaty, but said that he understood India's security needs and favored the removal of sanctions such as the ban on military sales and restrictions on the sale of so-called dual use technology items that had been put into place by the Clinton administration. Regarding the issue of Kashmir, which was a point of considerable contention with successive American administrations, he called for its resolution based on a negotiated settlement between India and Pakistan based on the Simla Accord. And when he finally took office, in his first State of the Union address he talked of erasing "old rivalries" with India to work for "peace and prosperity" (Saksena, 2002, 1). Such positive statements, although driven largely by strategic concerns and the administration's defense policy, which focused less on preventing the spread of nuclear weapons than on building defenses against rogue states, were widely welcomed by Indians. It appeared that there was finally an American president who was "bullish" on India and seemed to indicate a preference for this country rather than its traditional rival, Pakistan (Alden and Luce, 2001).

Then, in the wake of 9/11, India responded with immediate condemnation of the horrific events. As a content analysis of the major Indian newspapers (both English and regional language papers) indicated, the events were widely described as "terrible," "savage" and "vicious"—attacks against "democracy," "freedom," "humanity," and the "civilized world" that had been perpetrated by Islamic fundamentalists, notably those associated with Al Qaeda. Concurrently, the normally cautious Indian Government jumped in and offered its unequivocal help and support to the United States. In a widely publicized letter to President Bush, Indian Prime Minister Atal Behari Vajpayee wrote that the people of India and his government shared "the sense of outrage of the American people." He ended the letter by saying, "We stand ready to cooperate with you in the investigation of this crime and to strengthen our partnership in leading international affairs to ensure that terrorism never succeeds again" (Vajpayee, 2001). Similar sentiments were expressed by External Affairs Minister Jaswant Singh who said that India stood with the United States in the fight against terrorism and had offered operational help in mounting a strike against Al Qaeda. When asked by the press whether this meant that India would provide logistical help or a staging ground for a United States military operation, Singh replied with an emphatic "yes" (Rajghatta, 2001). This public offering of assistance to the United States clearly represented a significant foreign policy departure for non-aligned India which during the Gulf War in 1991 had only allowed American aircraft to refuel secretly in Mumbai, and when the facts became widely known, had ceased to do so (Joseph, 2003). Underlying this shift in the Indian position was the notion that tragic as the events of 9/11 were, they would unite India and America, both democratic nations, in the fight against global terrorism. As Prime Minister Vajpayee pointed out in a speech: "What the terrorists have done sends a strong message to democracies that we redouble our efforts to defeat this grave threat to our people, our values and our way of life" (Vajpayee, 2001). Echoing these views, Kanwal Sibal, India's Foreign Secretary addressing the Carnegie Endowment for International Peace stated: "International terrorism poses a grave challenge to both India and the United States ... the U.S. has no better partner than India in combating fundamentalist terrorism and the security challenges it poses. Our common experience and sufferings make us natural partners" (2001).

It was widely felt that having experienced the horrors of a terrorist attack on its soil, the United States would not only have a greater appreciation of the long struggle that India has waged against militant separatist groups, particularly in Kashmir, but that it would also be willing to use its influence to pressure Pakistan, which according to India, was the chief sponsor of terrorism on Indian soil. As Foreign Secretary Sibal described the situation: "India has been facing terrorism for many years, but it was considered our problem, a product of the unresolved India-Pakistan confrontation. Those behind it were not seen as a threat to the United States or the West and early signals that this insouciance might be misplaced were ignored. The dramatic events of September 11 drove home to the U.S. that those forces which did not want India to live did not want the U.S. to live either" (2001).

Having thus sought to make common cause with the United States, India was shocked and disappointed to find that the United States, although apparently appreciative of India's offer of help, had designated its *bete noire* Pakistan, as a frontline state in the war against terrorism. While the leaders of the BJP (Bharathya Janatha Party) government, notably the Defense Minister Jaswant Singh and National Security Adviser Brajesh Mishra tried to put on a brave face at the United States' action and argued that India's relationship with the United States was not hyphenated but independent of the latter's relationship with Pakistan ("India Says," 2001), popular opinion tended to see this decision as a slap in the face to India, which had gone all out to support the United States in its darkest hour, only to see the United States turning to its enemy.

While the choice of Pakistan could be justified as a tactical move motivated by its geographical and political links to Afghanistan, and would probably have eventually been accepted in India as a "necessary evil," it was America's non-committal response to India's efforts to highlight Pakistan's involvement in cross-border terrorism in Kashmir and its efforts to convince India to enter into dialogue with Pakistan, while itself prosecuting an aggressive war against terrorism, that became increasingly difficult to accept, especially for the educated middle class in India. The sense of resentment was further heightened after the attacks by militant groups on the legislature in Sringar, the capital of Jammu and Kashmir on October 1, 2001, and then the India parliament in New Delhi on December 13, 2001. The United States, while condemning the attacks, did not offer any public comment on the involvement of Pakistan in backing terrorist groups such as Jaish-e-Mohammad or the Lashkar-i-Toiba that were identified by India as responsible for these attacks (Rajghatta, 2001).

In separate statements, both United States Secretary of State Colin Powell and President Bush asked both "sides to come together in the campaign against terrorism," and said that the role of the United States as "a good friend of India, a good friend of Pakistan and a good friend of South Asia" was to help nations resolve their differences (Haider, 2001; Rao, 2002). The United States' position was expressed in Secretary Powell's interview to NBC News's Meet the Press in which he commented that "While the Indian government clearly has legitimate right to self-defense, we have to be very careful because if in this exercise of that right of self-defense we have states going after each other, we could create a very difficult situation which could spiral out of control" (Haider, 2001).

While some of the anger was directed internally against the BJP-led coalition government and its Defense Minister Jaswant Singh for failing to project India as a victim of cross-border terrorism sponsored by Pakistan and getting the United States' "war on terror" to focus on the issue of terrorism in Jammu and Kashmir ("Government Messed Up," 2001, 1), the major target was the United States whose behavior was seen as hypocritical and self-serving (Kagan and Reesa, 2001; Sanghvi, 2002). The predominant view, especially among the middle class and intelligentsia, was that while the United States talked of waging a "global war" against terror, in fact its principal concern was with its own military campaign against Osama bin Laden and Al Qaeda in Afghanistan, and that it was not only willing to ally itself with a state that harbored terrorists but that it did not recognize either the impact of terrorism on other countries or their need to act in their own defense (Aiyer, 2002, Ramachandran, 2002).

As one report in one of India's major English-language dailies *The Hindu* suggested: "The initial response to the September 11th attacks on America that at last terrorism had exposed its ugly face to the entire world, which would now be ready to listen to India's voice, has given way to despair and anger. It has become painfully obvious to even those in the saffron camp, who thought that the Vajpayee government had successfully weaned the U.S. away from its blind love for Pakistan, that India cannot depend on the U.S. or any other country to help fight its battle in Kashmir" (Vyas, 2001, 1). Similarly, another columnist writing in *The Hindustan Times*, one of the most widely circulated English dailies in India commented: "When the war against terror began in the immediate aftermath of the World Trade Center attacks, India cheered. We are also a democracy, the largest in the world in fact—and we have suffered because of terrorist violence ... Given that Washington and New Delhi have moved closer in recent years, we believed that this would be a war fought by the free world against all terrorists and dictators who sponsor them. We were wrong. Despite the rhetoric, the war is not about freedom and democracy. Rather than fight international terrorism, the U.S. seems to be concentrating on a single, limited objective ... We had hoped that the war against terror would treat all jihads on par but the U.S. has decided to ignore the one against India since it needs Pakistan as its strategic ally for its Afghanistan operation" (Sanghvi, 2001b). Yet another commented that America is interested only in its enemies and that "it has no time, energy or resources for the enemies of others … We Indians are really on our own" (Aiyar, 2002). Other reportage bemoaned the fact that "India was rapidly being relegated to the backwoods, in the selective struggle against terrorism being orchestrated by the United States" (Irani, 2001), that there was "no sign in the administration of any misgivings over Washington's support to a military regime in Pakistan committed to a militaristic agenda against India," "and that India could expect little from Washington aside from lip sympathy" (Rajghatta, 2001). Such news reports represented a clear shift from the sympathetic and supportive reaction that had been manifest in the immediate aftermath of 9/11, reflecting a change in the national mood that now appeared to have taken on an increasingly anti-American tone—a surprising development given the fact that historically, anti-Americanism was not particularly rooted or pervasive in the Indian context.

Despite the estrangement and policy differences that characterized the Indo-United States relationship for many years, the Indian people "have never particularly hated America" (Gupta, 2001, 1). A survey of the Indian electorate was conducted in 1999 by the New Delhi-based Center for the Study of Developing Societies (CSDS) in which respondents were asked whether they viewed the United States as an enemy or as a friend. Only 10 per cent saw it as an enemy, 27 per cent defined it as a friend, a little less than 30 per cent reported being neutral, and 36 per cent of those polled either had heard of the country or offered no opinion at all (Singh, Kumar and Yadav, 1999). As the well-known Indian editor and columnist Vir Sanghvi (2001a) explained: "For the first 40 years of our independence the Americans took the if-you-are-not-with-us-you-are-against-us line with New Delhi and refused to accept our claims to be non-aligned. But here's the funny thing: there's much less anti-Americanism in India than in all the countries that Washington helped, armed, financed and romanced … even when our Foreign Ministry cozied up to the Kremlin, educated Indians still looked to the West, and America in particular for our reference points. We valued the freedoms of the West … and recognized that as democracies India and America had much in common."

However, the general view of the United States was not necessarily positive. According to the CSDS survey in 1999, while Pakistan was viewed as an enemy by the vast majority of the respondents, and countries such as Russia and Nepal were rated quite positively, the United States fell somewhere in the middle, with a similar profile to China. Analyzing the CSDS survey data, McMillan wrote, "The contrast between the public perceptions of Russia, which is viewed almost universally as friendly, and the United States are striking. The fact that the U.S. had a similar profile to China, which has been at war with India, is a major arms supplier to Pakistan, and was described by the former Indian Defense Minister as 'threat number one' at the time of the 1998 nuclear tests indicates a high level of perceived hostility" (2002, 1).

The Roots of Indian Attitudes toward the United States

Although it has become commonplace to link instances of anti-Americanism to reasons such as a "clash of civilizations," or "envy of American values and institutions," or a generalized hostility to the United States military, cultural and economic hegemony, in the case of India, such an ideological opposition does not seem particularly apparent, except perhaps among the country's increasingly marginal left parties. According to a content analysis of the Indian press in the months following 9/11, a factor such as jealousy of the United States because it is "powerful, rich, modern or democratic," which was frequently cited by members of the Bush administration as a motivating cause for global anti-Americanism, does not figure in the public discourse about America, as reflected by the press. Instead, it would seem that it is America's response to India's concerns about cross-border terrorism occurring in Jammu and Kashmir and its continued relationship with Pakistan, whom India views as the chief sponsor of such actions, that lie at the heart of anti-American sentiment in India. This sentiment has been fueled further by American military operations in both Afghanistan and Iraq, which have been widely condemned in India. While the BJP-led Indian government has chosen to adopt a so-called "middle path," whereby it has opposed military action and called for UN involvement but avoided an explicit or public condemnation of the United States, reaction by both opposition parties and the general public has been much less restrained (Baruah, 2003).

In taking this rather cautious position, which represents a profound departure from India's response to the previous Gulf War when the government found itself on the losing side, the government has argued that alienation from the United States could lead to a compromise of national interests, especially if the latter took an anti-India position on the issue of Jammu and Kashmir at the United Nations (Mazumdar, 2003). But while the government has thus tried its utmost to avoid jeopardizing its bilateral relationship with the United States, opposition parties have taken a much stronger stand against the United States' actions in Afghanistan and Iraq, criticizing what one member of Parliament called the government's "unseemly haste" in unilaterally offering America the use of Indian facilities and airbases as well as its failure to "reactivate the non-aligned countries and the United Nations in dealing with the situation" ("Government criticized," 2001; "Centre should be," 2001).

This response has been very much in line with popular sentiment in India, which has been increasingly opposed to America's actions while pursuing the "war on terror." The content analysis cited above revealed that popular perceptions of the United States' war in Afghanistan were increasingly negative. In fact, almost 57 per cent of the articles related to the war in Afghanistan published in September, 2001, were critical of the United States, and by October the percentage had risen to 76 per cent, with the criticisms ranging from what was seen as the American callousness towards the destruction of Afghanistan and the loss of civilian lives, the ineffectiveness and indeed hypocrisy of the food drops and other humanitarian aid undertaken by it as well for its failure to better the lot of the Afghan people in any significant way. As one Indian columnist wrote: "Unequal adversaries have often fought wars but never has such a formidable superpower attacked a people so miserable and defenseless as the Afghans. No matter how many peanut butter and jelly sandwiches the U.S. drops along with less humanitarian aid like cluster bombs, this is a war in which civilians are going to be killed in large numbers. Already, more than 300 innocents have perished. No one is arguing that the U.S. has deliberately set out to kill civilians, like the monsters that attacked the World Trade Center did. But it is bombing Afghanistan with lethal ordnance in the knowledge that non-combatants will die even without missiles going astray" (Vardarajan, 2001).

If America's actions in Afghanistan were unpopular in India, the war in Iraq in 2003 was even more widely opposed. While the government continued to tread cautiously, the opposition parties unanimously condemned what they called the illegal and unjust war. They emphasized that the United States' actions in Iraq constituted a violation of international law and the national sovereignty of that country. Opposition leaders also criticized the BJP-led National Democratic Alliance government for failing to take a clear stand on the issue and in a statement issued after a joint meeting declared that the war "will create new tensions, which will threaten world peace. Already the stand of the United States has led to a wave of anger among the people in Arab countries. Use of brute military force will only strengthen the forces of terrorism. India's interests will seriously be harmed by such a war" ("Opposition forms," 2002). In a similar fashion, members of the Indian Parliament, including many belonging to the ruling BJP, also vociferously opposed the invasion of Iraq and demanded an immediate withdrawal of coalition forces from the country. "Expressing national sentiment, this House condemns the war in Iraq by the U.S.-led coalition. This is not acceptable," said a strongly-worded statement read out by Manohar Joshi, the speaker of the Lok Sabha or lower house.

National public opinion in India has been overwhelmingly against the war in Iraq. According to a poll conducted by the popular weekly newsmagazine *Outlook*, 86 per cent of Indians were opposed to the war and 69 per cent regarded President Bush as a "warmonger" (Lancaster, 2003a). A poll conducted by MidDay found that over 80 per cent of Indians were against the war. Despite the much-touted improvements in Indo-U.S. relations (Saksena, 2002) and the so-called Hindu nationalist wave that was supposedly sweeping through India and should have resulted in support for the United States against Muslim Iraq, there was little support for the American actions in Iraq within the great Indian middle class. As an editorial in the *Times of India* put it, "terrorism has nothing to do with Islam or any civilized code of conduct … indeed thanks to Washington's ill-judged vocabulary, terrorism has come to be seen as fundamentally associated with Islam, thus creating a grievous civilizational schism" ("War Without Frontiers," 2003).

A significant and sometimes impassioned opposition was extending across the spectrum of political opinions and manifesting in a series of antiwar rallies and demonstrations that took place across the country and involved tens of thousands of people. For instance, on March 2, 10,000 antiwar protesters marched in the Southern Indian city of Hyderabad carrying placards and banners reading "Drop Bush, not Bombs," and "No War." A week later at a rally that drew more than 20,000 people in Mumbai, in a dramatic gesture befitting his status as a former actor, MP Raj Babbar delighted the crowd by taking off his Nike shoes and burning them on the stage. On March 15, in New Delhi, thousands lined up in a human chain holding signs saying, "U-Ugly, S-Sadist, A-Aggressor," and "Bush learn to respect UN." Rallies and sit-in strikes were also held in cities such as Kolkata, Patna, Bhopal, Bangalore, Srinagar and Mysore ("Students rally," 2003; "Zee News TV," 2003; "Anti-war sentiment," 2003). The growing criticism of the United States was mounted on several levels. Many asserted that it was wrong of the United States to attack another sovereign nation and feared that it was intent on conquest. In numerous "man on the street" type interviews with journalists, ordinary Indians said that while they had felt compassion for America in the aftermath of 9/11, these feelings had all but vanished with the start of the war in Iraq (Murphy, 2003; McGivering, 2003; Lancaster, 2003a). As one respondent said, "Those feelings that were there after September 11 are gone. I think that they are gone for everyone now ... Who is to say that Mr. Bush will not like the leader here or somewhere else ... then he would just move in" (Murphy, 2003).

Others pointed out that the United States had attacked Iraq not because it posed an immediate nuclear threat to the world, but in pursuance of its own political ends (Kumar, 2003; Lancaster, 2003a). Representing this view on the editorial page of the *Times of India*, Siddharth Vardarajan wrote: "On the weapons issue, the dishonesty of the U.S. stand is self-evident. UN Security Council Resolution 687 mandates Iraqi disarmament and on April 13, 1998 the IAEA certified that Iraq had compiled a full, final and complete account of its previous nuclear projects and that there was no evidence of any prohibited activity ... The world has a right to demand that Iraq comply with its disarmament obligations but it must not legitimize U.S. contempt for international law ... The U.S. for its own domestic economic and political reasons wants to press-gang the world into war" (2002).

Others criticized the United States for operating with an incredibly simplistic and dangerous worldview (Sanghvi, 2003a). India's premier news magazine *India Today* pointed out a "startling simplicity in Bush's Manichaean world view that is both appealing and frightening. Like the third century A.D. Persian philosopher who preached dualism, Bush believes that there are Satanic forces represented by an "axis of evil" that are in a state of conflict with the good (i.e. the U.S.). As the aggressive U.S. leader battles for good over evil, pre-emptive strikes are in and old alliances are being recast" (Chengappa, Padmanabhan and Bhasi, 2003). Critics also expressed the fear that such actions could have potentially disastrous consequences across the world, including in India (Bidwai, 2003; Modi, 2003). In the words of K.P.S. Gill, a former director-general of police who played a key role in putting down separatism in the Indian state of Punjab: "The U.S. still remains substantially insulated from the consequences of instability and disorder in Asia ... If a particular situation remains 'messy,' or worsens further, withdrawal to the however imperfect 'fortress America' can still be contemplated. Those who are permanently located in this troubled neighborhood, however, do not have this option and would be required to deal with the chaotic impact of unfinished wars, collapsing states and a rootless, violent diaspora. These dangers are precisely what underlie India's disapproving line on Iraq ... that the destruction of an unsatisfactory but stable regime would plunge the entire region into disorder and would create wider spaces for the operation of the forces of extremism and terror" (2003).

People and pundits alike criticized what they perceived to be the double standards and inconsistencies in American policies, notably the fact that "Saddam Hussein was once favored and strengthened by the Americans" (Kumar, 2003). Others criticized the United States for quickly moving ahead with the war on terror while preaching restraint to India in its conflict with Pakistan, which is widely viewed in India as the primary sponsor of Islamic militant groups. Broadly speaking then, Indian public opinion has not accepted the American position on Iraq or more generally, on the war on terror. Consequently, as content analyses of the Indian press following 9/11 indicate, although there was considerable initial sympathy for America as well as a feeling that the attacks had been motivated by religious fanaticism, over time there was a growing sense that it was previous American actions and policies that had played a crucial role in causing the attacks. In other words, while the press was generally sympathetic with regard to the attacks and the resultant suffering of the American people, when it came to analyzing the causes underlying the attacks there was clearly a feeling that the Americans might have brought the attacks upon themselves.

While the reasons cited ranged from American arrogance in general, aspects of its foreign policy, particularly in relation to Israel and the Islamic World, its support of Osama bin Laden's operations in Afghanistan during the Cold War, there was clearly a rapid and significant transformation in the tenor of Indian public opinion. In fact, out of 207 articles that analyzed the root causes or conditions that led to the attacks of 9/11, almost 60 per cent attributed them to American actions or policies in some way, shape or form. Moreover, while there was an awareness that America needed to respond to the terrorist attacks on its soil, there was comparatively limited support for military action. And even this support, which was qualified by calls that it be limited to terrorist targets, declined over time. Instead, the majority of the 324 articles focusing on how America should react to the events of September 11 articulated alternative perspectives, ranging from those that opposed any type of military action (about 20 per cent) to those (approximately one third) that urged the United States variously to rethink its foreign policy, work with the United Nations and the international community to develop non military tactics to fight terrorism and finally to gather credible evidence regarding those believed to be responsible for the attacks of 9/11 and to avoid knee jerk actions motivated by anger and fear.

Out of a total of 79 articles analyzing American reasons for attacking Afghanistan, only about 6 (i.e. 8 per cent) accepted the American rationale that the military action in that country was motivated by the United States' efforts to fight global terrorism and an even smaller number (6 per cent) agreed with the view that America had mounted the so-called global war on terror in order to defend democracy and humanity. Finally, a substantial proportion of the articles also offered negative assessments of the war in Afghanistan, particularly in terms of the impact on the Afghan people. Thus even though India does not manifest the type of violent anti-Americanism that has been on display in many other parts of the globe, negative views of American actions following the events in Afghanistan and more recently, Iraq, have nevertheless become quite common. It was the pressure of public opinion polls which showed that 70 per cent people opposed sending Indian troops to Iraq, that played a critical role in the decision of the Indian government not to send an army division to aid in the stabilization effort, as requested by the Bush administration. While some in the government had "argued that for the deployment contending that a closer relationship with the United States would strengthen India's international position, particularly in relation to rival Pakistan," in the light of negative public opinion, the Indian cabinet voted not to send troops (Kifner, 2003).

What is particularly significant about the negative perceptions of the United States in India is that these views are not being articulated by the Indian masses in whose consciousness America barely registers, but by elites and members of the urban, middle class. While this response would appear to be in line with what Shlapentokh and Woods (2002) have found in countries such as Germany and Russia, in the case of India it is quite surprising since it is this very segment of society that has traditionally looked to America as an economic and cultural point of reference (Bhargava, 2003; Gupta, 2003, Sanghvi, 2003a). For example, the editor of *The Hindustan Times*, one of India's most circulated English dailies wrote: "Indians— and especially educated middle class Indians—like the United States. We see American movies, we eat American hamburgers (how significant that even McDonald's sent a letter to Hindustan Times distancing itself from the U.S.), we drink American colas, we like to go to the U.S. on holiday and we want to be able to afford to send our kids to American universities. The single greatest achievement of George W. Bush from an Indian perspective, is to have made us overcome our love of, and respect for, all things American and turned us into a nation that is solidly opposed to U.S. policy in the world" (Sanghvi, 2003b).

This mood would largely seem to be the result of disappointment at what is seen as "American double-think," notably its continued relationship with Pakistan and its decision to act against its own enemies while denying India the same right *vis-à-vis* Pakistan—a perception that was considerably strengthened by the United States Department of State's sharply worded response to the Indian government's attempt to assert the same right of preemptive war that the United States used to justify its invasion of Iraq (Lancaster, 2003b). Consequently, even though the Indian government has attempted to make the case that America's approach to South Asia is no longer hyphenated (that is, it does not see its relationship with India through the Pakistani prism and that some differences notwithstanding, the convergence of interests between the United States and India that emerged in the aftermath of September 11 remains intact), this view has found few takers at home. Instead, the pervasive feeling within the Indian middle class, as noted journalist Dilip Padgaonkar wrote, was that "no matter how much India and America strengthen their strategic partnership, it should accept the fact that the Bush administration in order to further its own interests, will not push General Musharraf beyond a point" (2003). In other words, the consensus was that while India might become a stop on the travel itinerary of American officials and there has been some acknowledgement of India's security concerns on the part of the United States, comparatively little has changed in fundamental terms. Commentators have pointed out that even though the Indian government has referred to India and the United States as "natural allies," the American government has been careful to reassure Pakistan that it remains "extraordinarily sensitive to its concerns" ("U.S. is," 2003). It is widely felt that if India is to protect its interests, it cannot rely on others and must chart its own course. Consequently, according to Sanghvi: "Indians have to come to terms with the truth. There is no global war against terror. We're on our own ... how credible can America's war against terror be when their principal ally is a man who sends terrorists across our borders? But that is only part of the story. Even if you take away our sense of hurt over Washington's willingness to pamper Pervez Musharraf and to let him keep his weapons of mass destruction, there is also bewilderment over what the U.S. thinks it achieved in its Afghan operation ... and we don't understand why Iraq is a target" (2003a).

Despite talk of a growing "strategic partnership" between the United States and India, manifested both in greater political, military and economic exchanges, the educated elites and middle class whose views essentially dominate public opinion in India, are quite disenchanted with the United States, primarily in response to its foreign policy actions. And it is such that alienation poses a fundamental problem for the United States. For if it is unable to garner support for its position from a group that has historically been favorably disposed to it, in a country that has clearly and unequivocally indicated an interest in developing a deeper, more constructive relationship with it, it is quite unlikely to convince those in countries where anti-Americanism is far more deeply entrenched. As a consequence, while it might command fear as the world's only superpower, at present it has few allies, and stands more isolated than at any time in its recent history.

Conclusion

Characterized until quite recently by wariness and a general lack of engagement, the relationship between the two estranged democracies of India and the United States has witnessed a sea change in recent years, with the emergence of a strategic dialogue between the two nations. The marked improvement of relations began in the latter months of the Clinton administration and accelerated after a November 2001 meeting between Indian Prime Minister Vajpayee and President Bush. This change was clearly reflected when, in the wake of the September 11 terrorist attacks on the United States, India took the immediate and unprecedented step of offering to the United States full cooperation and the use of India's bases for counter-terrorism operations. But even as the two countries have begun to explore the possibilities for a more normalized bi-lateral relationship over the last few years, the attitude towards the United States is far less positive than one might imagine given the strong support within India for the United States in the immediate aftermath of the events of September 11.

Although India has not manifested the anti-Americanism of the type that has become pervasive in many parts of the world, such as the Middle East, and the Indian masses remain relatively unaware of the United States (see CSDS survey, 1999), nevertheless there is disappointment with America's actions post-September 11, notably its continued relationship with Pakistan and its perceived failure to prevent the latter from aiding militant groups in Kashmir as well as its actions in Afghanistan and Iraq within the Indian establishment. This is especially true of segments of the educated middle class and the intelligentsia.

Thus even though the official tone towards the United States has generally remained moderate in the interests of maintaining the emergent relationship between the two nations, the Indian establishment has come to perceive the United States as operating with a set of double standards in the war against terrorism, one for itself and one for other nations such as India. Consequently, Indian suspicions regarding the United States appear to have been revived and this is clearly reflected in the attitudes towards the United States as reflected in the content analysis data.

* * *

Editorial Remarks

Since India gained independence from British colonial rule in 1947, two major themes influenced India's foreign policy as well as its people's attitudes to foreign countries including the United States. The first one was related to immediate security concerns in the presence of Pakistan and associated with serious territorial claims and related political problems between these two countries. For more than half a century the main conflict developed around Jammu and Kashmir, a province in India with a majority Muslim population. Violent resistance of the Islamic militant groups fueled by nationalists' rhetoric claiming the provinces' right to secede from India was met with a fierce resistance from New Delhi. For many years, India accused Pakistan of supporting the separatists and contributing to religious and ethnic clashes in Jammu and Kashmir and other places around the country. Therefore, supported by overwhelming domestic public opinion, India's democratically elected governments, regardless of their political composition, conducted foreign and military policies aimed at the reduction of the perceived threat from Pakistan. This has been a very sensitive issue, which was always taken into serious consideration by the United States because virtually any decision by the United States in this region was viewed in India as favoring Pakistan. For instance, not only direct arms sales to Islamabad were considered undermining India's national interests but also other actions including Washington's pressure on India to sign the Comprehensive Test Ban Treaty were viewed as weakening India's national security. There are more than a few examples from recent history, including several presented in this case, that prove how sensitive U.S.-India relations could be in the context of American policies toward Pakistan. In addition, according to the United States' law requiring sanctions against countries developing nuclear weapons, the United States placed economic and financial pressure on India, which put additional strains on the bilateral relations and worsened the image of the United States.

The second theme in India's foreign policy is closely associated with the country's independent status and the international role India has attempted to play for more than half a century. It was only natural for the country, free from colonial rule and eager to develop its own independent economic and social system during the Cold War, to distance itself from the world's superpowers, the Soviet Union and the United States. Moreover, in the eyes of many Indians, the United States remained a colonial power attempting to gain dominance around the world by new predatory economic and political means. Struggling for economic success while facing numerous social problems, including poverty and overpopulation, most Indian people perceived America as a rich and arrogant power disinterested in helping other nations in their struggle for survival and dignity. Such negative attitudes in the past were eagerly shared and encouraged by the leaders of the Soviet Union. The anti-American card has also been "played" by contemporary Russian policy makers, who constantly try to distance India from the United States in their own attempts to build up a strategic partnership in Asia.

Although these two major themes—the security concerns and the pursuit of an independent foreign policy—continue to shape India's foreign policy in the twenty-first century, new realities have come to play an increasingly important role in the relations between India and the United States. Despite the majorities of Indian people being in disagreement with American policies in Iraq in 2003–2004, there have been signs of change suggesting an improvement in bilateral relations between India and the United States and a potential for a change in the overall perception of America. The war on terror brought cooperation—in intelligence exchange and law enforcement in combating terrorism—to a new level. After 2002, United States defense sales to India have soared to hundreds of millions of dollars. By 2003, India became the second (after Mexico) greatest source of legal immigration to the United States, the single largest source of foreign students in America (more than 66,000), and the second (after Germany) as the country of choice for American senior scholars applying for government (Fulbright) grants to do research abroad.

Although, at this stage of history, strengthening of United States bonds with Pakistan as a key ally in the war against terrorism would definitely be viewed negatively in India, there is hope that both countries' shared democratic values, similar security concerns, and expanding economic, educational, and interpersonal ties will create a new foundation for stable and friendly relations between America and India.

Suggested Additional Literature

Limaye, S.P. (1993). *U.S.-Indian relations.* Boulder, CO: Westview Press.
Saha, S. (1990). *Indo-U.S. Relations 1947–1989. A Guide to Information Sources.* New York: Peter Lang.
Tahir-Kheli, S. (1997). *India, Pakistan and the United States.* New York: Council on Foreign Relations Press.

CASE 7
LITHUANIA

Public opinion polls consistently show Lithuania as one of the most pro-American countries in the world. In a poll conducted in September 1997 by Vilmorus, almost 78 per cent of respondents had indicated that they "have a lot of trust in" or "somewhat trust" the United States, and only 17 per cent had "little trust" or "no trust at all" in the United States. The September 11th, 2001 attacks only strengthened the pro-American views of the majority of Lithuanians. In a survey conducted by Gallup International on September 15–17, about 50 per cent of Lithuanians said that American foreign policies have a positive impact on Lithuania. This was the second highest result, lower only to that of Israel at 61 per cent. The world average was 32 per cent (Anonymous, 2001a).

Chapter 12

Lithuanian Media Coverage of the September 11th Events, and their Aftermath

Arunas Juska and Vladas Gaidys

The terrorism of Islamic countries began a war against the democratic and civilized world of which we are a part.

The Editorial Board of Lietuvos Rytas, *September 12, 2001*

The Americans and Taliban are both responsible for what happened. The United States should have dealt with the terrorists using the intelligence services. The bombing in Afghanistan will only increase the hatred of the United States among Muslims.

Viktoras Diavara, Musician, October 11, 2001

A Historical Context

Highly positive Lithuanian views of the Americans can in part be explained by the fact that since the early 1900s the United States has carried out a pro-Lithuanian foreign policy. American support was crucial for the creation and survival of the modern Lithuanian statehood, because both neighbors of Lithuania, Germany and Russia, had threatened and repeatedly occupied the country. Up to this day the geopolitical security of Lithuania, especially its integration into NATO, remains highly dependent on American policies in the region.

The United States' pro-Lithuanian stance can at least partially be attributed to Washington's moral and ideological commitments, such as those promoted by Woodrow Wilson's principles of self-determination of nations, which legitimized the creation of the independent Lithuanian state following World War I (Rauch, 1974). Since 1940, when the Soviet Union annexed the Baltic States, the United States followed the Stimson doctrine of non-recognition, denying the legitimacy of the Soviet Union's territorial acquisition through conquest (Kirby, 1978; Vitas, 1990). During the Cold War none of the Western countries was as forthright and consistent in its support of the Baltic peoples as the United States (Hiden and Salmon, 1994).

Besides moral considerations, favorable United States' policies toward Lithuania were also influenced by domestic as well as geopolitical considerations. During the Cold War, the Baltic people's case allowed the United States to challenge the legitimacy of the Soviet rule throughout Eastern Europe. For example, the successive American administrations supported diplomatic representation of the

163

independent Lithuania, Latvia and Estonia in the United States, creating a source of continuous embarrassment to the Soviet diplomatic services abroad. At the same time, such symbolic expressions of a pro-Lithuanian stance could not be possible without effective lobbying carried out by well-organized Baltic émigré communities in the United States (Penikis, 1991; Vitas, 1990). The American-Lithuanian diaspora was especially influential in shaping pro-American views in Lithuania. The 2000 United States Census lists 660 thousand persons of Lithuanian ancestry. It is estimated that more than 200 thousand individuals left Lithuania during the 1990s, a significant proportion settling in the United States. This is a relatively large group, considering the fact that Lithuania has a population of only 3.5 million. For a country emerging from more than a half century of international isolation, American-Lithuanians were one of the most important links to the Western world. Using their economic resources, education and status, the Lithuanian-American community has played a significant role in the politics of the homeland. Its influence was and continues to be manifold, especially in politics and culture, and, to a lesser degree, in the economy. For example, émigrés from the United States created and financed Vytautas Magnus University in Kaunas, the first private independent university in Lithuania. American-Lithuanians are occupying high posts in the Lithuanian government, military and various other state institutions. The current president of Lithuania, Vladas Adamkus, for most of his life lived in the United States, and served as a high-ranking administrator in the United States Environment Protection Agency, and in President Reagan's administration. Kazys Bobelis, the other influential American-Lithuanian, is a Chair of the Christian Democratic Party, and a member of Seimas (Parliament). In 1997–1999 the retired United States army battalion commander Jonas Kronkaitis served as a Vice Minister of National Defense of Lithuania.

Attitudes and Their Roots Prior to September 11th

Besides the socio-historical context of U.S.-Lithuanian relationships, socio-psychological factors have contributed and continue to play an important role in positively shaping views of America. Lithuanians perceive the United States not only as a rich country with plentiful opportunities for material prosperity and success, but also as a country that commands high respect because it creates wealth in a lawful way, without relying on cheating, stealing, or corrupt state officials and bureaucrats. The American dream of "making it" has a strong appeal to the majority of Lithuanians, especially for younger and better-educated individuals. Many hope of emigrating and finding work in America (Alksninis, 2002).

Despite the overall strong pro-American stance, there is a growing sense of ambivalence about the United States. Pursuing different goals, the various groups often have conflicting evaluations of the Americans. What is good for the individual (for instance, finding a job in the United States) might not be good for Lithuania as a country (perceived by many as the "brain drain"). Most importantly, the relationship that is evolving between the United States and Lithuania in the early 2000s is highly asymmetrical. Lithuania is dependent on American policies, but has little ability to influence them. It is believed that this asymmetry is so pronounced that the United

States does not even need to formulate specific policies toward Lithuania in order to influence its domestic developments.

Lithuanian public opinion was slow to react to the fact that differentiation among the subjects of cross-border interaction (among individuals and their families, non-government organizations, universities, cities, businesses and corporations, and governmental agencies) was often occurring on the basis of competing or conflicting interests, in which the American side had significant power and resource advantages. Gradually this led to a rather painful realization of the discrepancy between the Cold War rhetoric of morality and idealism, in the name of which the West fought the Soviets (extending freedom, prosperity, democracy, etc.), and the actual policies of the Americans and other Western countries. Governments and private businesses were seen as pursuing their own interests "at the expense" of the newly independent nations. Predictably, this produced a populist reaction. Overtly positive views of America became increasingly intermixed with a growing resentment.

Characteristic in this respect was a debacle with the privatization of Mazeikiai Nafta, a government-owned Lithuanian oil complex, which involved the U.S.-based Williams International Company. In 1998, an attempt was made to sell its majority shares to Williams, as opposed to Russian oil exporters such as Lukoil. The goal of privatization was economic and geopolitical. Besides modernizing its energy sector, the deal with Williams was aimed at strengthening Lithuania's ties with the West, and facilitating the country's entry into NATO and the EU. However, by 1999 Williams, despite its initial agreement with the Lithuanian government, refused to buy Mazeikiai Nafta unless the Lithuanian government agreed to pay the debts accumulated by the refinery. Such demands amounted to a pressure by Williams on the Lithuanian government to heavily subsidize the purchase of the refinery. The conservative politicians, including the president, forced the government to sell the refinery to the American firm at an enormous expense to Lithuanian taxpayers, calculated to be about $334 million (Clements, 2001). As a result, American control over Lithuania's energy sector was chosen over Russia's even at the price of doubling Lithuania's foreign debt.

The privatization of Mazeikiai Nafta produced a populist backlash against conservative politicians as well as against Williams International (and by extension, the United States). The purchase was widely perceived as unfair because of political pressure that this large American corporation had put on the government. Views of the United States soured as criticisms hardened. Many Lithuanians believe that if given the opportunity the United States will use its political power and influence for monetary gain at the expense of weaker and poorer nations. A public opinion survey conducted by Vilmorus in the immediate aftermath of the Mazeikiai Nafta privatization had shown that the number of those holding pro-American views declined dramatically. Only 33 per cent of respondents indicated that they trusted the United States, while 54 per cent said that they did not trust America.

Newspapers in Lithuania

The liberal mass media are dominant in Lithuania, while pro-communist media are virtually non-existent, and religious and nationalist newspapers are marginal and do not have a noticeable influence on society. The newspapers *Lietuvos Rytas* and *Respublika* that were chosen for this study can be characterized as liberal. They are also the two largest daily newspapers in the country with a circulation of 76 thousand and 45 thousand copies, respectively.

There are some differences in the styles of the newspapers. *Lietuvos Rytas* attempts to project itself as a solid and objective, while supporting the Liberal Party as well as the state's key aims (for example, the accession of Lithuania into the EU and NATO). This newspaper is close to the Liberal party. In contrast, *Respublika* openly cultivates the style of "the public taste." It publishes more sensational news, photos, and criminal stories. In general, *Respublika* puts an emphasis on the critique of power, irrespective of which party controls the government. *Respublika* more frequently expresses critical views toward Western societies and their culture, including the critique of the United States. However, criticism of the West in *Respublika* does not have an anti-Western character. Instead it is populist (speaking in the name of ordinary people against the powerful and influential) and mildly nationalistic (for instance, it sometimes criticizes policies of integration with the EU as disregarding Lithuania's interests).

The differences between *Lietuvos Rytas* and *Respublika* were also reflected in their news coverage of the September 11th events and their aftermath. *Lietuvos Rytas* proved to be more pro-American in its coverage than *Respublika*. Almost 80 per cent of the articles that appeared in *Lietuvos Rytas* in September through December 2001 were completely favorable toward the United States. The views in *Lietuvos Rytas* were closer to the official Lithuanian establishment than the stance taken by *Respublika*. *Respublika* did not shy from more controversial opinions and comments. Only 27 per cent of its articles could be characterized as completely pro-American, while a majority of opinions (64 per cent) were mixed, too difficult to judge, or neutral.

Major Interpretations of the Events of September 11th

Three periods of press coverage were studied. *Period I* (September 11th–17th, 2001) includes coverage of the terrorist attacks on New York and Washington D.C. and their immediate aftermath. *Period II* (October 8th–11th, 2001) consists of reporting on the initial stage of the U.S. military campaign in Afghanistan. *Period III* (December 9th–21st, 2002) represents coverage of the fall of the Taliban regime and the assertion of American military control over Afghanistan.

The Lithuanian press offered four types of explanations of the terrorist attacks on September 11th and America's subsequent responses, which are labeled here as psychological, institutional, geopolitical, and cultural. Each type of explanation provided a different description of the cause of the terrorist acts, as well as outlined a strategy and measures to be used to stop further attacks. Depending on the period of analysis and type of events covered, some explanations of the terrorism tend to prevail over others.

The first type of explanation is constituted by psychological accounts of the terrorist attacks. In these interpretations, the psychological makeup of terrorists such as Osama bin Laden and his co-conspirators is considered the most important reason that led to the attacks on New York and Washington D.C. It is claimed that such personal features as evil or insanity—or as a few commentators put it, a "genius of evil"—led Osama bin Laden and his henchmen to carry out the massacre of civilians (Anonymous, 2001b; 2001c). Similarly, *Respublika* characterized the terrorists as "fanatics who are motivated by only one goal, feeling and obligation in the name of which they scarify their lives" (Mickeviciute, 2001). Psychological interpretations of the September 11ᵗʰ events tend to demonize the terrorists and personalize the war against terrorism. From this perspective, military retaliation by the U.S. acquires "an eye for an eye" character, which has the ultimate goal of finding and punishing the culprits so as to serve justice.

The second type of explanation maintains that the attacks were caused by the failure of institutions to protect civilians from violence and terror. In this interpretation the blame is attributed to a combination of two factors. First, it is argued that September 11ᵗʰ represents a dismal failure or a breakdown in the work of the Federal Bureau of Investigation, Central Intelligence Agency, and the American government in general. Second, it is also emphasized that such large-scale killing and destruction was facilitated by characteristics of the societal infrastructure in the United States. More specifically, the tightly coupled and very large in scale infrastructure of the most developed country in the world enabled criminals to magnify impacts of their attacks manifold, as it happened when very large civil planes were converted into bombs. Thus, as *Lietuvos Rytas* observed, "The U.S. paid dearly so that the rest of the world could see that civil airplanes could be much more dangerous than bombs" (Vainauskiene, 2001; see also Anonymous, 2001d). If institutional failures are to blame for the terrorist attacks, then a solution to the problem of terrorism can be found in institutional reforms of the agencies responsible for the safety and security of the nation.

The third type of explanation is geopolitical and tends to see the terrorist attacks as caused by foreign polices pursued by the United States in the Middle East and the South Asian region. The terrorist attacks in New York represent a boomerang effect or blowback that the United States created by its own actions abroad. Therefore, to solve terrorism, the American foreign policy must be modified. As a columnist for *Lietuvos Rytas*, Ceslovas Ieskauskas, asserted, "Americans as of yet are not concerned about the causes that led to the terrorist attacks against their country. American domination was often based on selfish interests, and unbalanced foreign policy. The United States should not only find and punish the perpetrators of the terrorist acts," but also reform its foreign polices from being based on the principle of "the stick and carrot" to principles of justice and equal rights of other nations" (Ieskauskas, 2001). Similarly, in its editorial, *Respublika* claimed, "In its struggle with the former U.S.S.R., the United States brought up the army of the militant Islamists that now is turning against it" (Anonymous, 2001e).

The fourth and final type of September 11ᵗʰ explanation is a cultural one. From this perspective, the September terrorist attacks represent a clash of Western and Islamic civilizations and incompatible worldviews. "The terrorism of Islamic countries had started the war against the democratic and civilized world of which we are a part. Boundless hate of the Western world is a fertile and inexhaustible source of terrorism. We are confronted with a very different and hard to understand consciousness" (Anonymous, 2001f). Markas Zingeris, one of the leaders of the

Lithuanian-Jewish community and a former high ranking member of the conservative party, expressed similar views: "The wave of death bearing blows on U.S. cities came from the Muslim East. In burning centers of civilization is revealed the central collision of our age ... between a closed, totalitarian, and tribal mindset and ... an open liberal society" (Zingeris, 2001).

Adherents of the cultural interpretation argue that the September 11th events are an expression of the decline and failure of the Islamic civilization to modernize. For example, a well-known *Lietuvos Rytas* columnist Rimvydas Valatka argued that after the oil boom brought billions of dollars to Islamic societies, characterized by medieval order, it opened new possibilities for what he called the "geniuses of darkness and hate." According to him, the goal of Islamic terrorists is nothing less than to retake dominance in the world from the United States, which was also the goal of Hitler and Stalin. At the same time, the openness of the Western world, mass migration, and the rapid spread of new technologies created possibilities to attack the United States and Western Europe from within (Valatka, 2001). For "culturalists," the solution to terrorism lies in enacting broad polices of reform leading to rapid modernization and secularization in Islamic countries, thus bringing them into the "civilized world."

America as a Victim: Coverage of the September 11th Attacks (September 12th–17th)

In the week following the September 11th attacks, *Lietuvos Rytas* and *Respublika* published 76 articles devoted to these events. In addition, both newspapers provided to their readers extensive compilations of information selected from the foreign mass media and information agencies. Unquestionably, the September 11th attacks proved to be the most significant event of the year, attracting the considerable attention of the Lithuanian public. Thus, in the public opinion poll conducted in December 2001 by the Lithuanian and British polling firm *Baltijos Tyrimai*, 83 per cent of respondents identified the September 11th attacks in New York as the most important event of the year in the world. Second in importance was United States' war in Afghanistan (54 per cent) (Anonymous, 2001g).

The initial news from the United States caused an emotional shock in Lithuania mixed with an outpouring of compassion for the victims and a rising sense of anxiety and insecurity. These emotions were expressed on two levels: the individual, socio-psychological level, and the societal, national level. Both major newspapers provided accounts of the rising fear and distress among some individuals caused by the graphically depicted large-scale destruction in New York as well as advised on ways to deal with it. If the most powerful nation in the world proved to be completely unprepared and extremely vulnerable to terrorist attacks resulting in killings of thousands of civilians, what about the safety and security of a relatively poor Lithuania? Are we in danger? Are their terrorists lurking on every corner ready to blow up unsuspecting individuals? (Anonymous, 2001h; 2001i). In addition, the security and safety of the country's infrastructure was also scrutinized. Of special concern was the security of the nuclear power station as well as the safety of the other infrastructure, such as airports and railroads. Increasing attention was also paid to the very few Muslims who resided in Lithuania. Rising perceptions of Lithuania's vulnerability to international terrorism led to the strengthening of support in both newspapers for joining NATO and the European Union as a means of increasing the safety and security of the country (Anonymous, 2001i; 2001j; Ingnatavicius, 2001).

Among those who expressed their views were 57 per cent of journalists, 20 per cent politicians, 11 per cent intellectuals and experts, and 3 per cent clergy. In comparison with the reports on the Afghan war (periods II and III), the coverage of September 11ᵗʰ events proved to be more heterogeneous because it was constituted by opinions of representatives of more diverse social groups.

The predominant majority of views expressed in the coverage of the attacks were strongly pro-American: 50 per cent were completely favorable and 9 per cent mostly favorable toward America. Terrorism was unanimously condemned. Such pro-American sentiments can be in part explained by the surge of empathy for the horrible sufferings of thousands of innocent civilians. Newspapers recorded people spontaneously raising Lithuanian and U.S. flags with black ribbons, bringing flowers to the U.S. embassy and other places where Americans worked, and praying and holding masses in churches throughout Lithuania (Anonymous, 2001k; Cergeliene, 2001; Sakalauskaite, 2001). There were also personal and historical ties between two nations that elicited an emotional outpouring of support for the United States. An editorial in *Lietuvos Rytas* commented, "The U.S. is a second homeland for many Lithuanians. America supported our independence during the years of Soviet occupation" (Anonymous, 2001l).

At the same time, the analysis revealed a plurality of opinions regarding the causes of the terrorist attacks and ways to deal with this new threat. No one of the four explanation types we discerned dominated analysis of the September 11ᵗʰ attacks on New York. Psychological, institutional, and cultural explanations were each used 20 per cent of the time to account for the tragedy. Such heterogeneity of views can be explained by a combination of a few factors. The attacks were completely unexpected and initially information about the events was very limited, therefore all explanations seemed to be equally plausible. Furthermore, opinions were solicited and expressed by a wide variety of respondents. As all the attention centered on the spectacular events in the United States, only 7 per cent of respondents paid attention to the geopolitical context and the foreign affairs that might have contributed to the attacks.

America Retaliates: The Attack on Afghanistan (October 8ᵗʰ–11ᵗʰ, 2001)

Coverage in the press of the American response began to change after October 7ᵗʰ, 2001 when the United States began a military campaign against Afghanistan. The number of articles devoted to this event, compared with the September 11ᵗʰ aftermath, declined almost fivefold from 70 to 15. Unlike the spectacular attacks on skyscrapers in a city with a sizeable Lithuanian immigrant community, the war in Afghanistan lacked the element of drama that the readers could identify with personally. Afghanistan is a foreign country not only far removed from Lithuania geographically, but also culturally. Finally, unlike in New York, there were no correspondents from Lithuania to file reports from the war region. The decline in the number of articles proceeded simultaneously with fewer respondents outside the journalistic profession publicly analyzing and commenting on the new war. Journalists wrote 70 per cent of the articles published during this period of time.

Besides the decline in scope and heterogeneity of coverage, the focus of analysis in the Lithuanian press also began to change. No article during this period mentioned or discussed the institutional failures and mistakes made by the CIA or FBI in precluding the attacks in New York or Washington D.C. Instead geopolitical analysis became predominant. There was an increase from 20 per cent to 33 per cent of the total coverage, while use of cultural and psychological explanations declined from 20 per cent to 13 per cent each.

What factors may account for such changes? First, the furious investigation by the Americans produced evidence that connected the September 11th attacks to Middle Eastern terrorist groups. This new information led commentators to focus on the geopolitical situation in this region, and particularly on the role America played in it. Major stories included America's pro-Israel stance in the conflict in Palestine, the direct intervention in Iraq and Kuwait during the Gulf war in 1991, the stationing of the American troops in the region, and support of the authoritarian domestic regimes in the region. As a result, the September 11th attacks were increasingly seen as a continuation of terrorist activities committed by various Middle Eastern groups during the previous decade, such as bombings in 1998 of the United States' embassies in Africa and the World Trade Center in New York, and the attack on the *USS Cole* destroyer in Yemen in 2000. In other words, the new information about the perpetrators of September 11th acts diminished the validity of the psychological and cultural explanations, as the attacks increasingly looked like a spillover from the regional conflict in which the United States was directly involved (Anonymous, 2001m).

In addition, geopolitical explanations became prevalent because all Muslim countries, with an exception of the Taliban government in Afghanistan, distanced themselves from the terrorists. The Bush administration also was at pains to project its military campaign not as a conflict with Islam, but as a war against criminal terrorists and their supporters. Finally, since the most important goal of the United States actions was to depose the ruling Taliban regime in Afghanistan, the psychological interpretations of the conflict also seemed less relevant as the coverage focused on analysis of the military campaign.

Besides a change in the interpretations of the conflict, the pro-American stance of authors that dominated the coverage of the September 11th events began to show ambivalence and the first signs of mild dissent. On one hand, the predominant majority of commentators saw the United States bombing of Afghanistan as bringing justice and revenge for the killing of thousands of innocent civilians. It was a legitimate and justifiable attack by the Americans on a medieval regime harboring brutal and inhumane murderers. On the other hand, the majority of respondents, 62 per cent, also had mixed feelings and some reservations about the actions taken by the Bush administration. This mood of uncertainty and ambivalence was succinctly expressed by one of the most popular Lithuanian poets Justinas Marcinkevicius who wrote, "Where are the roots of terrorism? In Afghanistan? In the dark corners of the human soul? Or in an empty stomach? It seems that the Americans and their allies are not sure about this. Therefore they throw from airplanes first bombs, then food rations, and then proclamations. What should the local people think about all these 'gifts from the sky'? Probably, not much" (Marcinkevicius, 2001).

Uneasiness and reservations were especially noticeable on the pages of *Respublika*. They were caused, in part, by the still-vivid memories of the failed Soviet invasion in Afghanistan, which ended in a senseless killing of more than a million Afghan civilians and thousands of Soviet soldiers (including draftees from Lithuania), and plunged the country into an endless and brutal civil war. Doubts were also expressed in questioning broader American geopolitical objectives and the possible long-term impact of the attack on the region. Were Americans bombing Afghanistan to revenge the killings and restore justice, or were their motives more sinister, such as the goal of extending their military domination over South Central Asia? Were not Americans implicated in creating the mess in Afghanistan and destabilizing the region during the Cold War? Are Americans pursuing morally justified goals while at the same time engaging in compromising deals with corrupt and repressive regimes such as those in Pakistan and Uzbekistan? Alas, complained *Respublika* columnist Violeta Mickeviciute, Americans were not forthcoming with the answers to these questions. On the contrary, she argued, the United States government and military converted the coverage of the war in Afghanistan into a propaganda war. It imposed "restrictions on the freedom of the press that are exceeding the censorship of the previous wars" (Mickeviciute, 2001a). In her opinion, by engaging in such policies, the United States was undermining the values of the civilized world in the name of which Americans were fighting in Afghanistan (Mickeviciute, 2001b).

America as Victor (December 10ᵗʰ–12ᵗʰ, 2001)

In comparison with the first and second periods, the coverage of the Taliban collapse on December 9ᵗʰ, 2001 in both newspapers was least extensive. Only 12 original articles were published on the American victory and possible consequences that the end of hostilities could have for the region and the world. In part this can be explained by the remoteness of the region and the little direct impact that these events could have on Lithuania. The articles were written by journalists (75 per cent or the total) and experts on foreign affairs (25 per cent).

There was a noticeable increase in pro-American sentiments expressed by respondents. Seventy-five per cent of the articles written in the aftermath of the American troops' entry into Kabul were completely favorable toward the United States. Such a change of hearts occurred, in part, because of the unexpectedly rapid collapse of the Taliban regime. The fear that America would become bogged down in a guerilla war and thus destabilize the whole South Asian region was put aside. In addition, the White House managed to avoid large-scale civilian casualties that could have generated criticism. The change in tone confirms the truism that winners are rarely criticized or judged.

At the same time, there was a significant rise—from 13 per cent to 33 per cent—in the psychological interpretations of international terrorism. Two factors might have contributed to the increasing "psychologization" of this phenomenon. First, after the defeat of the Taliban, the United States began to focus on hunting down Al Qaeda and the remaining members of the Al Qaeda organization. Without an Afghan ruling regime able to protect the terrorists, the American military campaign was perceived as a police-type operation. Correspondingly, coverage of the developments in Kabul and its provinces took the character of reporting on a police operation that was closing in on the criminal fugitives. Thus, the notion of "Islamic terrorists," prevailed in the October 11th–15th, 2001 coverage, was increasingly replaced by simply "terrorists." Second, after the collapse of the Taliban, Osama bin Laden and his associates, running for their lives, became totally isolated and seemed increasingly powerless and irrelevant.

The other equally important part of coverage during this period was devoted to discussions on the geopolitical fallout resulting from the Taliban's collapse (33 per cent). The majority of commentators were preoccupied with speculation on whether the United States' victory and its rapprochement with Russia could dramatically increase the role of Russia in the Eastern Europe region and deter Lithuania's entry into NATO. Other possible influences on the South Asian region, including conflicts between Israelis and Palestinians and between India and Pakistan, were also extensively discussed (Radzivilovicius, 2001; Sabas, 2001; Smaizyte, 2001).

Conclusion

Lithuanian public opinion toward the United States in general, and views of the September 11th events in particular, can be characterized as mostly pro-American. The attitudes, however, contain some signs of tension and ambivalence. As the September 11th events changed countries' geopolitical and domestic contexts, views of America in Lithuania fluctuated between an overwhelming pro-American sentiment to a rather uneasy and critical stance. The almost instantaneous reporting of the events on television, radio, and the Internet facilitated the rapid shifts in public opinion.

The pro-American tone of Lithuanian public opinion expressed through polls and via mass media was rooted in the significant American contributions to the creation and preservation of the Lithuanian statehood, and the impact of the large and influential Lithuanian-American community, which is currently growing because of the latest wave of economic migration and settlement in the United States. The geopolitical context, especially Russia's constant attempts to regain influence in the countries of the former Soviet periphery, is also forcing the Lithuanians to look for support and protection from the United States. Finally, many Lithuanians, especially the younger and better-educated individuals, regard the United States as an open, prosperous, and welcoming immigrant society.

At the same time, there are clear signs of growing ambivalence, which can potentially evolve into various forms of anti-American resentment. Growing ambivalence is caused by a mixture of perceptions as well as by the intended and unintended consequences of American policies in other countries. In part it is a consequence of the overwhelming economic, political, and cultural power and dominance of the United States in the world. In such a world, the predominant majority of small countries such as Lithuania are dependent on American actions without having any meaningful influence in shaping them. Such a situation is ripe for generating anti-American populism, when fairly or unfairly, the United States' actions are perceived as bullying and meddling in other people's affairs. Anti-Americanism is also fostered by tensions and conflicts between idealism and pragmatism in the United States' foreign policies. For the majority of the population in Lithuania, the privatization of the national oil refinery by the American corporation Williams International highlighted these discrepancies. The declared principles of morality on which the United States' foreign policy is based were brushed aside for selfish acquisitions at the expense of the weak and poor.

The coverage of the September 11ᵗʰ events in Lithuanian newspapers was overwhelmingly pro-American. However, the sympathy for the victims was mixed with the rising fear and apprehension about personal and national security. By October 9ᵗʰ, 2001, when the United States launched an attack on Afghanistan, the conflict was defined as geopolitical in nature, that is, as a fight against Muslim terrorists and the theocratic regime that supported them. The strongly pro-American views predominant during the first stage of the conflict became more ambivalent and even critical when American bombs began exploding in Afghanistan. Finally, by December 9ᵗʰ, when the Northern Alliance supported by the United States troops overthrew the Taliban, the struggle with Islamic terrorism was redefined again, this time into a type of police operation being carried out against criminal killers. The American victory changed the tone of the war coverage from criticism and ambivalence into support of the victorious United States and its actions.

Public opinion in Lithuania in the near future will remain, most likely, pro-American, although from time to time there might be increases in anti-American sentiment. Swings from pro- to anti-American positions will be highly dependent on changes in the geopolitical context as well as on domestic developments. A rise in anti-American sentiment will, in all likelihood, not be prolonged. Past experiences show, for instance, that the fallout from the scandalous privatization of Mazeikiai Nafta by Williams International only temporarily raised anti-American sentiments in the country.

In September 2002, the Lithuanian Seimas by an overwhelming majority of votes decided to deploy a special military detachment in Afghanistan (Baciulis and Samuolyte, 2002). In November 2002, Lithuania was officially invited to join NATO, which it joined in 2004. The United States was instrumental in orchestrating the forthcoming expansion of the alliance as well as providing funding to the applicant countries, including Lithuania, to help meet NATO's conditions (Kaiser, 2002). In addition, for newcomers such as Lithuania, the leading role of the Americans in the alliance is extremely important because it provides some leverage in dealing with European capitals such as Berlin and Paris. Unquestionably, the extension of the American security guarantees to Lithuania will reinforce the traditional pro-American attitudes in the country.

* * *

Editorial Remarks

As in other chapters, the authors identified the link between the print media's characterization of the terrorists' motives and the general portrayal of the United

States. The Lithuanian press discussed four main causes of the September attacks. In the immediate aftermath, none of these explanations predominated. Commentaries explored the psychological qualities of the terrorists, labeling their acts as "horrible" and "terrible," or even "evil" and "insane." There were also several mentions of the cultural conflict between the Muslim world and the West, with which the Lithuanians identify. In addition, the press commonly criticized the United States' security forces and the inability of the FBI and CIA to protect their country. The most unfavorable explanation—that contentious American foreign policies had stimulated the attacks—was rarely proffered during this period. The print media's focus on either the negative psychological attributes of the terrorists, or the broader cultural conflict resulted in a predominantly favorable overall view of the United States in the Lithuanian press.

By October 2001, as the first bombs dropped in Afghanistan, the press coverage, like it happened in many other countries, lost some of its sympathy for America and increasingly framed the conflict in geopolitical terms. Many authors talked about the United States' policies in the Middle East, and explained the September events as a spillover from the regional conflict in which the United States was directly involved. This shift in content, coupled with the numerous reports on America's prodigious bombing campaign in Afghanistan, accounted in part for the print media's increasingly ambivalent and oftentimes negative assessments of the United States.

In the final period, although the press coverage declined considerably, another shift in Lithuanian views was discernable. Pro-American attitudes rebounded in December 2001 as the fall of the Taliban came unexpectedly quickly. The people's worries about a drawn-out war with heavy civilian causalities were abated and the conflict looked more and more like a police operation in which the criminals would in time be brought to justice.

The authors' underlying message reminds us that perceptions of the United States are unstable and often linked to current international events, including the actions of the United States. At the same time, the authors also stressed the importance of the historical context. They attributed the primarily favorable view of the United States in Lithuania, especially when compared to many other countries, to America's consistently pro-Lithuanian policy over the last decades as well as the common identification of the two nations with the Western mode of life.

Suggested Additional Literature

Clemens, Walter C. (2001). *The Baltic Transformed: Complexity Theory and European Security.* Lanham: Rowman and Littlefield Publishers.

Hiden, John, and Patrick Salmon (1994). *The Baltic Nations and Europe: Estonia, Latvia and Lithuania in the Twentieth Century.* London, New York: Longman.

Vitas, Robert A. (1990). *The United States and Lithuania: the Stimson Doctrine of Nonrecognition.* New York: Praeger.

Chapter 13

Concluding Remarks

Vladimir Shlapentokh, Joshua Woods and Eric Shiraev

In conclusion, let us summarize the findings from each national case. It can be seen from the previous chapters, that the media responses were very diverse and influenced by a wide range of domestic and international factors. Overall, international reactions can be described as occurring in stages in which the media changed the focus of analysis switching from immediate emotional assessments of the events of September 11th to more sophisticated comments on the U.S. response to the terrorist attacks, to wide-ranging evaluations about America, its government, values, and lifestyle in general.

The Reaction to 9/11

Right after the tragic attacks, the reaction of the world was almost uniform. The dominant morals and religions condemn killing. A majority of the comments described 9/11 in very emotional terms. Respondents who justified the action of the perpetrators, or wrote about their courage, or their status as victims of oppression, comprised no more than 5 per cent of the sample in any given country. Although the international press generally described 9/11 in condemning and negative terms, there were, however, some discernable differences in the proportion of condemnation between countries. At the two extremes, 86 per cent of the Lithuanian respondents characterized 9/11 in clearly negative terms, while only 54 per cent did the same in Egypt (see Appendix for the data in Figure 13.1 in table format). A considerable number of people in the international print media chose neutral terms, such as "well-organized," "shrewd," or "meticulous" to describe 9/11. As compared to the other project countries, the Egyptian respondents (41 per cent) led the way in the use of neutral terminology (India, 29 per cent; Germany, 27 per cent; Colombia, 23 per cent; Russia, 21 per cent; China, 15 per cent; Lithuania, 14 per cent).

While most people expressed feelings of horror, there were still those who gloated over the tragedy. (Chat rooms in Russia and Ukraine, for example, contained several posted "congratulations" addressed to terrorists; these messages, however, were vehemently criticized by the majority of people participating in online discussions.) In order to disguise their satisfaction, many people devised such phrases as: "We have sympathy for the Americans but not for America." This formula was particularly popular in Russia.

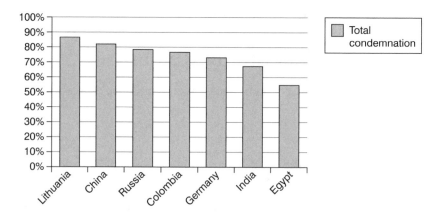

Figure 13.1   The Words and Phrases used to Describe 9/11

The Prime Suspect of 9/11

We should note the difference between the acceptance of America's view of the perpetrators as "Islamic extremists," and the more specific statement that the prime suspect was "Osama bin Laden." The degree of identification with America is much weaker in the first case than in the second. If we take the combined definition of the perpetrators (Osama bin Laden or Islamic extremists), only in China and Egypt the majority of respondents refused to accept America's prime suspects (see Appendix for the data in Figure 13.2 in table format).

In the fall of 2001 the absolute majority of the American people shared the views of the White House and the mainstream media, that Islamic extremist Osama bin Laden was behind the terrorist disaster. The German print media showed the highest level of identification with America in this respect. Eighty four per cent of the

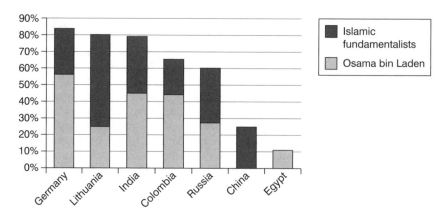

Figure 13.2   Prime Suspects of 9/11

German respondents named Osama bin Laden (57 per cent) or Islamic terrorists (27 per cent) as the perpetrators of 9/11. As one German observer wrote, "Osama bin Laden uses most of his money to finance his 'Holy War' against the West and in particular against America; he is the sponsor of terror" (Uhlemann, 2001). Second to the Germans, 80 per cent of the generally pro-American Lithuanians considered either Osama bin Laden (25 per cent) or Islamic extremists (55 per cent) to be the perpetrators of 9/11. Inspired by their own problems with fundamentalists, the Indians were also close to the Germans (45 per cent named Osama bin Laden, 34 per cent Islamic terrorists). As stated in the Hindi-language newspaper *Dainik Jagran*, "Evidence has come forward that Islamic terrorists were responsible for the attack on America" (September 13, 2001). The highest level of antipathy toward America was found among those who linked 9/11 to the U.S. (either to its government, or American radical groups). In Egypt, 47 per cent of the respondents named "America" as the perpetrator; in Russia, 16 per cent did the same. Egypt and Russia were the clear leaders in making this suggestion.

The Causes of the 9/11 Attacks

In the first few days after 9/11, one of the most salient topics in the international press was the question of "why" the U.S. was attacked. What were the root causes or conditions that led to 9/11? Within twenty-four hours of the attacks, President Bush gave his interpretation of such causes. Among other things, he talked about the terrorists' blind hatred of America. "These people can't stand freedom. They hate our values; they hate what America stands for" (www.whitehouse.gov, September 12, 2001). Another related issue was the political or religious motivation behind the attacks. In an address to the Congress and the American people on September 20, 2001, President Bush claimed that the terrorists practice "a fringe form of Islamic extremism." The president, however, was exceedingly careful not to associate 9/11 with what he repeatedly called "the peaceful teachings of Islam." For the president as

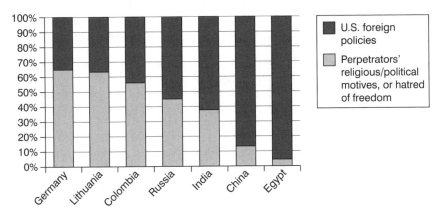

Figure 13.3   The Causes of 9/11

well as an absolute majority of Americans, there was no question that the ultimate blame for the attacks rested on the perpetrators alone.

Among foreign elites, there was little consensus on the issue of 9/11's cause, although the level of identification with the U.S. declined considerably in all the project countries in comparison to the two issues examined earlier. Three distinctive groups have formed. On one side of the spectrum, 65 per cent of the German elites, and 63 per cent of Lithuanians closely associated the cause of 9/11 with the perpetrators' religious or political motives, or hatred of American values. Colombia was close to the German/Lithuanian perspective. As one Colombian commentator wrote, "The attack was terrible, something unusual and cruel done by religious fanatics" (Abella, 2001). On the other side, only 4 per cent of the Egyptian elites and 13 per cent of the Chinese did the same. Russia and India assumed intermediate positions.

None of the countries in this study demonstrated responses of a particularly strong sense of identification with America on this issue. In the days immediately following the attacks many people pointed at American foreign policies as the root cause of the disaster. People in the Egyptian print media led the way in making this explanation. Among the Egyptian respondents who wrote about the cause of 9/11, 96 per cent of them blamed U.S. foreign policies; 87 per cent of the Chinese, 63 per cent of the Indians, and 55 per cent of the Russians said the same. "This terrorist attack is not an accident," wrote a respondent from Hong Kong. "It happened because President Bush offended many nations and organizations, such as Iraq and Palestine, with his foreign policies" (*Apple Daily*, September 13, 2001). Following the same line of thinking, an Indian author wrote, "Today's attacks are a result of America's policies in the Middle-East" (*Gujarat Samachar*, September 12, 2001). In Germany, 30 per cent of the respondents pinned the blame on American foreign policies. Our data are corroborated by the survey of opinion leaders (which are close to our conception of "elites") conducted by the Pew Research Center, which collected data in the aftermath of 9/11 (Pew, December 21, 2001).

Overall, the search for answers to 9/11's cause sparked criticism of the U.S. in all corners of the world, including Western Europe. In his recent book on anti-Americanism, Richard Crockatt (2003) discussed at length an issue of the *London Review of Books* (October 4, 2001) in which several British commentators, while expressing blunt denunciation of 9/11 and sympathy for the Americans, agreed that "the United States had it coming."

The respondents advanced several different variants of this critique, ranging from specific to general targets of criticism. General references to "U.S. foreign policies" as the underlying cause of 9/11 prevailed in most of the project countries. For instance, 72 per cent of the Chinese, 70 per cent of the Egyptians, 60 per cent of the Colombians, and 57 per cent of the Russians pointed to U.S. foreign policies or actions in general, without mentioning a particular nation or region in the world. The most salient "specific" policy critiques were directed at America's Middle East policies, particularly in regard to the Israel/Palestine conflict. As one Chinese columnist from Hong Kong wrote, "The root cause of 9/11 is that America is conducting a biased policy supporting Israel, while it suppresses the Third World, especially Arab and Islamic countries." Another relatively popular argument was that America had created its own enemy when CIA agents trained guerilla soldiers—

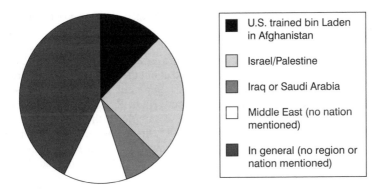

**Figure 13.4   The Types of U.S. Foreign Policies Blamed for 9/11 (combined %
from all project countries)**

mojahedin fighters such as Osama bin Laden—to fight the Soviet in the Afghan War
(1979–1989). Not surprisingly, this critique was somewhat popular in the Russian
press.

The elites in our study were generally more critical of America's foreign policies
than the masses. Polling data from the Fund of Public Opinion (May 2001)
corroborated this statement in Russia. Although the masses were influenced by the
media, on this issue they expressed less hostility, or disapproval toward American
foreign policies than people in the media. The Fund of Public Opinion survey,
conducted in May 2001, found that 60 per cent of "experts" said that the United
States played a negative role in the world, while only 49 per cent of the Russian
masses agreed with this claim.

Similar to the issue of the causes of 9/11 was the question of what type of words
should be used to describe the current global conflict. We considered four different
theses: 1) Bush's contention about "the struggle of good versus evil"; 2) the concept

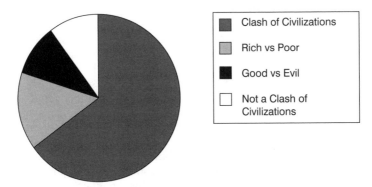

**Figure 13.5   The Global Conflict Brought to Light by 9/11 (combined % from
all project countries)**

of a "clash of civilizations" (see Chapter 1 of this book); 3) the Marxist conception of "rich versus poor;" and 4) an antithesis to Huntington that there is "no clash of civilizations." As our data showed, the clash of civilization thesis was clearly the most salient in the foreign press. Taking the average percentage across all seven countries, 64 per cent of the respondents talked about the "civilizational" character of the conflict (75 per cent of Egyptians, 74 per cent of Indians, 66 per cent of Colombians, 65 per cent of Germans, 54 per cent of Russians, and 50 per cent of Lithuanians). We did not include the Chinese sample in the average percentage mentioned in the text. Between September 12–15, there were no references to any of the conflict hypotheses. Even the more open newspaper from Hong Kong and the online forum avoided this issue completely (see Appendix for the data in Figures 13.3, 13.4, and 13.5 in table format).

Following the established trend, the Lithuanians (34 per cent) and the Germans (10 per cent) as well as the Indians (13 per cent) showed the most support for the official U.S. position (that is, Bush's "good versus evil" rhetoric), while the Egyptians demonstrated no patronage of this idea at all. The explanation of the war as a conflict between "rich and poor" was quite unpopular in India (0 per cent), Germany (5 per cent), and Lithuania (8 per cent), but fared better in Russia (23 per cent), where the influence of the Communist party remains strong. This idea was developed, with some reservations, by the leading Russian journalist Alexander Minkin: "The world is divided into rich and poor. The hatred of the poor is very strong. It's easy to lead the poor against the rich. And there are rich people who like to and know how to do that."

In most of the project countries there was an active debate over the credibility of the "clash of civilization" thesis. Some authors took an accusatory or conspiratorial tone. One Indian author discussed the idea as a "pitiful attempt to invent a post Cold-War enemy" (Bidwai, 2001). Another author found fault in the popularity of this thesis in the West: "Samuel Huntington's clash of civilizations thesis has been given currency by Western news networks. The 'Islamic world' is a myth ... no one calls the Western nations the 'Christian world'" (Baruah, 2001).

The Use of Military Force after 9/11

With lower Manhattan in ruins, not only President Bush, but almost all members of Congress, and a great majority of Americans believed that a military response to 9/11 was the proper course of action. Support for this idea around the world, however, was minimal. Germany and Lithuania, as usual, showed the most solidarity with the U.S. position. "Sometimes freedom must be defended using military force," wrote a German author (Rau, 2001). Yet, even in these countries no more than a third of the respondents declared their support. Among those respondents who discussed how America should respond to 9/11, only 15 per cent of Indians, 11 per cent of Russians, 5 per cent of Chinese, and 3 per cent of Colombians backed the idea of reacting with military force. Egypt followed its general pattern, showing no support at all for the U.S. stance. Not only was there a lack of support for a military response, but also most foreign elites made open demands on the U.S. to avoid a military confrontation. In the public discussions about how America should react to 9/11, critical views of its

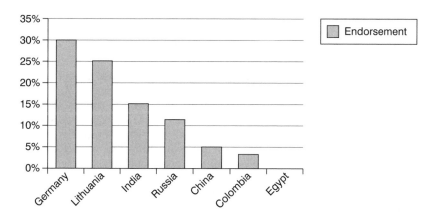

Figure 13.6   Endorsement of U.S. Military Actions Against the Terrorists

foreign policies also surfaced. As the prescribed response to 9/11, almost one-third of the Egyptian elites instructed America to change its foreign policies. This "solution" to the U.S.A.'s problem with terrorism was also quite popular in Russia (18 per cent) and India (19 per cent), while only 10 per cent of Germans, and 11 per cent of Colombians advanced the same critical advice.

The masses in foreign countries were much more supportive of a military response than the elites. A Gallup International poll conducted in late 2001 showed that 70 per cent of the Indian masses (compared to 15 per cent of elites), 65 per cent of the Germans (30 per cent of elites), 54 per cent of the Lithuanians (25 per cent of elites), 41 per cent of the Colombians (3 per cent of elites) and 39 per cent of the Russians (11 per cent of elites) "agree with the U.S. military action" (see the Gallup International Poll on Terrorism, September 2001, www.gallup-international.com). Although there are some methodological problems with comparing these data sources, the significant disparity between them is indeed noteworthy. The masses in foreign countries appeared to be several times more supportive of the official U.S. position than the elites.

The relative number of elites who showed willingness to help the U.S. in military actions was somewhat similar to the level of their general endorsement of these actions (though this issue did show, as expected, a relative decline). While 15 per cent of the Indians endorsed American military actions against the terrorists, only 11 per cent offered their country's aid to this mission. Showing a relatively high level of support for American military actions (11 per cent), the Russians, with their bad memories of their own Afghan war, were reluctant to offer material support; only 3 per cent were ready to pledge their country's involvement in a new war.

Germany, the American ally, represented a remarkable exception. The number of people who insisted on German participation in military operations increased in comparison to those who gave a general endorsement of the U.S. retaliation (from 30 to 52 per cent). The same increase occurred in China (from 5 per cent to 11 per cent). The extremely low level of material support offered by Lithuanians (0 per cent) and

Colombians (2 per cent) should be attributed more to their general lack of military infrastructure than an especially negative attitude toward the United States. Indeed, while 25 per cent of Lithuanians supported the idea of the U.S. conducting military operations, none of them offered their country's military aid.

Many elites contended that their governments should refuse giving any type of military support to the United States. In their minds, the proper course of action involved political, or diplomatic engagements, not military actions. A few days after the attacks, a commentator from China said, "Terrorism is not a military issue, but a political issue, therefore the elimination of terrorism should rely on political and diplomatic means" (Pei, 2001). While most elites supported the idea of offering various types of non-military aid (from diplomatic assistance to sharing information about terrorist organizations), this type of "help" was usually suggested as an alternative to President Bush's strong assertions that the U.S. military had "a job to do."

The reluctance of a majority of the elites to offer military assistance to the U.S. at this crucial moment in history contrasted with the statements of foreign leaders. President Bush declared that the U.S. had developed "a broad and strong coalition of countries who are *united with us* and involved in our campaign" (italics added). This was not an overstatement. Sixty-nine nations would come to support the global war on terrorism; 20 nations would deploy troops to the U.S. Central Command to aid the military actions in Afghanistan. At the leadership level, there was indeed a strong sense of ingroup identification, even if it was temporary and driven mostly by political considerations. Leaders from around the globe not only condemned the attacks, and accepted America's prime suspect Osama bin Laden, but even offered to support America's military response to 9/11 (see Appendix for the data in Figures 13.6 and 13.7 in table format).

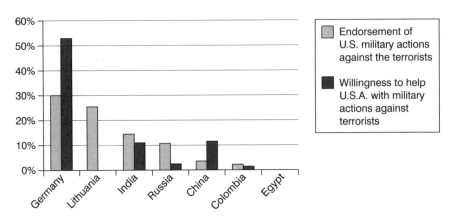

Figure 13.7   Endorsement of Military Actions versus Willingness to Help in Military Actions

How the World Characterized America after 9/11

One of the most apparent signs of the international elites' identification (or differentiation) with America was found in the words they used to describe the United States. It goes without saying that in the aftermath of 9/11, President Bush and other American politicians as well as mainstream journalists spoke, or wrote about the country, its people and institutions in glowing terms. The image of America abroad, however, varied quite dramatically from one nation to the next.

To compare the print media across countries, we comprised a list of forty codes. Twenty of these codes contained words or short phrases of a positive character, such as "brave, determined, united, freedom-loving and compassionate." The other twenty codes included a broad range of words and phrases with negative connotations, such as "warlike, revengeful, hypocritical, arrogant, cares only about its own interests, vulnerable, and materialistic" (see Appendix for the data in Figure 13.8 in table format).

The developments of September 11th have aroused debates about the world status of the United States. Among the 40 different images we considered, America's status as the "only superpower in the world" ranked overall as the most popular description of the U.S. in the international press. Five of the seven project countries including Colombia, Lithuania, Germany, Egypt, and India ranked this image first. The two countries with the most apparent global ambitions, China and Russia, invoked this image less frequently. The Chinese press ranked it seventh, and Russia ranked it eleventh, behind other popular images, such as "vulnerable," "arrogant," "warlike," and "tries to impose its will on other countries."

By and large, the foreign elites were fixated on America's puissance in their analysis of the events surrounding 9/11. For some, the idea that the U.S. has no major international opponent was simply treated as a given fact. For other respondents, America's status as the only superpower played a pivotal role in their particular messages.

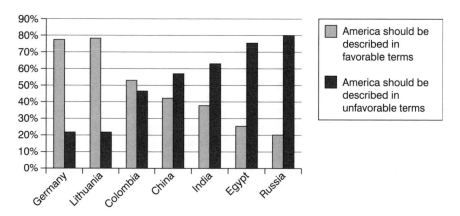

Figure 13.8   How America should be Described

Note: See the website for the most popular words and phrases used to describe America and for other materials.

Image of the Enemy and Attitudes about the United States

At least two interesting findings are evident in the analysis of the data. First, according to the two quantitative indicators, there is a positive association between each country's degree of concern about 9/11-like attacks, and its attitude about the United States. In general, higher levels of denunciation of the terrorist acts have been associated with higher levels of sympathy and support for the U.S. and its war against international terrorism. These data, however, as we have noted earlier, present evidence of an association, not a causation: it is not clear whether denunciation of terrorism actually affects directly attitudes about the United States. Although it was assumed that the large-scale attacks of September 11th would generate group identification with America, the opposite is also possible. That is, increased (or decreased) identification with the U.S. could cause greater (or lesser) levels of condemnation of 9/11 and its perpetrators. As another important clarification, alternative explanations for this relationship have not been statistically controlled. In fact, as discussed in the course of this book, several other factors of the U.S. image abroad seem plausible.

Second, while a majority of elites denounced the terrorist acts of 9/11, far fewer elites identified with the U.S. on the major issues surrounding 9/11 such as explaining the reasons for such attacks and suggesting a response. In each of the seven countries, the proportion of respondents who "identified" with America was significantly smaller than the proportion of those who "condemned" 9/11-like terrorism (the difference of proportions in Germany, .24; Lithuania, .42; Colombia, .42; India, .48; Russia, .50; China, .36; Egypt, .26). These differences can be attributed to several factors, not least of which is the emotional nature of people's evaluations of 9/11. Most foreign elites watched the shocking images and felt emotionally compelled to condemn the terrible acts and sympathize with its victims. However, this emotional salience weakened when elites speculated further about the U.S. and its responses to the attack.

While the common threat of international terrorism has the power to bring countries together, there are several other factors that can tear them apart. Russia is an interesting case in point. It might be expected that the dramatic attacks by Chechen terrorists in Moscow and other regions of the country would lead directly to increased group identification between Russia and the United States. To some extent, this is indeed what happened. Several analysts have pointed out that for a brief period following 9/11 the problem of terrorism bolstered Russian-American relations. President Vladimir Putin's initial reaction to 9/11 was, by all accounts, sympathetic, and his solidarity with the U.S. was strong. Russia quickly became a member of the international anti-terrorist coalition, several measures were taken to allow U.S. troops in Central Asia, and official relations between the U.S. and Russia were warmer than at any time since WWII. However, there were many other factors that countered this growing relationship. Actions such as the expansion of U.S. influence within countries formerly controlled by Moscow, the inclusion of Baltic countries in NATO, envy of U.S. economic success, the nationalists and communists' loathing of American society or capitalism, and the necessity of the Kremlin to find a scapegoat for its failed economic reforms have all caused conflict and controversy.

The U.S. position in the world will, at least to some extent, depend on how foreign countries perceive the United States and what policies are conducted based on such attitudes. Negative attitudes about America grow an adversarial climate in which terrorists can find support among ordinary people; foreign intelligence agencies are less willing to share information with their U.S. counterparts, and U.S. military operations are impeded. It also generates political capital for the opposition in countries where the leader cooperates with America. Our findings, as we have hoped, could further stress the importance of perception and image in international affairs. A loss of credibility or respect, or a failure to convince other countries about particular issues including the imminence of a global threat ultimately leads to a less predicable and safe world.

After the 9/11 attacks on America, few topics in the contemporary world gained similar attention than the war on terror led by the United States. In many foreign countries, the initial "flood of sympathy" for America's tragedy soon dried up and was followed by a wide range of opinions. The assessments of the events and the actions undertaken by Washington have become increasingly polarized. Some opinion leaders maintained that a sovereign nation has the right to defend itself whereas others deemed the U.S. as a "cowboy" nation—quick-tempered and bent on unilateralism—whose "manipulative corporations" and "military adventurism" had brought the terrorist actions upon itself. Some national media sources and political leaders put the entire blame on terrorists for the murder they committed while others were looking for more complex explanations. Overall, the reactions to the events in the United States and its actions in 2001 and after revealed an incredible amount of information about the domestic political and cultural influences that determined support and sympathy as well as criticism and animosity toward the United States and its policies.

As our analyses have shown, there can be few analytical tasks more complicated than tracing the origins of people's views of other countries. The task is especially difficult in the case of the United States, a country with high visibility in foreign affairs, no military or economic equals in the world, and an infinite number of international contacts. Most critics point out the shortcomings of U.S. actions in the international arena, while many others refer to political, psychological, or cultural circumstances in foreign countries that contribute to the attitudes. Considering the arguments on both sides and using the common enemy paradigm to analyze the materials obtained by this study, we believe we have clarified a few main assumptions about and international image of the United States and the possibilities for its improvement.

Appendix: Graphic Displays in Table Format (in %)

Figure 13.9   The Words and Phrases used to Describe 9/11

	Lithuania	China	Russia	Colombia	Germany	India	Egypt
Total condemnation	86	82	78	76	73	67	54

Figure 13.10   Prime Suspects of 9/11

	Germany	Lithuania	India	Colombia	Russia	China	Egypt
Osama bin Laden	57	25	45	44	28	0	11
Islamic fundamentalists	27	55	34	22	32	25	0

Figure 13.11   The Causes of 9/11

	Germany	Lithuania	Colombia	Russia	India	China	Egypt
Perpetrators' religious/political motives, or hatred of freedom	65	63	56	45	37	13	4
U.S. foreign policies	35	37	44	55	63	87	96

Figure 13.12   The Type of U.S. Foreign Policies Blamed for 9/11 (combined % from all project countries)

U.S. trained bin Laden in Afghanistan	14
Israel/Palestine	22
Iraq or Saudi Arabia	8
Middle East (no nation mentioned)	12
In general (no region or nation mentioned)	44

Figure 13.13   The Global Conflict Brought to Light by 9/11 (combined % from all project countries)

Clash of Civilizations	64
Rich vs Poor	14
Good vs Evil	12
Not a Clash of Civilizations	10

Figure 13.14   Endorsement of U.S. Military Actions Against the Terrorists

	Germany	Lithuania	India	Russia	China	Colombia	Egypt
Endorsement	30	25	15	11	5	3	0

Figure 13.15   Endorsement of Military Actions versus Willingness to Help in Military Actions

	Germany	China	India	Russia	Colombia	Lithuania	Egypt
Willingness	52	11	11	3	2	0	0
Endorsement	30	25	15	11	5	3	0

Figure 13.16   How America should be Described

	Germany	Lithuania	Colombia	China	India	Egypt	Russia
Using favorable terms	78	78	53	42	37	25	20
Using unfavorable terms	22	22	47	58	63	75	80

References

Abella, Arturo (2001). *El Nuevo Siglo.* September 15.

Abrahamian, Ervand (1993). *Khomeinism: Essays on the Islamic Republic.* London and New York: IB Tauris.

Abrams, D. and Hogg, M. (1988). Comments on the motivational status of self-esteem in social identity and intergroup discrimination. *European Journal of Social Psychology,* 18, 317–334.

Agre, P.E. (2002). Real-time politics: the Internet and the political process. *The Information Society.* 18: 311–331.

Ahmed, Ahmed and Hamza, Mamdouh (ed.). (2003). *Sinâ'at al-karâhiyya fî l-'alâqât al-'arabiyya al-amrîkiyya.* Al-Ahrâm Al-tijâriyya: Qleeob.

Aiyar, M.S. (2002). From 9/11 to 12/13. *United Press International.* December 26.

Alden, E. and Luce, E. (2001). A new friend in Asia. *The Financial Times* (London edition). 16.

Alexeyev, Yury (2001). Russia's participation in anti-terrorist operation in Afghanistan may be substantial; non-military Russian experts believe that active participation of Russian secret services in operation may ensure its success (www.strana.ru). September 18.

Alksninins, Gintautas (2002). Lietuvius vel masins zaliosios korteles. *Lietuvos Rytas.* September 30.

Al-reefy, Mohammed (1983). *Al-mawqif al-amrìkì wal-wâqi'al-'arabì.* Al-mansha'a Al-'âmma: Tripoli.

Alterman, Eric (2003). USA Oui! Bush Non! How Europeans See America. *The Nation.* Issue: February 10.

Al-Zayyat, Montasser (2004). *The Road to al-Qaeda: the story of Bin Laden's Right-Hand Man.* Translated by Ahmed Fekry and edited by Sarah Nimis. London and Stering, Virginia: Pluto Press.

Anonymous (2001a). Lietuviai nelike veltis i JAV kova su teroristais. *Lietuvos Rytas.* September 21.

Anonymous (2001b). Laiko zenklai. *Lietuvos Rytas.* December 27.

Anonymous (2001c). Pasaulio savaite. *Lietuvos Rytas.* December 29.

Anonymous (2001d). Laiko zenklai. *Lietuvos Rytas.* September 15.

Anonymous (2001e). Rusijai naudingas karas. *Respublika.* October 11.

Anonymous (2001f). Laiko zenklai. *Lietuvos Rytas.* September 12.

Anonymous (2001g). Apklausos veidrodyje – ir Lietuvos, ir pasaulio ivykiai. *Lietuvos Rytas.* December 31.

Anonymous (2001h). Geriausi vaistai nuo panikos-ramus darbas. *Lietuvos Rytas.* September 13.

Anonymous (2001i). Nuo panikos ir nerimo gelbeja tvarkinga kasdienybe. *Lietuvos Rytas.* September 14.

Anonymous (2001j). Antiteroristiniame sajudyje – ir Lietuva. *Lietuvos Rytas.* September 15.

Anonymous (2001k). Mintyse ir maldose – su uzpulta amerikieciu tauta. *Lietuvos Rytas.* September 17.

Anonymous (2001l). 'Lietuvos Ryto' savaite. *Lietuvos Rytas.* September 15.

Anonymous (2001m). 'Lietuvos Ryto' savaite. *Lietuvos Rytas.* October 15.

Anonymous (2002). Skandalas del 'Williams' pagausino euroskeptiku gretas. *Lietuvos Rytas.* September 18.

Anti-war sentiment palpable in Mysore (2003). *The Hindu* (online edition). March 22.

Arbatov, Alexei (2001). Press Conference with Vice Chairman of State Duma Committee for Defense. *Federal News service.* (www.fednews.ru). September 18.

Arbatov, G. (1992). Rescue Russia, or Else! *Newsday.* October 25.

Arbatov, Georgi (1987). It Takes Two to Make a Cold War. *New York Times.* December 8.

Aznarez, Juan Jesús (2002). Las FARC crecieron un 32% en la zona de distensión. *El País.* (España). January 15.

Baciulis, Audrius and Vaida Samuolyte (2002). Misija Afganistane. *Veidas.* September 26.

Baluyevsky, Yuri (2001). An interview. Equal Russia-US partnership an earnest of global stability. *Krasnaya Zvezda.* No. 227, December 9.

Baruah, Amit (2001). *The Hindu.* October 11.

Baruah, Amit (2003). War should be last option. *The Hindu.* February 20.

Bauman, Z. (1987). *Legislators & Interpreters: on modernity, post-modernity and intellectuals.* Ithaca, N.Y.: Cornell University Press.

Bavin, P. (2003). Russians about America and Americans about Russia: A comparative analysis of survey results. (www.fom.ru).

Bayat, Asef (1998). Revolution without Movement, Movement without Revolution: Comparing Islamic Activism in Iran and Egypt. *Comparative Studies in History and Society.* Vol. 40, No. 1 (January), 136–169.

Bayat, Asef (2000). Activism and Social Development in the Middle East. *Interdisciplinary Journal of Middle East Studies.* 34/1.

Belluci, Paolo, and Isernia, Pierangelo (2003). Massacring in Front of a Blind Audience? Italian Public Opinion and Bosnia. In R. Sobel and E. Shiraev (eds.). *International Public Opinion and the Bosnia Crisis.* Penn State University Press.

Bezlova, Antoaneta (1999). Stand on Yugoslavia Shows Shift in Foreign Policy, *IPS.* April 21.

Bhargava, T. (2003, accessed online in April). India's new Anti-Americanism (http://www.opendemocracy.net/themes/article-3-1160.jsp).

Bidwai, P. (2003, accessed online in February). India should oppose the war on Iraq, but will it? (http://www.antiwar.com/bidwai).

Bimber, B. (1999). The Internet and citizen communication with government: does the media matter. *Political Communication.* 16: 409–428.

Bitsoyev, Said (2001). How we fight wars and how they do it. *Novye Izvestia.* December 28.

Bogaturov, Alexei (2001). Love's comeback: Russia's second attempt at partnership with the West. *Vek.* No. 38, September 28.

Brook, T. and Frolic, B.M. (eds.). (1997). *Civil Society in China.* Armonk, NY: M.E. Sharpe.

Brooks, Jeffery (2000). *Thank You, Comrade Stalin!* Princeton, New Jersey: Princeton University Press.

Brownfield, William R. (2001). Scene-Setter for Secretary Powell's Trip to Colombia. U.S. Department of State website. (http://www.state.gov/p/wha/rls/rm/2001/4867htm).

Buchanan, William, Cantril, Hadley (1953). *How Nations See Each Other.* Urbana, Illinois: University of Illinois Press.

Bull, H. (1984). The Revolt against the West. In H. Bull and A. Watson (eds.). *The Expansion of International Society.* New York: Oxford University.

Bush, George W. (2003, accessed online in January). State of the Union. (http://www.whitehouse.gov/news/releases/2003/01/20030128-19.html).

Bushnell, David (1992). *The Making of Modern Colombia: A Nation in Spite of Itself.* Berkeley: University of California Press.

Caballero, Antonio (2001). El siglo XXI. *Semana.* September 13. (http://www.semana.com/archivo/articulosView.jsp?id=18698).

Cambio (2003). Un país endurecido. No. 515, May 12–19.

Ceaser, James W. (2003). A Genealogy of Anti-Americanism. *The Public Interest.* 152.

Center should be alert to situation (2001). *The Hindu* (online edition). November 23.

Cergeliene, Rasa (2001). Amerikieciai patyre mazeikieciu atjauta. *Lietuvos Rytas.* September 13.

Chan, Joseph and Jack Qiu (2002). China: Media Liberalization under authoritarianism. In Monroe Price, Beata Rozumilowicz and Stefaan Verhulst (eds.). *Media Reform: Democratizing the Media, Democratizing the State.* New York: Routledge.

Chang, Tsan-kuo (1993). *The Press and China Policy: The Illusion of Sino-American Relations, 1950–1984.* Norwood, NJ: Albex.

Chari, P.R. (1999). Indo-US Relations: Non proliferation concerns. In G.K. Bertsch, S. Gahlaut and A. Srivastava (eds.). *Engaging India.* New York: Routledge.

Chary, M.S. (1995). *The Eagle and the Peacock: U.S. Foreign Policy Towards India Since Independence.* Westport, CT: Greenwood Press.

Chengappa, R., Padmanabhan, A. and Bhasi, I. (2003). U.S. Policy: The World According to Bush. *India Today* (online edition). August 28.

Chomsky, Noam (2001). *9–11.* New York: Seven Stories Press.

Clack, George (2003, accessed online in September). Introduction. *Writers on America.* (http://usinfo.state.gov/products/pubs/writers/homepage.htm).

Clemens, Walter C. (2001). *The Baltic Transformed: Complexity Theory and European Security.* Lanham: Rowman & Littlefield Publishers.

Cohen, J. (1960). A coefficient of agreement for nominal scales. *Educational and Psychological Measurement.* 20, 37–46.

Comisión Fulbright-Colombia (2003). Historia del Programa. (http://www.fulbright.edu.co/historia.html#ingles).

Coser, L. (1965). *Men of Ideas: A Sociologist's View.* New York: Free Press.

Crandall, Russell (2002). *Driven by Drugs: U.S. Policy Toward Colombia.* Boulder, CO.: Lynne Rienner Publishers.

Crockatt, Richard (2003). *America Embattled: September 11, anti-Americanism, and the global order.* New York: Routledge.

Davis, R. (1999). *The Web of Politics: The Internet's Impact on the American Political System.* Oxford: Oxford University Press.

Daweesha, Adeed (1997). *Egypt, in Sayigh and Shlaim, The Cold War and the Middle East.* Oxford: Clarendon Press.

Dessouki, Ali E. (1984). *The Primacy of Economics: The Foreign Policy of Egypt.* In Bahgat Korany and Ali E. Dessouki (eds.). *The Foreign Policy of Arab States.* Boulder, Colo.: Westview Press.

Deuze, M. (2003). The web and its journalism: Considering the consequences of different types of news media online. *New Media & Society.* 5(2), 203–230.

Ding, X.L. (2002). The challenges of managing a huge society under rapid transformation. In J. Wong and Y. Zheng (eds.). *China's Post-Jiang Leadership Succession: Problems and Perspectives.* Singapore: Singapore University Press.

Dugas, John C. (2001). Drugs, Lies, and Audiotape: The Samper Crisis in Colombia. *Latin American Research Review.* 36(2): 157–174.

Dugas, John C. (2004). The Colombian Nightmare: Human Rights Abuses and the Contradictory Effects of U.S. Foreign Policy. In Cecilia Menjivar and Nestor Rodríguez (eds.). *When the State Kills.* Austin: University of Texas Press.

Dugin, Alexander (1998). *Osnovi Geopolitiki.* Moscow: Arktogea.

Dugin, Alexander (2001). An Interview. *Nezavisimaya Gazea.* September 13.

Eagly, Alice H., and Shelly Chaiken (1998). Attitude Structure and Function. In Daniel T. Gilbert, Susan T. Fiske and Gardner Lindzey (eds.). *The Handbook of Social Psychology.* Boston: McGraw-Hill.

Ebeid, Mona (2002). At the roots of legitimate anger. *Al-Ahram Weekly Online,* January 24–30.

Editorial (1949). *New York Times.* October 16.

El Espectador (2002). Reacciones de candidatos presidenciales. January 10.

Embassy of Colombia (2002). Colombia: 40 years of experience fighting terrorism. (http://www.colombiaemb.org/terrorism.htm).

Embassy of Colombia (2003). Trade: Colombia wants jobs, not drugs. (http://www.colombiaemb.org/trade.htm).

Ermarth, Michael (2004). Counter-Americanism and Critical Currents in West German Reconstruction 1945–1960: The German Lesson Confronts the American Way of Life. Alexander Stephan, ed., *Americanization and Anti-Americanism. The German Encounter With American Culture After 1945.* New York: Berghahn Books.

Farag, Fatema (1998). Eye on Scandal. *Al-Ahram Weekly.* September 23 (http://weekly.ahram.org/1998/395/frn.htm).

Fedorov, Andrei (2001). Russia is facing a difficult choice. *Nezavisimaya Gazeta.* September 14.

Felgenhauer, Pavel (2001). Bin Laden Best Left to Rot. *Moscow Times.* September 20.

Felgenhauer, Pavel (2001). U.S. Faces Costly Stalemate. *Moscow Times.* October 25.

Fernández de Soto, Guillermo (2001). Intervención de Canciller Fernández de Soto en reunion de la OEA. (http://www.colombiaemb.org/Doc_Terrorism/CANCILLER-TERRORISMO.pdf).

Fewsmith, J. (2000). Discovering nationalism in China (book review). *Political Science Quarterly.* 115(2), 306–308.

Fochkin, Oleg (2001). Water supplies could be contaminated. *Moskovsky Komsomolets.* September 13.

Friedman, Thomas (2002). Let them Come to Berlin. *New York Times.* November 7.

Fuller, Graham E. (1990/1). The strategic irrelevance of Israel. *The National Interest.* No. 22, Winter.

Fundación Social-UNICEF (2002). *Vigía del Fuerte – Boletín sobre la situación humanitaria.* Bogotá, Colombia, December.

Fung, Anthony (2002). One City, Two Systems: Democracy in an Electronic Chat room in Hong Kong. *Javnost: the Public.* 9(2): 77–94.

Fung, Anthony and Chin-Chuan Lee (1994). Hong Kong's Changing Media Ownership: Uncertainty and Dilemma. *Gazette.* 53: 127–133.

Fung, Anthony and Chin-Chuan Lee (2002). Market and Politics: Hong Kong Press During Sovereignty Transfer. In Xing Lu, Wensha Jia, D. Ray Heisey and Lucy Lu (eds.). *Chinese Communication Studies: Contexts and Comparisons.* Westport, CT: Albex.

Gahlaut, S. (1999). Re-energizing the debate: Indo-US nuclear issues. In G.K. Bertsch, S. Gahlaut and A. Srivastava (eds.). *Engaging India.* New York: Routledge.

Gaidys, Vladas (1994). Russians in Lithuania. In V. Shlapentokh, M. Sendich and E. Panin (eds.). *The New Russian Diaspora.* New York: M.E. Sharpe, Inc.

Gallup International (2001). Gallup International poll on terrorism in the U.S. September.

Gallup Organization (2002). View of Foreign Nations. *The Gallup Poll: Public Opinion 2001.* Wilimington, Del.: Scholarly Resources.

Gassert, Philippe (2001). Antiamerikanismus. In Detlef Junker (ed.). *Die USA und Deutschland im Zeitalter des Kaltes Krieges, 1945–1968. Ein Handbuch.* Vol. 1. Stuttgart: Deutsche Verlagsanstalt.

Gill, K.P.S. (2003). The world outside the castle walls. *Asia Times Online.* February 12.

Glad, Betty and Shiraev, Eric (eds.) (1999). *The Russian transformation.* NY: St. Martin's Press.

Goethe, Johann Wolfgang von (1948). To America. Trans. Stephen Spender. Thomas Mann (ed.). *The Permanent Goethe*. New York: Dial.

Goldman, M., Cheek, T. and Hamrin, C.L. (eds.) (1987). *China's Intellectuals and the State: In Search of a New Relationship*. Cambridge: Harvard University Press.

Gornostaev, Dmitry (2001). Will Bush see that his myths are dispelled? (www.strana.ru). September 13.

Government criticized for unseemly haste (2001). *The Hindu* (online edition). September 28.

Government messed up terror campaign (2001). *Indian Express* (online edition). November 22.

Grayson, George. W. (1985). Anti-Americanism in Mexico. In Rubinstein and Smith (eds.). *Anti-Americanism in the Third World: Implications for U.S. Foreign Policy*. New York: Praeger.

Grieder, B.J. (1981). *Intellectuals and the State in Modern China: A Narrative History*. London: The Free Press.

Grushin, Boris (1994). *Is peace at all possible in today's Russia? Mir Mnenii i Mnenia o Mire*. December 8–12.

Gupta, S. (2001). India, Pakistan and two Americas. *Indian Express* (online edition). October 27.

Habermas, Jürgen (2003). Unsere Erneuerung. Nach dem Krieg: Die Wiedergeburt Europas. *Frankfurter Allgemeine Zeitung*. May 31.

Haider, M. (2001). U.S. stresses restraint. *Dawn* (online edition). December 17.

Hale, E. (2002). Global warmth for U.S. after 9/11 turns to frost. *USA Today* (online edition). August 14.

Harding, H. (1991). *A Fragile Relationship: The United States and China since 1972*. Washington D.C.: Brookings Institution.

Harris, Lee (2003). The Intellectual Origins of America-Bashing. *Policy Review*. January, Issue 116.

Harwit, E. and Clark, D. (2001). Shaping the Internet in China: Evolution of political control over network infrastructure and content. *Asian Survey*. 41(3), 377–408.

Haseler, Stephen (1985). *The Varieties of Anti-Americanism: Reflex and Response*. Washington, D.C.: Ethics and Public Policy Center.

Haugaard, Lisa (2002). Blunt Instrument: The United States' punitive fumigation program in Colombia. Washington, D.C.: Latin America Working Group. (http://www.wola.org/Colombia/fum_LAWGFumigationReport.pdf).

Heider, Fritz (1946). Attitudes and cognitive organization. *Journal of Psychology*. 21, 107–112.

Heider, Fritz (1958). *The Psychology of Interpersonal Relations*. New York: Wiley.

Heikal, Mohammed (1978). Egyptian Foreign Policy. *Foreign Affairs*. 56: 4, 1–14.

Heine, Heinrich (1985). Ludwig Börne: A Memorial. In Jost Hermand and Robert C. Holub (eds.). *The Romantic School and Other Essays*. New York: Continuum.

Hiden, John, and Patrick Salmon (1994). *The Baltic Nations and Europe: Estonia, Latvia and Lithuania in the Twentieth Century*. London, New York: Longman.

Ho, Leung-mau (2003). Chinese senior officials: they don't ignore online users anymore? *Ming Pao Daily News*. June 11.

Hollander, Paul (1992). *Anti-Americanism: Critiques at Home and Abroad, 1965–1990*. New York: Oxford University Press.

Hollander, Paul (1995). Introduction. *Anti-Americanism: Irrational and Rational*. New Brunswick, NJ: Transaction Publishers.

Horowitz, Irving Louis (1985). Latin America, Anti-Americanism, and Intellectual Hubris. In Rubinstein and Smith (eds.). *Anti-Americanism in the Third World: Implications for U.S. Foreign Policy*. New York: Praeger.

Human Rights Watch (HRW). 1998. *War Without Quarter: Colombia and International Humanitarian Law*. New York: Human Rights Watch.

Huntington, Samuel P. (1993). The Clash of Civilizations. *Foreign Affairs*. Vol. 72, No. 3, Summer.

Ibrahim, Ibrahim I. (1986). The American-Israeli Alliance: Raison d'etat Revisited. *Journal of Palestine Studies*. Vol. 15, No. 3, 59 (Spring), p. 25.

Ieskauskas, Ceslovas (2001). Aklas kerstas gali stumti i suirute. *Lietuvos Rytas*. September 17.

India News (2000). President of the United States to visit India. March.

India says relations with U.S unaffected by aid to Pakistan (2001). *The Business Recorder* (online edition). October 18.

Ingnatavicius, Tadas (2001). Tarptautiniu teroristu pedsakai-ir Lietuvoje. *Lietuvos Rytas*. September 13.

Irani, C.R. (2001). Losing the high ground. *The Statesman* (online edition). October 7.

Jian, An (1999). China Turns to Russia for Strategic Partnership. *The Strait Times*. July 31.

Joffe, Josef (2002). The axis of envy: why Israel and the United States both strike the same European nerve. *Foreign Policy*. September–October.

Kagan, D. and Ressa, M. (2001). India accuses Pakistan of terrorism, U.S. of hypocrisy. *CNN Live at Daybreak*. October 25.

Kagan, Robert (2003). *Of Paradise and Power: America and Europe in the New World Order*. New York: Alfred A. Knopf.

Kagarlitsky, Boris (2001). A need for honest answers. *Moscow Times*. October 30.

Kagarlitsky, Boris (2001). Bin Laden? Better Be Sure. *Moscow Times*. September 18.

Kaiser, Robert (2002). NATO ready to admit 7 Eastern Bloc countries. *Washington Post*. September 26.

Kapur, D. (2000). India in 1999. *Asian Survey*. 40(1), 195–207.

Katouzian, Homa (1990). *Musaddiq and the Struggle for Power in Iran*. London and New York: IB Tauris.

Keller, Suzanne (1963). *Beyond the ruling class; strategic elites in modern society*. New York: Random House.

Kennedy, J.F. (1960). *The strategy of peace*. New York: Harper & Row.

Kepel, Gilles (1984). *Muslim Extremism in Egypt: The Prophet and the Pharaoh*. Al Saqi Books: London.

Khakamada, Irina (2001). An interview. (www.strana.ru). September 14.

Khamrayev, Victor (2001). The Duma against carpet bombings: The lower house of parliament discusses the latest developments Vremya Novostei (www.wps.ru/eindex.html). September 20.

Kifner, J. (2003). In rebuff to U.S., India says it won't send troops to Iraq. *The New York Times* (online edition). July 14.

Kirby, D. (1978). Morality or expediency? The Baltic question in British-Soviet relations, 1941–1942. In Vytas Stanley Vardys and Romuald J. Misiunas (eds.). *The Baltic States in Peace and War, 1917–1945*. University Park: Pennsylvania State University Press.

Kirk, Robin (2003). *More Terrible than Death: Massacres, Drugs, and America's War in Colombia*. New York: Public Affairs.

Kissinger, H. (1979). *White House Years*. Boston: Little Brown.

Ko, S.B. (2001). China's pragmatism as a grand national development strategy: Historical legacy and evolution. *Issues & Studies*. 37(6), 1–28.

Kovalev, Nikolai (2001). An interview. (www.pravda.ru). December 6.

Kovalev, Nikolai (2001). The U.S. would thus repeat the bitter experience (www.strana.ru). September 14.

Kristiansen, Wendy (2002). Islamists Divided. *Le Monde Diplomatique*. September.

Kronstadt, K.A. (2003). *Indo-U.S. relations: An issue brief for Congress*. Congressional Research Service, The Library of Congress.

Kuhn, R.L. (2000). *Made in China: voices from the New Revolution.* NY: TV Books.

Kukharkin, Alexander (1974). *Po tu storony rassveta.* Moscow: Politicheskaya Literatura.

Kumar, K. (2003). Liberal delusion. *The Hindu* (online edition). May 3.

Kurginian, Sergei (1992). *Sedmoi Stsenarii.* Parts 1–3. Moscow: Eksperementalty Tvorchesky Tsentr.

Kux, D. (1994). *India and the U.S.: Estranged democracies 1941–1991.* Washington D.C.: National Defense University Press.

Lacorne, Denis, and Rupnik, Jacques (1990). France Bewitched by America. In Denis Lacorne, Jacques Rupnik, and Marie-France Toinet (eds.). *The Rise and Fall of Anti-Americanism.* New York: St. Martin's Press.

Lagos, Marta (2003). Terrorism and the Image of the United States in Latin America. *International Journal of Public Opinion Research.* Volume 15, No. 1.

Lagos, Marta (2003). Terrorism and the Image of the United States in Latin America. *International Journal of Public Opinion Research.* 15(1): 95–101.

Laitin, David D. (1998). *Identity in Formation: the Russian-speaking Populations in the Near Abroad.* Ithaca: Cornell University Press.

Lancaster, J. (2003a). In New Delhi, Hindus take a dim view of America. *The Washington Post.* April 3.

Lancaster, J. (2003b). Mulling action, India equates Iraq, Pakistan. *Washington Post.* April 11.

Latynina, Yulia (2001). Plato on Fate of Modern Civilization. *Moscow Times.* September 19.

Lau, Tuen-yu, Anthony Fung and Michael Ji (2003). E-government in China: Keeping up with the Joneses? China and the Internet: Technology, Economy and Society in Transition, organized by Benjamin N. Cardozo School of Law, Yeshiva University, UC Berkeley Graduate School of Journalism, School of Journalism and Communication, Peking University, Stanhope Centre for Communication Policy Research, UK, May 30–31.

Lee, Pat Fong (2003). Media self-censorship, scholars angry. June 16. A24.

Li, Tzu-ching (1997). CPC said to Expect Eventual Sino-U.S. War. *Hong Kong Cheng Ming.* No. 235, as translated in *World News Review*, May 8.

Lietuvos Statistikos Departamentas (2001). *Lietuvos Gyventoju ir Bustu Surasymas 2001. Lietuvos Gyventojai Pagal Tautybes.* http://www.std.lt/Surasymas/Rezultatai/Tautybes.htm.

Limaye, S.P. (1993). *U.S.-Indian relations.* Boulder, CO: Westview Press.

Lippmann, W. (1922). *Public Opinion.* New York, Harcourt: Brace and Company.

Londoño, Jorge (2003). Así vemos a los gringos. *Cambio.* No. 511, April 14.

Marcinkevicius, Justinas (2001). Kam skabina varpai. *Respublika.* October 10.

Markov, Sergei (2001). A War Has Been Declared! Who Is the Enemy? (www.strana.ru). September 22.

Markov, Sergei (2001). Opinion by this newspaper's experts. *Nezavisimaya Gazeta.* No. 197, October 23.

Markov, Sergei (2001). Society Writes Mandate for Putin: Bush-Putin summit of unprecedented importance. (www.stana.ru). October 24.

Mazumdar, A. (2003). India won't jeopardize relations with US over Iraq. *Times of India* (online edition). May 23.

McFaul, Michael (2001). Thank You Russia. *Vremya-Novosti.* September 17.

McGivering, J. (2003, accessed online in April). Kashmir anger over Iraq war. (http://news.bbc.co.uk/1/hi/world/south_asia/).

McMillan, A. (2001). Attitudes towards the United States amongst the Indian Electorate. Unpublished manuscript.

Meyer, Gail. E. (1980). *Egypt and the United States: The formative years.* Associated Press: New Jersey.

Mickeviciute, Violeta (2001a). Senos modernaus XXI amziaus karo klaidos. *Respublika.* October 15.

Mickeviciute, Violeta (2001b). Tiesa apie Afganistana skilda legendomis. *Respublika.* October 12.

Minkin, Alexander (2001). *Moskovskii Komsomolets.* September 13.

Modi, O.P. (2003). American aggression. *World News Connection.* August 17.

Mohammed, Zainab (1997). *Al-siyâsa al-misriyya tijâh al-wilâyât al-muttahida al-amrîkiyya.* Dirâsât al-wahda al-'arabiyya: Beirut.

Moore, R.R. (2001). China's fledging civil society: A force for democratization. *World Policy Journal.* 18(1), 56–66.

Muker Ji, C. and Simon, B. (1998). Out of the limelight: discredited communities and informal communication on the Internet. *Sociological Inquiry.* 68(2), 258–273.

Murphy, C. (2003). Compassion for America curdles abroad. *St. Petersburg Times.* April 1.

Murphy, Caryle (2002). *Passion for Islam: Shaping the modern Middle East, the Egyptian experience.* Scribner: New York.

N.A. (2003). Beijing banned Fortune Magazines: Naming and Criticizing ten publications. June 25. A 21.

Nehru, J.L. (1949). A voyage of discovery. Speech delivered to U.S. Congress. October 13.

Nemtsov, Boris (2001). An interview. *Moskovsky Komsomolets.* September 13.

Nietzsche, Friedrich (2001). *The Gay Science.* Cambridge: Cambridge University Press.

Nikonov, Vyacheslav (2001). Partnership or renunciation? Russia risks assuming the whole burden of the operation in Afghanistan. *Trud.* October 27.

No Author (1952). Our Country and Our Culture. *Partisan Review.* 19.

No Author (2001). 'Anschläge gegen uns alle gerichtet.' Bundeskanzler Schröder spricht in einer Regierungserklärung von einer, Kriegserklärung an die freie Welt. *Süddeutsche Zeitung.* September 12, 2001.

No Author (2002). *The National Security Strategy of the United States of America.* September 17 (see http://www.whitehouse.gov/nsc/nss.html).

No Author (2003, accessed online in September). What We're Fighting For. *Preamble, Institute for American Values.* (http://www.americanvalues.org).

No Author (2003a, accessed online in September). A World of Justice and Peace Would be Different. A Response to the Manifesto 'Propositions: What We're Fighting For' by 60 American Intellectuals. *Institute for American Values.* (http://www.americanvalues.org).

No Author (2003b, accessed online in September). In the 21st century, there is no longer any justification for war. Second reply by the Koalition für Leben und Frieden to the 'What we are fighting for' group of the Institute of American Values. *Institute for American Values.* (http://www.americanvalues.org).

No Author (2003c, accessed online in September). Is the Use of Force Ever Morally Justified? A Response from Americans to Colleagues in Germany (August 7, 2002). *Institute for American Values.* (http://www.americanvalues.org).

Norris, P. (1999). Who surfs? New technology, old voters and virtual democracy. In E.C. Kamarck and J.S. Nye, Jr. (eds.). *Democracy.com? Governance in a Networked World.* Hollis, NH: Hollis.

Office of Immigration Statistics (1999). *1999 Statistical Yearbook.* (http://www.bcis.gov/graphics/shared/aboutus/statistics/ybpage.htm).

Office of Immigration Statistics (2001). *2001 Statistical Yearbook.* (http://www.bcis.gov/graphics/shared/aboutus/statistics/ybpage.htm).

Opposition forms panel against war on Iraq. (2002). *The Hindu* (online edition). November 5.

Osipov, Georgy and Palshin, Kirill (2001). Russia invited to participate in the new split of the world, but will it get anything out of it? *Izvestia.* October 2.

Ovcharenko, Elena and Yevgenii Umerenkov (2001). Those who bombed Moscow have reached the United States. In a new era, the world realizes that terrorism is no joke. *Komsomolskaya Pravda.* September 12.

Owen, John M. (2002). Transnational Liberalism and U.S. Primacy. *International Security.* Volume 26.

Padgaonkar, D. (2003). American double-think. *Times of India.* November 16.

Pan, Z. (2000). Improvising reform activities: The changing reality of journalistic practice in China. In C.C. Lee (ed.). *Power, Money, and Media: Communication Patterns and Bureaucratic Control in Cultural China.* Evanston, IL: Northwestern University Press.

Pankov, Yuri (2001). The United States is not ready to fight international terrorism. *Krasnaya Zvezda.* September 18.

Papacharissi, Z. (2002). The virtual sphere: the Internet as a public sphere. *New Media & Society.* 4(1), 9–27.

Patterson, Anne W. (2001). Embassy Thanks Colombians for the Expressions of Support Following Terrorist Attacks in the U.S. (http://usembassy.state.gov/posts/col/wwwsa013.shtml).

Pavlovsky, Gleb (2001). Are we prepared to wait until the enemy hits us as it hit America? (www.strana.ru). October 24.

Pavlovsky, Gleb (2001). Terrorists' aim is world war. (www.strana.ru). September 12.

Pei, Minxin (2001). *Apple Daily.* September 15.

Penikis, Janis (1991). Soviet views of the Baltic Emigration: From reactionaries to fellow countrymen. In Jan Arveds Trapans (ed.). *Toward Independence: The Baltic Popular Movements.* Boulder, CO: Westview Press.

Polumbaum, J. (2001). China's media: Between politics and the market. *Current History.* 100(647), 269–277.

Pombo, Mauricio (2001). Los Budas y las Torres. *El Tiempo.* September 13.

Pomfret, John (2001). In China, Anti-U.S. Sentiment Unfettered. *Washington Post.* September 14.

Postmes, T. and Brunsting, S. (2002). Collective action in the age of the Internet – mass communication and online mobilization. *Social Science Computer Review.* 20(3): 290–301.

Powell, Colin L. (2001). Designation of the AUC as a Foreign Terrorist Organization. (http://www.state.gov/secretary/rm/2001/4852.htm).

Primakov, Evgeny (2001, 09/15). An interview. *Moskovsky Komsomolets.* No. 205, September 15.

Primero Colombia (2002b). Resistencia civil organizada para proteger a la población civil propone òblvaro Uribe. April 10.

Pronina, Lyuba (2001). Fired Up About Arms. *Moscow Times.* September 24.

Ptichkin, Sergey (2001). Is Kremlin Protected Against Air Attack? *Rossiyskaya Gazeta.* September 14.

Pushkov, Aleksei (2001). Host of the television program *Postskriptum* quoted by www.smi.ru. September 15.

Qiu, L. (1999/2000). Virtual censorship in China: Keeping the gate between the cyberspaces. *International Journal of Communication Law and Policy.* 4: 1–25.

Radzivilovicius, Tadas (2001). Pasaulio savaite. *Lietuvos Rytas.* December 22.

Rajghatta, C. (2001). U.S. condemns attack on J&K assembly. *The Times of India* (online edition). October 2.

Ramachandran, S. (2002). Pressure on US to broker peace. *Asia Times Online.* May 24.

Randall, Stephen J. (1992). *Colombia and the United States: Hegemony and Interdependence.* Athens, GA.: University of Georgia Press.

Rao, P.V. (2002). Powell fails to see India's point of view. *Financial Times* (online edition). July 29.

Rau, Johannes (2001). *Die Tageszeitung.* October 10.

Rauch, Georg von (1974). *The Baltic States: The Years of Independence. Estonia, Latvia, Lithuania, 1917–1940.* London: C. Hurst.

Registraduría Nacional del Estado Civil (2002). Informe de Votación – Corporación: Presidente – Votación a nivel nacional. (http://www.registraduria.gov.co/2002PRP1/).

Rivlin, Paul (2003). Egypt's Demographic challenges and economic responses. *MERIA Journal.* Vol. 7, December, 1–13.

Robertson, J. (2003, accessed online in January). The Anti-American blowback from Bush's policies. Foreign Policy in Focus Policy Report. (http://www.fpif.org).

Rogozin, Dmitry (2001). An interview. *Nezavisimaya Gazeta.* September 13.

Rose, R. (2002). *A Bottom up Evaluation of Enlargement Countries. New Europe Barometer 1.* Glasgow: University of Strathclyde.

Rubenberg, Cheryl (1986). *Israel and the American national interest: A critical examination.* University of Illinois Press: Urbana and Chicago.

Rubinoff, A.G. (2001). Changing perceptions of India in the U.S. Congress. *Asian Affairs: An American Review.* 28(1), 37–61.

Rubinstein, Alvin Z. and Smith, Donald E. (ed.) (1985). *Anti-Americanism in the Third World: Implications for U.S. foreign policy.* Praeger Publishers: New York.

Rubinstein, Alvin Z. and Donald E. Smith (eds.) (1985a). *Anti-Americanism in the Third World: Implications for U.S. Foreign Policy.* New York: Praeger.

Rubinstein, Alvin Z. and Donald E. Smith (1985b). Anti-Americanism: Anatomy of a Phenomenon. In Rubinstein and Smith (eds.). *Anti-Americanism in the Third World: Implications for U.S. Foreign Policy.* New York: Praeger.

Ryurikov, Dmitry (1999). *Russia Survives.* Washington DC: Nixon Center.

Sabas, Rytis (2001). Pasaulio savaite. *Lietuvos Rytas.* December 15.

Safonov, Anatly (2001). Interview of Deputy Minister of Foreign Affairs to *Moskovskie Novosti.* October 23.

Safran, Nadav (1978). *Israel: The Embattled Ally.* Presidents and Fellows of Harvard College: U.S.

Saha, S. (1990). *Indo-U.S. Relations 1947–1989. A Guide to Information Sources.* New York: Peter Lang.

Sakalauskaite, Ramune (2001). Prie JAV ambasados – geles ir maldos. *Lietuvos Rytas.* September 13.

Saksena, R. (2002). Love is in the air. *The Week* (online edition). February 10.

Samper Pizano, Ernesto (2000). *Aquí estoy y aquí me quedo: Testimonio de un gobierno.* Bogotá: El òbncora Editores.

Sanghvi, V. (2001a). India and America: Love's Labor Lost. *The Hindustan Times* (online edition). October 24.

Sanghvi. V. (2001b). The U.S. is ignoring India's war on terrorism. *Time Asia* (online edition). November 5.

Sanghvi, V. (2002). U.S. since 9/11: Lessons and conundrums. *The Hindustan Times* (online edition), September 14.

Sanghvi, V. (2003). The loneliness of America. *The Hindustan Times.* March 30.

Santos, Francisco (2001). La partera de la historia. *El Tiempo.* September 12.

Sardar, Ziauddin, and Davies, Merryl Wyn (2003). *Why do People Hate America?* Disinformation Books.

Schoultz, Lars (1998). *Beneath the United States: A History of U.S. Policy toward Latin America.* Cambridge, MA: Harvard University Press.

Search and Investment Consultancy Company (2003). 57% Chinese support backing North Korea against the US again. *Ming Pao Daily News.* June 17.

Semana (1999). Exodo. 895, July 26.

Shebarshin, Leonid (2001). A war for an audience. *Vremya MN.* October 17.

Shelia, Vakhtang (2001). The wrong war. *Novaya Gazeta.* No. 74, October 11.

Sherif, M. (1966). *Group conflict and co-operation: Their social psychology.* London: Routledge and Kegan Paul.

Shiraev, Eric (1999). The Post-Soviet Orientations toward the United States and the West. In Shiraev, E. and Glad, B. (eds.). *The Russian Transformation*. New York: St. Martin's Press.

Shiraev, Eric and Bastrykin, Alexander (1988). *Moda, Kumiry, I Sobstvennoye Ya*. Leningrad: Lenizdat.

Shiraev, Eric and Terrio, D. (2003). Russian Decision-making Regarding Bosnia: Indifferent Public and Feuding Elites. In R. Sobel and E. Shiraev (eds.). *International Public Opinion and the Bosnia Crisis*. Lexington Books/Rowman and Littlefield.

Shiraev, Eric and Zubok, Vlad (2001). *Anti-Americanism in Russia: From Stalin to Putin*. New York: St. Martin's Press/Palgrave.

Shlapentokh, Vladimir (1986). *Soviet Public Opinion and Ideology: The Interaction Between Mythology and Pragmatism*. New York: Praeger.

Shlapentokh, Vladimir (1986). *Soviet Public Opinion and Ideology: Mythology and Pragmatism in Interaction*. New York: Praeger.

Shlapentokh, Vladimir (1988). The Changeable Soviet Image of America. *The Annals*. Vol. 497, May.

Shlapentokh, Vladimir (1988). The Changeable Soviet Image of America. In T. Thornton (ed.). *Anti-Americanism. The Annals of the American Academy of Political and Social Science*. Vol. 497, 157–171. Newbury Park: Sage Publications.

Shlapentokh, Vladimir (2001). Is Putin a pro Western Lone Ranger? *Johnson's Russia List*. No. 5609, December 20.

Shlapentokh, V. and Woods, J. (2002). Views of world elite at core of U.S. problems abroad. *USA Today* (online edition). December 29.

Shlapentokh, Vladimir and Joshua Woods (2003). Foreign Attitudes toward the USA after 9/11: America as Victim.

Shusharin, Dmitry (2001). The president's loneliness: President Putin has the courage to make unpopular decisions. *Vremya MN*. October 26.

Sibal, K. (2001). Meeting emerging security challenges. Address delivered to Carnegie Endowment for International Peace, Washington D.C.

Siebert, S.F. (1956). *Four Theories of the Press: The Authoritarian, Libertarian, Social Responsibility and Soviet Communist Concepts of What the Press Should Be*. Urbana: University of Illinois Press.

Sindeikis, Algimantas (2002). Dar vieno 'absurdo spektaklio' pabaiga. *Veidas*. August 22.

Singh, V.B., Kumar, S. and Yadav, Y. (1999). *Surveying the Indian electorate*. New Delhi: Center for the Study of Developing Societies.

Smaizyte, Vytaute (2001). Pasualio savaite. *Lietuvos Rytas*. December 29.

Sobel, Richard and Shiraev, Eric (eds.) (2003). *International Public Opinion and the Bosnia Crisis*. Lexington Books/Rowman & Littlefield.

Solovei, Valerii (2001). Hands United? *Vek*. No. 37, September 21.

Sozhenitsyn, Alexander (1998). Ugodilo Zernishko promezh dvukh zhernovov. *Novy Mir*. No. 9, 47–125.

Stebbins, R.P. (1953). *The United States in world affairs*. New York: Harper & Brothers.

Stepanov, Andrei (2001). Russian public opinions in new political realities. *Vremya MN*. No. 14.

Students rally against war on Iraq. (2003). *The Economic Times* (online edition). March 14.

Tahir-Kheli, S. (1997). *India, Pakistan and the United States*. New York: Council on Foreign Relations Press.

Thibault, D. (2002). Global survey shows growing anti-Americanism. *CNSNews.com*. December 6.

Thom, Francoise (2003). Deux points de vue critiques sur la diplomatie francaise. La cpitulation preventive. *Le Figaro*. May 6.

Thornton, Thomas (ed.) (1998). *Anti Americanism: Origins and context*. The Annals of the American Academy of Political and Social Science: Washington D.C.

Tickner, Arlene (2003). Colombia and the United States: From Counternarcotics to Counterterrorism. *Current History.* 102(661): 77–85.

Tokatlian, Juan Gabriel (1997). Colombia-Estados Unidos: Una relación hipernarcotizada. In Luis Alberto Restrepo (ed.). *Síntesis '97 Colombia.* Bogotá.

Tretiakov, Vitaly (2001). An interview with *Rossiyskaya Gazeta.* September 13.

U.S. Census Bureau (1996). *Population.* (http://www.census.gov/prod/2/gen/96statab/pop.pdf).

U.S. Department of State (2001). *Patterns of Global Terrorism: 2000.* Washington, D.C. (http://www.state.gov/s/ct/rls/pgtrpt/2000/).

U.S is extraordinarily sensitive to U.S. concerns. (2003). *Indiainfo.com.* October 6.

Uhlemann, Godehard (2001). *Rheinische Post.* September 12.

Ulyanov, Nikolai (2001). Russia will not actively participate in new Afghan war. (www.strana.ru). September 19.

United Nations High Commissioner for Human Rights (UNHCHR) (2002). Report of the United Nations High Commissioner for Human Rights on the human rights situation in Colombia. United Nations Economic and Social Council (E/CN.4/2002/17, February 28).

Uribe, òblvaro (2002b). Manifiesto Democrático: 100 puntos – òblvaro Uribe Vélez. (http://www.presidencia.gov.co/documentos/documen.htm).

Uzelac, Ana (2001). Terror May Be Tie That Binds. *Moscow Times.* September 13.

Vaicius, Ingrid, and Adam Isacson (2003). *The "War on Drugs" Meets the "War on Terror."* Washington, D.C.: Center for International Policy.

Vainauskiene, Brone (2001). Vel – vertybiu perkainojimo metas. *Lietuvos Rytas.* September 17.

Vajpayee, A.B. (2001). Letter to President Bush. (http://meaindia.nic.in). September 11.

Valatka, Rimvydas (2001). Naujasis Amerikos karas – ne tik jos. *Lieuvos Rytas.* September 17.

Van Hollen, C. (1980). The tilt policy revisited: Nixon-Kissinger geopolitics and South Asia. *Asian Survey.* 20, 341–360.

Vardarajan, S. (2001). An ignoble war, earn your peace prize, Mr. Annan. *Times of India* (online edition). October 28.

Vardarajan, S. (2002). Stand by Iraq, say no to Bush. *Times of India.* September 12.

Vasiliev, Evgeny (2001). Moment of Truth. The Kremlin had better revise its foreign policy and defense doctrines. *Vremya MN.* September 14.

Vasiliev, Nikolai (1955). *Amerika s chernogo khoda.* Moscow: Molodaya Gvardiya.

Vidal, Gore (2002a). *Perpetual war for perpetual peace: how we got to be so hated.* New York: Thunder's Mouth Press/Nation Books.

Vidal, Gore (2002b). *Dreaming war: blood for oil and the Cheney-Bush junta.* New York: Thunder's Mouth Press/Nation Books.

Vitas, Robert A. (1990). *The United States and Lithuania: the Stimson Doctrine of Nonrecognition.* New York: Praeger.

Vries, de B. and Zwaga, W.E.R. (1997). Legislators or interpreters? On the relationship between journalists and their readers. *Media, Culture & Society.* 19(1): 67–82.

Vyas, N. (2001). War helping Pakistan, says BJP. *The Hindu.* October 8.

Wang, Anran (2001). *Apple Daily.* October 8.

Wang, G. (1995). *The Chinese Way: China's Position in International Relations.* Scandinavian University Press.

War without frontiers (2003). *The Times of India* (online edition). November 26.

Washington Office on Latin America (WOLA) (2002). Taking Stock: Plan Colombia's First Year. *Colombia Monitor.* Vol. 1, No. 1 (March). (http://www.wola.org/Colombia/monitor_may02.pdf).

Weber, I. (2003). Localizing the Global: Successful Strategies for Selling Television Programming to China. *Gazette.* 65(3), 273–290.

WPS Media Monitoring Agency (2001). Political forecasts. (www.wps.ru). October 31.

Wyman, M. (1997). *Public Opinion in Postcommunist Russia*. London: Macmillan Press.

Xian McDonald Bombing, Kentucky received bomb threats (2003). *Ming Pao*. June 17, A22.

Xu, H. (2000). Morality discourse in the marketplace: Narratives in the Chinese television news magazine Oriental Horizon. *Journalism Studies*. 1(4), 637–647.

Yang, G. (2003). The co-evolution of the Internet and civil society in China. *Asian Survey*. 43(3), 405–422.

Yavlinkky, Grigory (2001). Russia May Play its own Game. A selection of comments. *Nezavisimaya Gazeta*. September 15.

Yi, See Mun (2003). The country America cannot see. *New York Times*. August 27.

Zakaria, Fareed (2003). The Arrogant Empire. *Newsweek*. March 24.

Zee News TV (2003). Demonstrations against attack on Iraq. *BBC Monitoring International Reports*. March 20.

Zeldin, Theodore (1990). Foreword. In Denis Lacorne, Jacques Rupnik, and Marie-France Toinet (eds.). *The Rise and Fall of Anti-Americanism*. New York: St. Martin's Press.

Zhao, Y. (1998). *Media, market and democracy in China: Between the party line and the bottom line*. Urbana: University of Illinois Press.

Zheng, Y. (1999). *Discovering nationalism in China*. New York City: Cambridge University Press.

Zhirinovsky, Vladimir (2001). An interview (www.strana.ru). September 14.

Zhou (sic), Y. (2000). Watchdogs on party leashes? Context and implications of investigative journalism in post-Deng China. *Journalism Studies*. 1, 577–597.

Zingeris, Markas (2001). Teroro idejos yra pavojingesnes net uz ginklus. *Lietuvos Rytas*. September 14.

Zweig, Stefan (1984). Is there a Newspaper Novel? Anton Kaes, Martin Jay and Edward Dimenberg (eds.). *The Weimar Republic Sourcebook*. Berkeley: University of California Press.

Zyuganov, Gennady (2001). An interview. *Nezavisimaya Gazeta*. September 13.

Zyuganov, Gennady (2001). An interview. (www.strana.ru). September 14.

Index